'A' IS FOR ANAKTUVUK:

TEACHER *to the* NUNAMIUT ESKIMOS

NAOMI GAEDE-PENNER

The story of Anna Bortel Church

'A' IS FOR ANAKTUVUK:
TEACHER *to the* NUNAMIUT ESKIMOS

To Iris — who has her
own adventures —
be sure save
your own identity
stories.
Naomi Gaede-Pen

TATE PUBLISHING
AND ENTERPRISES, LLC

Published by Tate Publishing & Enterprises, LLC
127 E. Trade Center Terrace | Mustang, Oklahoma 73064 USA
1.888.361.9473 | www.tatepublishing.com

Tate Publishing is committed to excellence in the publishing industry. The company reflects the philosophy established by the founders, based on Psalm 68:11,
"The Lord gave the word and great was the company of those who published it."

Book design copyright © 2013 by Tate Publishing, LLC. All rights reserved.
Cover design by Kristen Verser
Interior design by Blake Brasor
Alaska map by Barbara Spohn-Lillo
Photos from Anna Bortel Church collection and Elmer E. Gaede collection. Front cover photo from Anna Bortel Church collection.
Songs Copyright © *Anna Bortel Church*

Published in the United States of America

ISBN: 978-1-61777-756-1
1. History, United States, State & Local, West (Ak, Ca, Co, Hi, Id, Mt)
2. Biography & Autobiography, Educators
13.01.08

DEDICATION

To all children who desire to know their ethnic traditions, history, forefathers and foremothers, and to the people who provide them the reading and writing tools to do so.

APPRECIATION

Anna wrote weekly letters to her parents, who saved those diary documentations of her life in Alaska. She herself saved newspaper clippings, letters from her supervisors, and other scraps of communication. Over the years, handwritten and typed letters, photographs, and newspapers have faded, and memories have grown fainter, too. In crafting and documenting Anna's astonishing story, supplementary data was valuable and much appreciated. Here are some of the history reservoirs that contributed to *A is for Anaktuvuk: Teacher to the Nunamiuts.*

Dr. Elmer Gaede, Public Health Services physician at Tanana, Alaska (1957-1959) flew his Piper PA-14 to Anaktuvuk Pass in 1959 for a medical field trip. The outcome of his offer to Anna Bortel to "come along" was greater than he could ever imagine. Anna Bortel received permission from the Territorial Education Department to accompany him, along with instructions to conduct an educational assessment. Elmer Gaede's recount of the experience was written in his letters to his parents as well as in *Alaska Bush Pilot Doctor* (previously *Prescription for Adventure: Bush Pilot Doctor*), all of which supplemented details in this book.

Ruby Gaede's letters to and from Anna, and Ruby's letters to her parents-in-law following a Gaede family trip to Anaktuvuk Pass to visit Anna, added to the writing.

Reverend John Chambers's personal letters to Anna and his book, *Arctic Bush Mission: The Experiences of a Missionary Bush Pilot in the Far North,* were wonderful resources in confirming and affirming interactions between the Presbyterian missionaries and the Nunamiut village as well as with Anna. These provided photo memory-joggers, specific names, and bits of history.

Nicolas Gubser, a Yale student, lived among the Nunamiut at the same time Anna was teaching. His ethnographic research culminated in *The Nunamiut Eskimos: Hunters of Caribou,* which was another source for verifying facts and cross-checking observations.

Michael Cline taught in Anaktuvuk from 1967 to 1969. His teaching and his study of this group of people resulted in *Tannik School: The Impact of Education on the Eskimos of Anaktuvuk Pass.* His painstaking documentation provided a fallback when questions arose of "What about this custom/living arrangement/family/location?"

In John Martin Campbell's books *In a Hungry Country: Essays by Simon Paneak* and *North Alaska Chronicle: Notes from the End of Time,* pictures and notes enhanced descriptions of people, lifestyle, and locations described in Anna's story.

Sarah Pat Quigley edited the original version of this manuscript; Sally Dolan scrupulously read for flow, accuracy, and congruency; and Marianna Gaede and Jack Neff responded as typical readers. I could not confidently write about Alaska without my Alaska editor, Jan O'Meara. Thank you, James Bare, my Tate editor, for walking with me through my string of *Prescriptions for Adventure* books.

All in all, it has been a widespread and decades-long group endeavor.

RECOGNITION
AND REAL NAMES

This book adds to the stories of early educators and broadens the personalities of scientists, teachers, and healthcare workers who are referred to in other books as "a teacher," "the doctor," "a nurse," "the scientist," or "one of the Natives." Real names have been used, whenever possible, with the intent of providing characters with clear identities and, subsequently, recognition. Apologies are extended for errors that can occur due to erosion of facts or perceptions over time.

In regards to the Native people, it is my hope that by using actual names, their specific history will be documented by the state of Alaska as well as within villages and that this history, in story form, will be more easily remembered and transferred to future generations. Alongside history-telling, portraying specific people bestows honor and tribute to the living as well as to the startling number of babies who died in Anaktuvuk Pass.

A portion of the royalties for this book will go to the Simon Paneak Museum in Anaktuvuk Pass, Alaska.

TABLE OF CONTENTS

BEHIND THE STORY

In 1957, my physician father took a position at the Tanana Public Health Services Hospital along the Yukon River in Interior Alaska. The Athabascan Indian village was home to three hundred people. I joined forty-eight Native and non-Native boys and girls at the Tanana Day School, grades one through eight. Miss Bortel taught first and second grades and was my teacher. I thrived in the learning environment of seasonal bulletin boards; government subsidy snacks of cheese and snow-cold powdered milk; story time; and activities such as pet shows, holiday programs, and an Easter egg tree.

My family left Tanana and Alaska briefly, and we went south, but the territory-turned-state wouldn't release our family to a common and comfortable existence. With a gleam in his eye, my father responded to a plea for medical assistance on the Kenai Peninsula, and we returned to the Last Frontier, where we rolled up our sleeves to homestead outside of Soldotna.

Anna left Tanana, too. She went north, to Anaktuvuk Pass. We flew in our family cruiser to visit her, and decades later, I made two more trips to Anaktuvuk Pass, even though by that time, Anna had left. Our worlds stayed connected.

Anna wasn't as enthusiastic as I about writing her stories. I kept nudging her. Finally, she dug into her letters and photos and started reminiscing and writing. My unrelenting research added more geographical, historical, and character formation. Her sharp memory kept adding details. Stories were crafted into a book, in her voice.

When I've had the opportunity to visit Anna in her retirement home in Oregon, we hark back to our experiences at Tanana, granted with generational differences. To this day, I am spellbound by her stories. Listen now as she shares them with you.

PREFACE

....

'A' is for Anaktuvuk: Teacher to the Nunamiut Eskimos is not meant to compete with the stringent and remarkable research by Gubser, Cline, and Campbell, which supports their ethnographic and anthropological perspectives. The purpose of *this* book is to tell a story, a story of following God's call, growing relationships in an unfamiliar culture, and thriving in a physically hostile environment. It is intended to inspire, not inculcate, and, while doing all this, even put a smile or two on the reader's face.

PART I

1923-1954

GROWING INTO A
SCHOOL TEACHER

Alaska 1960

Needed:

School teacher for Anaktuvuk Pass, Alaska, located above the Arctic Circle, for nomadic tribe of approx. 96 Nunamiut Eskimos. People desire education but prior attempts of setting up school have not been successful. Until recently, people have continually migrated and are currently dependent on caribou for shelter, clothing, food, tools; minimal cash income. Qualifications:

- familiar with the primitive living conditions in the interior of Alaska
- prepared to sacrifice personal comfort for the good of the school
- intimately acquainted with the ways of the Native people and their attitudes towards learning
- able to adjust to adverse living conditions without sacrificing teaching efficiency

No school building, tent or sod house available for teacherage, no roads to transport building supplies, no wood for fuel except willows, no public services besides post office. Sporadic bush pilot services. Presbyterian Church with itinerant minister. Severe winters.

This advertisement did not actually appear in print but was adapted from a 1961 speech presented by Mr. Ernest Gruening, state senator, at an Alaska senate meeting where he described the dilemma Alaskan educators faced and the determination of the Native people to obtain an education. In this same speech, he praised my work of pioneering the first school for the last nomadic group of Eskimos in Alaska, in the remote village of Anaktuvuk Pass.

...the revelation of so many problems did not dampen the enthusiasm of the folks of the village (Anaktuvuk). For they persuaded Anna Bortel, who had been head teacher at Tanana School, to teach them in their church. In Miss Bortel they had found the ideal teacher, one able to comprehend their problem, one kind and sympathetic, and above all one able to adjust to all conditions that might face her." 1961 Congressional Record— Senate, #13201 by Mr. Gruening, "A Unique American Educational Venture in Alaska's Far North."

ABC

On that first morning, the boys and grade school students ran around outside the chapel while they waited to be summoned inside. I opened the door and surveyed the scene before me. The older boys wore tall, black rubber boots with their pants more or less stuffed inside. Some of the young girls wore full skirts with white anklets, their bare legs tempting mosquitoes. The others wore traditional cotton atigas and mukluks. Teenage girls, their heads covered with wool or cotton scarves, whispered and chatted in huddles. Two girls had walked nineteen miles to be on time for opening day.

Behind the students stood a twenty-one-year-old girl who desired to attend school but, at her age, wasn't sure she'd be accepted. Pushing close beside her, a group of preschoolers felt left out and giggled with dirt-creased grins as they pretended to shoot me with their slingshots. Several were barefoot. An older boy was educably handicapped. Altogether, twenty-six students, ages six to eighteen, crammed themselves into the makeshift classroom.

Children who had sat on the willow-boughed dirt floors all their lives experimented with sitting in desks. In self-conscious silliness, they slid in their desk seats and giggled; and then peeked beneath their desks, as if something unknown was hiding beneath. These pieces of typical school furniture appeared high on their list of novelties.

The three teenage girls who had attended up to three years at the boarding school, were quite advanced and could speak English easily. Children age nine and younger had never attended school, and some of the first-graders could not speak a word of English.

My Scott Foresman textbooks were definitely not written for these children. What did they know about oak and fruit trees, zoos, farms, pet cats, or homes with davenos and refrigerators? What would they think if I told them the color red was like cherries and fire engines? Or *A* was for *apple*. I'd have to say red was like cranberries, blue was like the summer sky. The traditional *A* is for *apple* would have to be changed to *A* is for *Anaktuvuk, Alaska, Ahgook, Anna*; and *B* is for *baby, bear, Bortel*; and *C* is for *caribou*. Instead of 2 cats + 2 cats = 4 cats, I'd need to make worksheets with

2 fox + 2 fox = 4 fox

1 ptarmigan + 4 ptarmigan = 5 ptarmigan

But here I was, about to teach school in the small chapel and living in a one-room sod house. Indoor plumbing was unheard of. A gas lantern offered flickering light.

What power or drive had compelled me to leave the comforts and familiarities of my home in Ohio; more so, my teaching job in an enviable state-of-the-art school?

ABC

In the fall of 1929, I was six years old—old enough for first grade at South Main Street Grade School in Bowling Green, Ohio. Now I could go to the bus stop with my sister, Millie, and brother, David. Our mother, Myrtle

Crosby Bortel had filled us with a hearty breakfast before waving us out the door. Our father, Clifford Bortel, was already off to work at the wallpaper and paint store he co-owned.

I'd anticipated this momentous day of *real* school and felt very grown-up. I'd known school was coming since I'd seen the fall clothes in the J.C. Penny store windows when Millie and I had walked downtown with Mother. We only window-shopped. Instead of a store-bought dress for school, Millie and I choose fabric, and Mother sewed us dresses. Millie, sixteen months older than me, had been through this before and made her decision more easily than I. I ran around the store, tugged on my mother's arm, pulled on corners of fabric, and scampered off to other bolts of prints.

Before I bounded out the door on that first school day, Mother tried to straighten my out-of-control hair, which had turned from blond to light brown and was cut short with high bangs. Impatiently, I waited in my new blue print dress with puffed sleeves, hopping on one foot, trying to catch sight of the school bus.

"Your banana will squash your sandwich," warned Millie as my decorated tin lunch bucket slipped out of my hand and banged to the ground. She was always serious, sensible, and definitely not silly.

David was three years older than me and loved trains. His bedroom was a museum of sorts. Although his room was shrouded with the warning of *No Trespassing by Sisters*, I'd been known to sneak down the hall, look in both directions, and then furtively turn the brass door knob and peer with one eye into this forbidden zone. Many of his treasures were railroad tables and paperwork filled out by brakemen. We lived near the train tracks, and David's room was on the second-story and had an airing deck outside. He'd rigged a block signal with red, amber, and green lights. When a train clattered by at night, awakening David, he'd flick the switch on and off, and the engineer would "toot" back a greeting. I grew up with the mournful sound of a train whistle.

At last the bus rumbled into view and we climbed up the steps.

As is often the case, I looked up to my older brother, and to begin with, I relied on him to protect me from any disturbances at the bus stop or the bully on the bus ride. As I grew more confident, I stood up for myself and enjoyed my independence.

ABC

I loved my sister dearly, even though our temperaments were different. Millie didn't have to experiment as much as I did. Before I was even school age, I tried smoking. When the corn stood ripe in the field with golden-brown silk, two neighbor children and I decided to try our hand at roll-your-own cigarettes.

"I can find matches and newspaper in the kitchen," I volunteered. "Then let's climb up on the building behind the garage."

We took along newspaper and carefully formed our cigarettes with corn silk from the adjoining corn field. Furtively, we lit our clumsy rolls, coughed, and sputtered.

"Anna! Come down at once." My father's firm voice interrupted our concentration.

We looked at each other in astonishment. How did he know we were up there? Rubbing out and smashing our cigarettes, we quickly climbed off the hot, rough roof. Instead of delivering the anticipated lecture on smoking, Daddy expressed concern over fire and the safety of the buildings. This was the beginning and end of my smoking habit. My knack for improvising and experimenting would become a useful trait, but down the road, when it didn't include newspapers and corn silk.

ABC

As an early grade-schooler, I didn't understand why teachers viewed my focused, bookworm sister as a model student but knew me to be mischievous—a student more interested in socializing and motivated by curiosity. In any case, I believed teachers were an unfriendly lot, with the primary purpose of popping the balloon of children's fun. Regardless, I raised my hand frequently when the teacher asked for a volunteer.

One day this resulted in tragedy. It was my turn to clean the fish bowl that held a school of guppies swimming blithely around in circles. Another student and I carefully carried the bowl to a dimly lit basement room. Brooms, mops, and cleaning supplies stood at our sides as we made our way toward a deep sink. Tipping the bowl on its side, we conscientiously held our hands over the lip as the water slowly flowed through our fingers.

When we refilled the bowl, I suddenly noticed in horror and exclaimed to my classmate, "There are only three fish left! What happened to the others?"

We trudged sadly back to the classroom. "What will we tell teacher?" I whispered. Tears filled my eyes; I felt sure that I could never be trusted again.

The guppy tragedy was heartbreaking, but another school recollection was devastating. I was to give an oral history report in front of class. My heart beat so loudly that I knew my classmates could hear it. When I finished, the teacher ridiculed the report and pointed out the deficiencies. Cringing in mortification, I wanted to run home and fall into my mother's arms, but all I could do was to put my head down on my desk. My hands felt cold and clammy. I squeezed my eyes shut and tried to hide within myself. I thought I would faint, which would have been a relief.

If anyone would have told me I would become a school teacher, I would *never* have believed them. Except for the opportunity to socialize with my friends, I didn't care for school, or in many cases, my teachers. I couldn't imagine anyone spending his or her life in a classroom by choice. A teacher role fit Millie, who was the studious one, but David and I were content to receive average grades, and it was obvious to my teachers that I enjoyed my classmates much more than times tables and writing essays. And I preferred spending time outdoors rather than inside sitting still.

ABC

In my preteen years, I looked forward to caring for babies while their parents attended the services at Portage Camp. When I played with these real-life baby dolls and hugged them close, I would pretend some of them were my very own. In those years, girls often married right out of high school; but this didn't happen to me, and after graduating from high school, I worked for a year in a variety store and as a nanny, and then I went to college at Spring Arbor Junior College, Spring Arbor Michigan, followed by Bowling Green State University.

During this time there was a desperate need for teachers across the United States. Consequently, potential teachers could take specific classes and achieve temporary teaching certificates, if they then agreed to complete their course work and obtain a degree. Therefore, while completing my college work, I applied for a teaching position at Crissey, Ohio, twenty-two miles from Toledo, and promptly signed a year's contract for $1150. How thrilling to have a real job, real money, and the bonus of my older sister, Millie, as the principal of the same school!

On that first sunny September day of school, I walked up the sidewalk to the classroom feeling nine feet tall. I was the teacher, not a student! I thought of my own negative experiences as a grade-schooler and hoped to furnish my students with more positive memories than I had. My multiracial first- and second-grade students flocked in from an area on the outskirts of Toledo. What a challenge to keep these rambunctious children busy, and I wondered if my teachers had felt the same way about me. During evenings, I industriously designed lesson plans that I hoped would be interesting and at the same time stimulate their learning.

The second year, Millie and I accepted teaching positions at Monclova School in Monclova, Ohio. I then took off a year from teaching to complete my senior year of college at Greenville College. After graduating, I applied in Pekin, Illinois, where a friend was teaching. The interviewing process went smoothly and the school board was eager to hire anyone willing to teach—that is, after I promised I would not marry during the 1947–1948 school year. I signed the contract without hesitation. My supervisor informed me that as soon as the new Wilson school was built, I would be teaching in it. Until then, I would be teaching at the Franklin School, on the banks of the Illinois River.

A number of the children attended our school from the district where a new million dollar school was to be constructed. The buses were overly packed with children, and children became uncomfortably warm on the buses, which functioned as incubators. By the time the children tumbled off the bus and walked into the school yard, some who had appeared to be perfectly healthy when they left home exhibited symptoms of having been exposed to measles or chicken pox. Packed into the sweltering buses hastened the rashes. Soon it became standard procedure to check children's faces, arms, and chests for spots as they took off their coats in the coat room. Miraculously, amidst all this, within a few weeks, order took shape and the children learned to print their names, read, and count.

Two years later, Wilson School was completed. It was the most modern school in Illinois, and every teacher's dream. Teachers traveled from all over the state, including Chicago, to tour the facility. Adjoining my large classroom was an activity room which provided abundant space for learning projects. Rows of spacious cupboards stored class materials and the children's projects, and at one end, restrooms flanked a workspace, which included a large sink. The newspaper carried up-to-the-minute reports and photographs of the classroom activities and field trips of this model school. At age twenty-eight, I had settled into an enviable professional position.

PART II

....

1954 - 1957

THE TRAIL NORTH

··

At age thirty-one, I found myself on the Alaska-Canada (Alcan) Highway, which twisted and cut across northwestern Canada and chopped a crude 1,520-mile path through the massive, unchallenged wilderness from Dawson Creek, British Columbia, to Alaska. Since the highway's inception in 1942, it had tested the endurance of travelers and their vehicles—and it would test mine.

I'd read books and articles about that distant and mysterious American territory. My heart and mind surged with excitement as I learned about freezing-cold back country that was accessible only by dogsled or perhaps a small airplane; a vast, unknown country with remote Eskimo villages, polar bears, and the Northern Lights sweeping across the Arctic sky. And then, one winter night in early 1954, I knelt beside my bed with hands folded on the patchwork blanket top. I sensed God s presence and a very real command to go to Alaska, despite the fact that I didn't have a teaching position there.

Many people thought this was a strange and illogical decision. The fact that Wilson School had just offered me a substantial increase, a $200 per year raise for the following year, was only one of these.

Colleagues at school raised their eyebrows.

"Will you live in an igloo?" one individual queried.

"The sun never shines in the winter," another declared.

"And there's snow all the time," added another.

All the same, on June 14, 1954, I closed the door of my light-green 1951 Styleline Chevrolet and backed out the driveway of my parents' home. Mother stood weeping and waving. Daddy had left quietly for work without saying good-bye. He feared he'd never see his daughter again.

ABC

Twelve days later, with 4,408 miles between my Ohio home and my Alaska destination, my driving companion, Dorothy Fisher, and I drove into Valdez, tucked into one of the many bays within the large Prince William Sound.

I'd learned about the small town through church officials who put me in touch with Wilson and Jay Stein, a young couple who were starting a Free Methodist church in Valdez. My correspondence with Jay painted reality into my mental picture of Valdez and heightened the allurement of Alaska:

> Do you know that snow piles up to 300 inches?! Then you'll need rain gear, too, for the wet spring and fall. We really can't buy much here, in the way of clothes, but we order from Sears & Roebuck out of Seattle...

Dot had been handy with map-reading and calculating miles; not only that, her take-it-in-stride attitude helped get us through situations where a person alone might have crumpled over the steering wheel in tears. She didn't fret or complain when we found a log across the road, faced a treacherous and muddy descent and ascent around a buried-in-the-mud semi-truck, fought off ferocious attacks by mosquitoes, cooked simple meals on a Coleman stove, and endured more dust and bumps than we cared to remember.

Now we were here. I'd anticipated going directly to Wilson and Jay Stein's; however, they were temporarily back in Missouri. Not one to let a detail slip, Jay had written directions to lead me to our greeting committee, Andrew and Louela Taylor.

"You made it!" drawled Andrew. His handshake was slow and firm.

He stood back and Louela entered the narrow doorway of the tiny trailer.

"Come on in," she said. She was neat as a pin with her hair pulled up and looked no worse for the wear of coming to this last frontier.

They acted as though they'd just been waiting for us, and as if we were long-lost friends or relatives. Down the short hallway, their two preschool boys peeked from behind a door. We sat down nearly knee-to-knee. The conversation turned immediately to stories about surviving the Alaska highway. It hadn't been that long since they'd driven up from Louisiana. Ohio and Louisiana are not similar in culture or geography, but we shared the commonality of having made it up *that* road. "You, too?" and "Oh, I remember *that* detour!" were mixed with what were anxieties then, but humor now: flat tires, running out of gas, not knowing if there'd be a mechanic in the next town or what the night's lodging might bring. As aggravating as it had been to have no running water and no electricity, we all laughed now.

Dorothy, or Dot as she preferred to be called, had ambitions for the summer only, but for Andrew, Louela, and I, we believed that with hope, hard work, and prayer our individual long-term Alaska dreams could be realized.

The trailer was warm from the high evening sun, as well as something very delicious baking in the oven. By this time, the two boys, James and Roy, had emerged, clutching trucks and cars, still not saying a word. I'd never met a child I couldn't befriend.

"Hey, show me what you've got there," I said. I held out my hands.

That's all it took.

In the tight space of the trailer, it made more sense for me to remain sitting than to help Louela pull out supper makings. The tantalizing smell had been red salmon baked whole. That was the first of many meals—both salmon meals and meals with the Taylors.

I'd been cooped up in a car for so many days and was itching to walk around and explore my new hometown. Back from the docks lay a carefully laid out town with straight gravel streets. Various businesses lined McKinley Street, and several churches were among the houses in the square-grid settlement. Keystone and Alaska Avenues ended at the docks with nearby salmon fisheries. Seagulls flapped, shrieked, and fought over dead fish, either on the shoreline or floating. Sharing wasn't something they'd ever learned. In town and tucked into outlying forested areas, six-hundred people lived in winter and 1,400 in summer.[1]

Dot and I found only the bare necessities at Bill Egan's Valdez Supply and Gilson's Mercantile.[2] These two grocery stores carried a variety of canned goods and produce at varying prices. A bank, a gift shop, two restaurants, the Pinzon Bar, a drugstore, a dry cleaner, a post office, a gas station, and a hospital rounded out the minimal services. No five-and-dime, shoe, or clothing store.

"Nothing to waste our money on here," said Dot.

It wouldn't be long before I'd discover that not only were mainstay provisions reduced, but communication with the outside world was very limited as well. The *Valdez News,* a news-sheet, was printed and posted randomly on the store windows, and public notices were tacked to a wall at the post office. The few radio connections to the United States, or even to Anchorage, were often frustrating static on the sporadic evening reception.

But, on that day, I'd been dazzled by the thundering, frothing water-falls and long-fingered glaciers edging down the towering mountains in Keystone Canyon, and the enormous bay upon which boats rocked gently. To a girl from Ohio, I was in a wonderland and I floated euphorically above these minor inconveniences, which even seemed amusing.

ABC

Within weeks, heavy clouds rolled down the encompassing mountains, obscuring the sky and replacing the soaring sun that had welcomed us. Pressed in by surrounding mountains, a flat sky above, and a large body of water before me, I felt an uneasy confinement, and it dawned on me why the local people referred to traveling to the lower United States as going "Outside." When I'd first heard that term, I thought it meant "going out-doors." I was learning that it referred to returning to fully-stocked grocery shelves, sprawling green lawns, cheaper gasoline, paved streets, and sources of entertainment and refinement. I suspected that it might also mean a respite from countless days without energizing sunshine.

This was only mid-summer. This was not even winter. The unquestionable call to Alaska went round and round in my head.

Added to this gloom, I had no job, except for volunteering at the El Nathan Children's Home. Louise Segerquist and Esther Peterson held together the Home with frugality, rolled-up sleeves, and love. The children called them Aunt Louise and Aunt Pedo. Both they and the children welcomed me into their content and active life. I enjoyed every minute with the Aleut (AL-lee-OOT), Indian, and part-Polish children, and I filled the hours with baking cookies, cutting hair, and reading stories, which, while I was paid in snuggles and giggles, wouldn't pay my bills.

Dot searched for work.

"What did you find today?" I asked over a simple supper of grilled cheese sandwiches.

"Maybe some babysitting. Maybe some ironing. Maybe weeding a garden."

She picked up a short-term job and volunteered wherever she could. By the end of summer she was ready to fly back to be with her boyfriend. Aunt Louise, Aunt Pedo, and I drove her to Anchorage and said our farewells. Dot had been a tie to my life in Ohio. Now I was alone.

ABC

Alone didn't last long. As much as I was at loose ends to begin with, life in Valdez came together. I finally met face-to-face with Wilson, Jay, and their young son Clovis, who had been the first people I'd associated with Valdez.

"Well, did I give you enough information before you arrived?" asked Jay.

Her hospitable concern brought to life the friendship seeds sown in her letters.

"If there's anything you ever need fixed or looked at, I'm here to help," added Wilson.

The sincere look on his face confirmed that he wasn't just being polite.

The Steins, Taylors, and I became a close-knit group; a family away from family for holidays and times when we struggled with how different Alaska was from the environments we'd come from.

At long last, a teaching contract came through too, but rather than simply teaching one or two elementary classes, I had a composite of kindergartners in the morning, a general music program, and clerical work in the office. This diverse list of responsibilities surprised me, as did the stunningly high salary of $5,180 per year with future raises implied.

As it turned out, my first year was a hodgepodge of teaching:

Kindergarten	9-11 a.m.
(In a small room adjacent the superintendent's office)	
Secretarial work	11:30 - 12:00
8th grade reading	11:15-1:45 p.m.
(In the former jail building)	
7th grade reading	1:45-2:15 p.m.
High School typing	2:15-3:15 p.m.
Choir/Chorus	3:15-4:00 p.m.

I hadn't expected to sprint between classes. When I heard rumors that when the new hospital opened, I might find my students in an old hospital ward, I wondered, *Could these unusual environments be educationally stimulating?* As odd as this teaching arrangement was, I adored my kindergartners and became so tickled with what they'd reveal, seriously, at daily sharing time. Each day I awoke with anticipation of spending the morning with them, seeing life through their innocent eyes, and teaching the alphabet, primary colors, and numbers one to ten.

ABC

Valdez boasts more snow than anywhere else in Alaska. Three-hundred inches is normal. In 1954 and into 1955, we would be exceeding that statistic. The Indians and Eskimos refused to live in Valdez—they declared it to be too windy and too snowy. They were right. I managed fairly well with chains on my tires and ban-ice in the car's gas tank. I also kept the snow brushed off my car when it was parked, lest I lose it and never find it until spring. Already, several cars had been damaged when snowplows attempted to remove what looked like a snow pile. Around town, the snow, pushed high on either side of the streets, resulted in driving tunnels. Cars could not be seen in advance, and drivers approached corners cautiously.

Regardless of my fill-in-the-gaps teaching schedule and the fathomless snow, I adapted to Valdez. Social by nature and fond of music, my natural bents were embraced by the barebones village, where everyone had to pitch in and work together.

For Thanksgiving 1954, the churches combined services and I was asked to facilitate the musical numbers. The *Valdez News, (Nov. 29, 1954)* wrote up the event in this way:

Union Thanksgiving Service Scheduled

The second annual Union Thanksgiving Service will be held at 1 p.m. in the Episcopal Church. This will be the first time that four clergy have participated in such a service for a good many years. Churches represented will include Free Methodist, the newest group in town, the Baptist, the Assembly of God, and the Episcopal Church. Preacher for the service will be the Rev. Ralph Wilson pastor of the Valdez Gospel Chapel, Assembly of God. Prayers will be led by the Rev. James Rose, pastor of the 1st Baptist Church, and the scripture will be read by the Rev. Mr. Taylor, pastor of the Free Methodist Church. The Rev. Robert Grumbine will be in charge of the service. The offering will be given to the Valdez Community Hospital. Miss Duane White will be the organist for the service. Anthems will be provided by the High School chorus under the direction of Miss Anna Bartel (sic.) Due to the limitation of the space in the Church, only six girls will sing in the chorus.

The third year, my responsibilities included teaching both kindergarten and music classes. The music instruction spanned the entire grade school, including full-blown musical performances and an operetta with little girls dressed in frilly dresses and looking like dainty butterflies, even though they'd worn snow boots between home and the school auditorium.

ABC

In no uncertain terms, Valdez was isolated and rugged compared to where I'd come from, but I'd done quite well for three years. I'd grown solid and supportive friendships with Wilson and Jay Stein, Andrew and Louela Taylor, and other members of the first Free Methodist church in Alaska. Louise Segerquist and Esther Peterson had always enfolded me in their El Nathan family. The school and community provided numerous opportunities to use my passion for music. But I'd heard stories of what lay farther north: Interior Alaska, Indians and Eskimos, villages with no roads that connected them to any other civilization; places, that in comparison, made Valdez look modern and well-supplied with conveniences.

PART III

··

1957 – 1960

FARTHER NORTH

In late August of 1957, I flew with a bush pilot to Tanana (TAN-na-nah), Alaska, at the confluence of the Yukon and Tanana Rivers. The riverbank village was about an hour's flight west-northwest of Fairbanks, and had half the population of Valdez's winter residents: 300 people. After statehood, the Yukon River would rank as the third longest river in the United States. Its width was nothing common either. Tanana Day School looked across a half-mile expanse to a large island, behind which the river spread even farther. Whereas, in Valdez, my daily landscape was that of tall mountains cupped around the bay, here, the river would be the captivating force. Mountains didn't grow around Tanana, and at first, I missed what had become a safe, cocooned feeling; but over time, my fascination with the water highway changed my perspective and my appreciation, especially after all my belongings and a year's worth of groceries chugged downriver on a flat river barge.

The amenities were less than half those of Valdez: the Northern Commercial Company (NCC) store, hospital, school, post office, three small churches, and a landing strip.

"Most of the children will be Athabascan (ATH-uh-BAS-kuhn), that is Indian, not Eskimo," Mr. Robert Isaac, from the Territorial Education Office in Juneau, had informed me when I'd been interviewed for the job.

Tanana Day School was the only school in the Territory with a dual teaching system. The Bureau of Indian Affairs (BIA) hired the head teacher for the Native children, who would be Florence Feldkirchner in the coming year. I was hired by the Territory of Alaska for the non-Native children. Even though two teachers were hired, one for the Native and one for the non-Native children, the classes would be mixed together and not segregated. The remote village schools provided only grades one through eight. If students wished to receive more education, they had to go to boarding school, typically Mount Edgecumbe in Sitka.

Forty students were anticipated for the 1957 fall semester, of which twelve to fifteen would be non-Native children from the Civil Aeronautical Authority (CAA) families or the Public Health Services (PHS) Hospital personnel. I would be teaching the first and second-graders.

When I arrived, Florence had already moved into the teacherage, which was in the white-frame Knights of Columbus building where the two-room school was also situated. It didn't look unique to Alaska, nor did the square, two-story clapboard CAA buildings or the long, one-story, red-shingled hospital buildings with basements. Then again, the buildings on Front Street resembled any aging Frontier town with their tall, square storefronts. The Natives' one and two-room log cabins were set away from these areas. Mixed in were sled dogs chained to their houses; sleds; end-of-season purple-pink fireweed that had started to seed out in cottony strands; and odds and ends of wooden boxes, tin cans, and such stuff tossed here and there, and piles of grown-old sawdust. Dirt paths ran through tall grass and between cabins and outhouses. At that time of year, the air only hinted slightly of woodstove smoke.

After the winter would set in firmly, I'd think back to my village wanderings and how I hadn't seen many wood piles stacked tall in anticipation of winter. I'd wonder why the Natives waited until it was bitterly cold, and then I'd learn they believed that if they chopped too much wood ahead of time, they might die and all their efforts would be in vain; or, other villagers would see an ample supply of chopped wood and want to borrow some. The best way to avoid such problems was to chop wood as needed, even if it was so cold outside that their eyelashes would nearly freeze together by the time they accomplished the task.

Florence was in her mid-fifties and wore her dyed hair parted down the middle and secured in a tight bun at her neck. Everything about her was no-nonsense and controlled, from her black pumps to her perfect posture. She carried an air of formality, but it wasn't as if she was unfriendly. There was a resoluteness about her, which was comforting, and I figured I could count on her no matter what happened.

The teacherage itself was modernly furnished and had hot and cold running water, an oil furnace that heated the entire building, an indoor toilet and a bathtub, electricity, and a refrigerator. I expected to be comfortable when the temperatures plunged to below 50 degrees, which Mr. Isaac had warned happened here in the Interior.

A new PHS physician, Dr. Elmer Gaede (GAY-dee) and his family arrived a few days behind me. I met them one Sunday morning at the Arctic Missions Chapel. Roy Gronning, the missionary man, was a tall, blond Scandinavian and filled up the doorway as well as towered over most everyone, and more so his wife, Margie, who was under five feet tall.

"Anna, I'd like you to meet Elmer and Ruby Gaede. These are their children, Naomi, Ruth, and Mark." His voice boomed, but his smile was pleasant and demeanor gentle. His wife, Margie, was the firecracker.

The Gaedes had come from Anchorage, where Elmer had served at the Anchorage Alaska Native Service Hospital for two years. Prior to that, they'd driven up the Alcan from their Mennonite roots in the wheat fields of Kansas. Elmer exuded energy and looked as if he never sat still long enough to gather any weight on his slim frame. Ruby smiled easily and did her best to hang on to Mark, their toddler, who kept trying to grab her glasses. The short introduction was the start of a lifelong friendship. Naomi and Ruth were second and first-graders in my class. Naomi was the more outgoing of the two and loved creative projects, especially with crayons, and reading storybooks. Ruth, who was slower to warm up to new situations and her classmates, would become a straight-A student with perfect attendance.

My class was filled out with blonde, fair-skinned girls from the CAA families, dark-eyed Athabascan children, and even some Native children with red hair. I liked the composite and hoped they would meld together, learn from one another, and all be richer because of the differences. As it turned out, pet shows, Christmas programs, cutting and pasting construction paper Valentines, and playing together at recess brought out the fact that they were all children with similar needs and frustrations, and complementary interests and abilities.

A few weeks after school started, the Gronnings, Gaedes, and I got out of town, which, if a road was followed, could only be eight miles at the most. I had been told I would not need my Chevy, and neither the Gaedes nor the Gronnings had vehicles. Unless a truck was used for hauling something, there was seldom a vehicle on the dirt Front Street, on which everyone walked. Doc, as we soon referred to Dr. Gaede, brought out the red Jeep-turned-ambulance, and we all piled in.

We joggled along, trying to keep Mark and almost-three-year-old Chris Gronning from toppling into the cardboard box full of hot dogs, potato salad, canned peaches, and cupcakes. Baby Bethel Gronning hid her face in Margie's shoulder. Our destination was Picnic Point, about a mile and a half downriver and on a high bluff overlooking the Yukon.

A two-by-four-and-plywood table held our food, and we sat cross-legged on a blanket atop the thick moss; that is, when someone wasn't jumping up to keep a toddler from getting too close to the riverbank or the fire. Mark in particular seemed bent on crawling into the fire and screamed until his father held him nearby and let him throw in twigs. The fire crackled, and the smoke carried the aroma of cooked meat. I knew I'd like it here.

Picnic Point, Tanana, Alaska, Alice Peters, Margie Gronning, Roy Gronning with Bethel and Chris, Naomi Gaede, Ruby Gaede with Mark, Elmer Gaede, Ruth Gaede, 1957.

ABC

Ruby and I both desired relationships with the people in the village and an understanding of their culture. This part of Alaska was even more different from my upbringing in Ohio than was Valdez. We couldn't naturally meet neighbors by hanging out our laundry, going to the end of a driveway to pick up the morning paper—of which there was neither a driveway nor a paper—or bumping into someone in a drugstore or coffee shop. I met children's parents. Doc met sick or injured people. Ruby met the hospital staff.

In an attempt to get acquainted, Ruby and I walked to village homes, most along Back Street that ran parallel to Front Street, and knocked on doors. There were no telephones to call ahead; we could only hope the villagers were as interested in meeting us as we were them. In most cases, we were welcomed with bashful smiles—Ruby as the doctor's wife and I as the school teacher.

The cabins had low ceilings that helped contain the heat from the wood stoves, which were fashioned from 55-gallon oil barrels placed on their sides, fitted with metal legs, and cut open at one end for a door. Babies often swung from a hammock in a corner, whereas other family members slept together in beds along the side walls. When an infant fussed in the hammock during our conversation, the mother would give the suspended bed a gentle push, which would sway, and often the child would be lulled back to sleep. The plank floors were cold, so the children played on the beds. The aroma of wood fire, a cup of tea, and conversations that women of any place and culture could have about children, cooking, shopping, and homemaking tasks, made our visits fun and fulfilling.

Ruby was a nimble seamstress and stitcher and was particularly intrigued by the Athabascan beadwork. One cold, snowy day, she and I visited an older Indian woman we affectionately called Grandma Elia, who was making moose-skin slippers with decorated beaded tops for Ruby.

When we approached Grandma Elia's cabin, we spotted her sawing wood.

"Grandma, it is so cold out here," I called ahead. "Why don't you go inside and we will finish this for you?"

Ruby was a handy farm girl, but this was the initial experience for both of us with a cross-cut saw. First off, the saw bit into a log and got stuck. With some careful tugging, we managed to extricate the blade and start over.

"This is harder than I thought," said Ruby.

What a sight we novices must have been with our starts and stops and when, after much exertion and puffs of breath in the frosty air, we really hadn't done much more than make uneven scratches. Grandma Elia, who had been watching out the window, came out with instructions to help *us* as we struggled to help *her.*

I was glad the villagers accepted me. One intriguing village event was the potlatch, which took place after a successful hunt, in recognition of a person, or in connection with a funeral. I was eager to experience this and instructed to bring along my own bowl, a pie tin for meat, an eating utensil, and a small knife. I excitedly stepped out into temperatures that hovered around minus 40 degrees, switched on my flashlight, and walked to the community hall near the center of the village and down Back Street.

At this temperature, the dry-packed snow squeaked beneath my feet, and the hair in my nose stiffened. Axes and chainsaws were silent, and husky dogs lay curled into balls, their noses tucked into their tails. The snow glittered in the crystal-clear moonlight. I felt profoundly alive. In the consistent flow of letters from home, my parents expressed their amazement that, regardless of the temperatures, I continued to make my way outdoors. I noticed how the nurses who complained about the long, dark, cold winter frequently stayed in their rooms and battled depression. I figured a walk in the dim midday sunlight or the startling moonlight would have done them good. (In the future, this condition would be recognized as seasonal affective disorder (SAD), a contributor to mental and physical health problems of people in the North.)

When I entered the building, I spotted the Gaedes and the Gronnings sitting on the floor in one corner. The room was humid with the smell of wet moose-skin mukluks and cigarette smoke blended together with that of heating soup. I recognized students' parents and then found myself tugged on by children who wanted me to sit with them. It was a good feeling to be greeted so affectionately.

By the time the evening was out, I'd learned how to carve off bite-sized pieces of meat from the meat-and-bone portion I'd been given by the servers, who walked straight down the oil cloth on the floor; and I made a mental note to next time bring a salt shaker for the soup, which was a thick blend of vegetables, macaroni, and moose meat, but a bit flat and could have used some enhancement.

ABC

In spring, the village was rocked by earthquake after earthquake. With alarming frequency, we might have six to eight tremors in one day. The cracking and groaning sent shivers up my back and made my heart thump in my ears. The villagers said they'd never experienced so many before, which was no comfort to the rest of us. In my classroom, I noticed dust sifting through the air after a jolt, and I wondered about the effect on the building. In short order, Mr. Windsor, the BIA supervisor, flew into the village. I expected that he and Florence needed privacy for conducting business, so I went about straightening up my classroom. It wasn't long before Florence marched in.

"Miss Bortel, would you please come into my living quarters?" she said stiffly. "I think you'll be interested in what Mr. Windsor has to say."

When I entered the kitchen, Florence had a strange look on her face. Without any social preface, Mr. Windsor stood up, shook my hand, and tersely announced, "The school is condemned and, therefore, closed."

Neither Florence nor I could utter a word. Everyone knew that the antiquated building needed foundation repairs, but to close on such short notice and with six more weeks in the semester seemed impossible. I felt as though I'd been slapped in the face, and I stood there, blinking my eyes.

Florence regained her composure before I did. She replied firmly, "We cannot close school this quickly. We must have school on Monday so we can pass out grade cards."

Following this unexpected turn of events, I never knew what the mail would bring. The commissioner wrote that he didn't know the school had been closed without prior notice. He assured me that the Territorial Department of Education would protect me and that I'd still be paid for the final six weeks. A letter from the certification supervisor followed with this information:

> At a recent supervisory meeting the closing of the Tanana Day School and your reassignment for the coming year were discussed. We have recently received notification of a vacancy at the Bettles Field School. Because of the new building which is to be constructed this summer, with a one bedroom school apartment, this is considered a choice assignment. The building is scheduled to be completed by October 1. There will be an approximate enrollment of seventeen. If you accept this assignment, please let us know as soon as possible and an amended contract will be made for you.

I knew that $98,000 had been appropriated for the Bettles school, which was directly north, on the Koyukuk (KOY-yuh-kuck) River, and just into the Arctic Circle. The new venture was enticing, but the end of the story had not been written.

Before I flew back to Ohio for the summer, Dr. Gaede and Mr. Isaac had put their heads together to figure out how to make school happen not only for the Gaede girls but the rest of the village. Doc had discovered that Quonset huts, which functioned as barracks for the workers who had installed a Defense Early Warning (DEW) system on the hill behind the village would be available.

When I returned in autumn, five of these road-wide structures had been transported down and positioned on the vacant lot between the school and a neighboring house. The windowless 24-by-18-foot, khaki-colored, semi-cylindrical shelters had doors at each end, but no plumbing, no wiring, and no heat. They really weren't much more than tents.

Prior to my leaving in May, Florence had taken a teaching position in Barrow. Subsequently, Mr. Isaac had offered me the position of head teacher for the Tanana school with the responsibility to hire two more teachers. He had also shown me the architectural plans for the new school. But, for this time, I had to magically make an educational facility rise up from the dust. Fortunately, the extreme pioneer setting didn't daunt my new co-teachers, and with humor and fortitude, they jumped in beside me.

The previous year, Miss Feldkirchner had persuaded me to start a school newspaper, which was actually the only newspaper for the village. In October 1958 issue of *The Northern Lights*, student writer Larry Grant introduced the teachers:

Meet the Teachers

Miss Harriet Amundson is from McGregor, Minnesota and is a graduate of Greenville College, Greenville, Illinois. She made her first trip to Alaska when she came to Tanana August 30. She thinks winters here will be like winters in Minn. She teaches 3rd and 4th grades during the day and works on the school stoves in the evening.

Mr. Herman Romer is from Bethel, Alaska. Last year he taught in Naknek. Mr. Romer attended school in Texas and is a graduate of the University of Alaska. Mr. Romer teaches the upper grades during the day and works on school stoves in the evenings.

Neither of the fresh-faced teachers in their early twenties was unfamiliar with brutal winters, hard work, or difficult situations that required digging deep within oneself for resources to survive. Before the new school was completed, these character traits were severely tested.

Inadequately designed narrow three-quarter-inch copper tubing carried the oil from the outdoor tanks into the huts and to the stoves. When temperatures sunk to 30, 40, and 50 degrees below zero, the oil thickened and would eventually freeze.

"We have to tap the lines to keep the oil flowing," I told my colleagues. "And we have to do this every few hours."

Sometimes we all bundled up, stumbled out into the bitter darkness, shuffled through deep snow, and pounded together. Other times, we set our alarms and each took a shift. For me, the New Year did not start with a celebration but with body-shaking tears. At 3:00 a.m., I collapsed in bed, chilled to the bone and utterly worn out. I had reached the end of my rope and had no reserve to cope with one more minute of this pioneer life. Harriet numbly struggled with the lines at 4:00 a.m. Temperatures were freezing outdoors and now sunk lower inside our Quonset. She desperately fought to restore some heat. Herman quietly carried our potatoes and onions to his place, which still had heat, to keep them from freezing. Our fortitude was freezing to a standstill in the winter battle.

ABC

1741	Russian navigators, Chirikov and Bering, discover Alaska
1784	First settlement on Kodiak Island
1867	Russia sold Alaska to the United States for $7,200,000
1848-1914	Gold strikes and rushes
1959	Statehood, January 3

"The new school windows are here, and Alaska is a state!" I hurried into the hut. The floor shook beneath my feet.

Harriet steadied her cocoa.

"Let's have a party!" The good news about both these events rejuvenated my spirits.

On February 1, 1959, our frantic and all-consuming attention to staying warm in the tent encampment ended. I stood inside the sparkling new teacherage, overcome with emotion, and even though my smile stretched well into my cheeks, I felt my eyes tear up from both relief and exhaustion. Before me were double kitchen sinks, Formica countertops, a floor that was level and solid, real cupboards, and a utility room with a washer and dryer.

The following day, the children carried their school supplies from the dark, dusty Quonsets to their never-before-used school desks in the modern school. They walked silently into the school, and, awestruck, they whispered softly as they appraised their spacious, tall-ceiling classrooms. Herman, Harriet, and I each had our own room with windows across one side and a blackboard with bulletin boards stretching across the other. The rooms were joined end to end, and Herman's and Harriet's were connected by accordion-folded partitions that, when pulled back, transformed their classrooms into an auditorium. Across the hall, the boys and girls each had their own *indoor* bathrooms. I had my own office and would no longer share a teaching space with office supplies and files.

Parents toured the new facility, pulled along by their children, and the building became a regular stop for visiting health care officials. There weren't many places to go or see in the village besides another person's home, so this fresh construction, which changed the landscape of Tanana, became both a getaway and a sightseeing destination.

On one such occasion, Mary Ann Burroughs, the director of nurses, introduced me to Barbara Reid, the new public health nurse, who, along with her supervisor, Fran, traveled among the villages. We like-minded, independent women who had sought out life in the Last Frontier had a stimulating conversation, the kind that goads one in positive directions.

Ever since I'd come to Alaska, I'd wondered what lay farther north. At first, *farther north* meant north of Valdez; now, *farther north* meant up where Eskimos lived. Fran told me about Anaktuvuk (An-ak-TU-vuk) Pass, an area so remote that not only were there no roads leading to it, but no river or ocean access. A bush pilot could take his chances in the summer, or wait until winter when a small, nearby lake froze. That part of the Arctic Circle didn't exactly invite anyone to come and live; well, anyone who relied on transportation other than his or her own feet or a dog sled.

Her gleaned information came from proposals for medical research of those people. Apparently, there were several nomadic groups totaling around a hundred Nunamiut (NOON-a-mute) Eskimos who followed migrating caribou herds in the pass. These inland people had only been discovered recently, during the war years, and were unique because the majority of Eskimos lived along the coast.

From what I gathered, the landscape was barren, with no trees or much vegetation. Fran wasn't sure what the people lived in since there were no logs for cabins. Perhaps they used sod. There was no school, but some of the children had been sent to a boarding school in Wrangell, in southeastern Alaska. After witnessing how homesick their children became and how vulnerable they were to outside influences, such as alcohol, the parents stopped sending them away for education. They desired their own school. Even though there were numerous unknowns, these details and images widened the gap for me to see an opportunity to teach farther north.

ABC

With the relocation from the shelter wells to the state-of-the-art (for Alaska) school and teacherage, I consciously appreciated the conveniences, warmth, and ease of teaching in Tanana. Ironically, my interest of teaching in a place with no actual accommodations and in a location so remote that even when it was a destination for a scientist or hunter, it could easily be flown over because it was so invisible in the wilds, did not subside. It didn't help that Fran had recognized my aspiration to go to Anaktuvuk Pass and, before she'd left, she'd suggested, "Why don't you join me and another nurse, Beverly, when we assist Dr. Gaede on his medical field trip? You can fly with Dr. Gaede and cook for our team."

When I asked Doc, he welcomed the company. "Just think what an adventure it would be." That pretty well summed up how he framed everything in life. His prescription for adventure was being a bush pilot doctor in Alaska.

When I requested a leave of absence, Mr. Isaac granted it with a telegram.

> Administrative leave authorized; Employ substitute if possible. Please submit report on number, names, ages, grades of pupils available for a school in Anaktuvuk Pass. Also any information pertinent to starting a school.

Now, not only was I compelled by personal curiosity, but I had an assignment. My questions grew each day. I learned that Reverend John Chambers, the Presbyterian missionary in Barrow, flew in, weather permitting, to hold church services at Anaktuvuk Pass. I wrote him and explained my educational interests. He responded, "In July, we expect to complete the floor in a newly constructed log church Perhaps this would be suitable for secondary use as a school."

ABC

Finally, April 21 arrived, the day to fly farther north, in fact, 180 miles north of the Arctic Circle. I bundled up, carried a compact bag of personal items, and met Doc at his red Family Cruiser on skis, which was parked below the riverbank in front of the hospital. He stood awkwardly, with most of his weight on his right leg, and shoved a pair of crutches behind the backseat. Ruby stood nearby, her lips tightly closed. She glanced at me and shook her head

"Doc, how are you going to fly with your pain?" I asked.

"I guess you'll have to take over if there's a problem." He pasted a grin on his face and tried to minimize the seriousness of the situation.

He'd been plagued with sciatic nerve flare-ups and had struggled to simply maintain a normal work week at the hospital. To get any relief, he had to lie completely prone. Now, he'd be tucked into a seated position—if he could even get into the plane. He turned away from us and struggled to lift his leg to the step-rung. I couldn't fathom how he'd walk in snow with crutches.

We flew to Bettles Field, approximately 125 miles directly north, where Doc refueled and checked on weather conditions at Anaktuvuk.

"Andy Anderson, who built this lodge and is a bush pilot who frequently flies this area, says there's a plane missing out there," reported Doc. "So, keep an eye out. He also says to watch carefully for the village or we'll mistake the houses for clods of dirt."

Only 100 miles and we'd get to this mysterious spot that wasn't more than just another mountain pass on the maps.

The winding John River guided us north to the entry of the Brooks Range, which opened to a valley several miles wide. Trees disappeared, and all that remained were shadowy patches of willows. Granite mountains with icy peaks rose on either side. No spruce covered, or softened their raw edges. My adrenalin raced and I sat transfixed at this very new world in front of me.

At about 10:30 a.m., Doc dipped the plane wing. "I think we've found our village," he said over the engine's roar. "Let's look for a place to land."

Anaktuvuk Pass (village), Alaska, 1959.

All I could see were smoke spirals from what looked like softened cupcakes.

He made a low pass over the settlement and opened the throttle. People popped out everywhere at the roar overhead.

"They're pointing," said Doc. "The landing area must be over there. The lake."

The plane bobbed in the wind.

"Could be a rough landing."

I hung on, but was too excited to be afraid. After several sharp jolts we slid to a stop.

ABC

Adults and children arrived, panting from the exertion of pushing against the wind. The stark setting was punctuated by their rosy-cheeked smiles and the Eskimo women and children's colorful cloth-covered parkas. Everyone's fur-edged hoods blew this way and that in the stiff gale.

Doc reached across and opened the door. I swung one leg over the door jamb to the hooked rung before pulling myself out. Doc followed hesitantly, sucking in his breath several times. Once on the ground, he smiled genially and awkwardly moved toward the small group.

"I am Doctor Gaede." He pronounced the words slowly and pointed to himself. "This is Anna Bortel."

I nodded and then reached into the backseat to haul out his medical bag and other supplies. Two men and an older boy reached forward to carry the boxes.

We followed our welcoming committee to a nearby Quonset hut that had been erected by the Air Force Medics. I had no idea how it had shown up here.

A generator produced flickering light from the bulbs hanging from the ceiling, and a space heater brought up the temperature to *only* chilly. The floor moved up and down whenever anyone moved.

Fran and Beverly, who had arrived earlier, had already given skin tests for tuberculosis. Fran appeared as if she was working in a city clinic and wore smart winter boots with short heels. Never mind the uneven plywood floor, canvas walls, and a spindly folding table for supplies; she was dressed as a professional and went about her work quietly.

Beverly was more practical. Her reddish-brown hair was pulled into pigtails, and she wore flat-bottomed leather boots. She engaged the patients. Even though most of them couldn't understand English, they could interpret her motions and exaggerated faces. She was having fun.

Several wide-planked benches were against the rounded walls, but as patients arrived, many chose to sit on the floor. They watched us curiously, leaned toward one another, and interspersed giggles in their soft murmurings. Fran and Beverly prepared to administer polio shots. Doc got busy behind an area partitioned with a hanging blanket.

"Hey, Anna," said Beverly, looking over her shoulder. "Lend us a hand. You can practice your cursive on these immunizations cards."

I tried to communicate with everyone, even if they couldn't understand my English words or I their Eskimo. They laughed easily and often and seemed to take this new experience in stride.

One older Eskimo woman, Mae Kakinya (Kaa-KIN-yah), and her husband, Elijah, who lived farther north, heard that the doctor was coming and traveled miles by dog sled for a medical examination. Elijah spoke some English and explained this to us when they walked in, speckled with snow.

"Hello," I said to Mae. "It's cold out there, isn't it?"

Elijah and Mae Kakinya, Anaktuvuk Pass, Alaska, 1959.

She stared at me blankly and then faced her husband. Elijah spoke to her in Eskimo. Without hesitation, she pulled her heavy caribou parka over her head and sat down to wait. Beneath this outerwear, she had on a dark, floral cotton dress open at the neck. When her turn came to be examined and she was asked to remove her dress to facilitate the examination, she glanced from Doc to me and then, apparently not comprehending what we had said, took hold of either side of the neckline and, in one swift motion, ripped the dress apart from top to bottom. My jaw dropped in astonishment. Doc didn't miss a beat and acted as though this happened every day. He pressed his stethoscope to her chest and continued with his exam.

ABC

The sixty-something year-old trader from Canada, Pat O'Connell, the only white person living in the village, had invited us over for Irish stew. Fran was worn out from the day and wanted to climb into her sleeping bag with a book. Beverly hovered over the camp stove with a can opener, deciding what she might throw into the skillet. Doc and I could not pass up the opportunity to see more of Anaktuvuk Pass, even if he had to limp and grimace to get here. At least the wind was at our backs. We set out for the village.

Pat's one-room house was three-quarters of a mile south of the Quonset and on the north edge of the village, just across a frozen creek. A kerosene lamp provided the only light in the small confinement, and the corners of the room retreated into dimness. It was probably better that way since there were cardboard and Blazo boxes helter-skelter with ammunition, books, worn-out magazines, dirty clothes, and indiscernible items made of caribou. In spite of his housekeeping clutter, his cooking skills excelled, or at least the pot with caribou, potatoes, and onions did.

"Of course it's made from caribou!" Pat laughed at our question.

We savored every morsel of the tasty dinner while he talked without stopping. We were fascinated by his tales of survival of the fittest. This immense Brooks Range dared men to research and hunt, and then either swallowed them into the infinite and identical valleys or sucked life out of them with bitter winds and slow starvation.

"When that bear finished him off, there was nothing left. Not a bone. Nothing." Pat took a spoonful of stew. "Now, would you like some more coffee?"

His stories sent chills down my back, but at the same time I wanted to hear more.

"Hey, Pat." A voice and a rap at the door brought in another guest.

The man stood with shoulders hunched as if he was frozen to the core. "Do you have some coffee?"

He was dressed from head to toe in animal skins, and at first glance, he appeared to be one of the Natives. But, when he pushed back his parka hood, we could see that he was as white as we were; and when he spoke, he was undeniably educated outside the village.

Pat introduced him as a scientist from Arctic Research who had just arrived by dog team. "Boyd's been around these parts for the past ten years, checking out wildlife and taking reports to Anchorage."

Once Boyd had a chipped coffee mug in his hand, he elaborated on his work. In a momentary pause, he turned to me and asked, "So, Anna, what do you do when you're not assisting Dr. Gaede?"

"Actually, I'm a school teacher in Tanana, and right now, I'm doing a survey about potential students here in Anaktuvuk," I explained.

He might have been doing the same thing for ten freezing years, but his fervor had not chilled. When he found out I was a school teacher, he and Pat tangled into a debate.

"The BIA says it is too inaccessible to put a school here," said Pat. "Besides, they doubt they could find anyone to teach."

"They can always send their children to boarding school," Boyd reminded us.

"That's true, but when they've done that, their kids have been exposed to liquor, which the adults all oppose," argued Pat. He acted as though these people belonged to him and he knew what was best for them.

"But one has to wonder about starting a school if the people keep following the caribou rather than settling into one place," said the scientist.

A noise outside interrupted the conversation. It was Simon Paneak, the leader of the village. His glasses steamed up when he entered the room, and he pulled them from his face. The large-boned man moved straight toward me and held out a letter.

"You read," he said, and then he didn't say another word.

I read it aloud. The letter informed the village that there was no room for their children at the boarding school in Wrangell.

Simon Paneak looked at me. "We have twenty to thirty children. No school. We want school. You tell Department of Education we want school. Maybe they listen then. Maybe you come teach?"

I sat, stunned. *Could I make it in such an isolated village? And how did he know I was a school teacher?*

Boyd continued his argument. "How can supplies be brought in? Only small planes can land on the frozen lake in the winter or with floats on the lake in the summer."

"We want school. Our children need education," Simon said, unwavering.

Simon had a distinct presence. He spoke with authority and didn't argue but wouldn't back down either. I found out later that scientists who visited the village routinely hired him to teach them about the Nunamiut culture and traditions as well as wildlife in the Brooks Range.

"Okay, Anna. You go write a report to the Department of Education, and I will build a schoolhouse," said Pat.

Once again, Boyd vigorously protested.

Pat barged in. "We have to plan ahead. There are trees about forty miles away, and they need to be cut when the sap is running, say about

June or July. Then they have to season until winter. Since we couldn't get them anyway until dog sleds could haul them back, that would work out just fine."

My mind reeled. I felt as though I'd been flooded with a month of information, and even so, the day was not over.

ABC

Rev. John Chambers's trip to Anaktuvuk Pass coincided fortuitously with ours, and a church service was to be held in the chapel that evening. Doc and I climbed a hill to the log church, which was an anomaly in the conglomeration of thick sod houses we saw everywhere else. The silver corrugated-metal roof was topped with a thin, white wood cross that shivered in the wind, but had somehow been anchored securely, so there was no danger of it flying from its prominent position. This could not have been an afterthought. The wind had blown noticeably and forcefully since we'd arrived, and Doc expressed concern frequently for his airplane.

We entered the church through a porch-like room. In small communities, word of a newcomer travels faster than the wind, and here the wind blew with vigor. The people inside could guess immediately that we were the doctor and teacher who had just flown in. By the same token, we didn't have to guess who the white man near the pulpit was either.

"Hi. Anna Bortel and Dr. Gaede?"

"Hello. Reverend John Chambers?

We shook hands and laughed at the obvious. The flying missionary was cordial, unassuming, and around thirty years old.

Between thirty and forty adults and children crowded into the tight quarters. Doc and I didn't see any chairs or even perimeter benches like those in our Tanana community hall. Willow branches were scattered on the floor. People smiled at us, spoke some words in Eskimo, and then sat down on the branches. We glanced at each other and followed suit, which was easier for me than for Doc, with his sciatic affliction, but he managed.

The service began with a familiar hymn, and hearty singing filled the room.

Who taught these men to sing bass? I wondered. *And their brown hymn books look just like the ones I grew up with!*

Apparently, it had been months since the itinerant minister had been there, and the service was a catch-up of infant baptism, adult baptism, communion, and church membership. Although absorbed in the fervency of the experience, when the service concluded at 10:30 p.m., we stiffly stretched to an upright position. So far, Doc hadn't needed crutches, which was an answer to *our* prayer.

Doc and I left the church just as the sun settled behind a mountain range, leaving behind a trail of pink. From the opposite range, an enormous, full, silvery moon glided into view. I felt dwarfed by the magnitude of the mountains and the breadth of the pass.

That night, I couldn't fall asleep, and it wasn't only the unusual accommodations. What bothered me were the swarming thoughts and arguments I couldn't seem to stop.

Why am I drawn to this village? I love Tanana and my friends there. But this village needs a school teacher, and I'm acquainted with bush teaching. I'm even accustomed to crude conditions. Yet, I would be so alone here with no white women to share with. What if I got sick in this isolated place? Where does God want me? Near dawn, I relinquished my anxiety to the Almighty.

The next day, the medical team continued examinations and I talked school business with Pat. As before, we discussed the building material problem. He pointed out that the only growing shrubbery around Anaktuvuk was the shoulder-high willow bushes that the Eskimos depleted for firewood, their only source of heat.

Doc completed his work, and I visited homes to obtain the requested educational information. Fran and Beverly had arranged for a chartered bush pilot to pick them up, and we said good-byes. Doc and I wandered through the village and snapped pictures before our own departure. A man saw us and invited us into his sod house. The low ceiling, dirt floor with willow branches, pile of caribou skins, and small stove provided the very basic of necessities to stay warm and out of the elements.

The little children, who knew few English words, appeared wherever I walked and called out in sweet voices, "You teacher! You teacher!" I fought against letting my mind wander into the "what if?" but all the same—I couldn't help but love these cheerful prospective students who appeared untouched by the world's superficial distractions and undesirable habits.

The adults seemed pleased to show off their culture. Mothers carried their babies on their backs, inside their cozy, fur-lined parkas. A belt, on the outside of the mother's parka, and below the baby's bottom, kept the child warm and secure above her waist line, I asked a mother to demonstrate taking her little one out of this cocoon and took a movie of the procedure. In a smooth motion, she gracefully leaned over from the waist, reached back and guided her baby up her back until his little head poked out of by her parka hood. She then moved into a squatting position and swung the little guy out and around to her lap. We gasped. He was naked from the waist down. The tyke blinked in the sunshine and the brisk wind as the mother wiped caribou hair from his face.

"Put him back. Oh, put him back," I exclaimed.

She reloaded him by bending over to let gravity help him slide up her back.

Pat caught up with us before we started the mile walk to the airplane.

"The children who have gone out to school have received excellent grades," said Pat. "They're a smart group, and they'd work hard for a teacher. Think about it, Anna."

From conversations the previous evening and the visits in the homes, I was convinced that a school was crucial. But could I *live* here? By most standards, Tanana was in the sticks, but this place didn't even have many sticks. I'd seen firsthand what it was like: nothing more than sod houses and meat caches suspended on stilts. No school, no FAA, no medical facilities. I'd asked questions. Pat's trading post randomly stocked rolled oats, flour, sugar, tea, coffee, Pilot Boy crackers, and canned milk. Every now and then, a jar of peanut butter or box of cornmeal showed up, or perhaps a jar of jam. Homer Mekiana's (Mek-ee-ANA) home-based post office received and sent mail whenever a bush pilot showed up, which was not more than once a week. What Anaktuvuk Pass *did* have was a group of people who were highly motivated to support my efforts.

The logical facts of impossibility aligned themselves on one side of my mental ledger, yet when adults and children jostled around us, I was swayed to the illogical.

Just as the villagers had braved the chill to greet us, so they also accompanied us back to the plane. Their faces were blushed from the cold and wind, but their dark eyes were warm. "You a teacher," echoed in my ears as I climbed into the airplane. I'd wanted to go north, but could I make it this far north?

Future scholar at Anaktuvuk Pass, Alaska, 1959.

ABC

When we arrived back at Tanana, I headed straight for my bathroom with running water, flush toilet, and bathtub. What luxuries!

And then I wrote Mr. Isaac with the offer to open a school for the Nunamiut Eskimos in Anaktuvuk Pass. He contended that after my year assembling a tent village school, living in drafty huts, and working on obstinate fuel lines, I should just rest. As much as I protested that I'd fully recovered from that trauma, he wouldn't budge. "No frontier experiences for you right now. You need a rest. Stay with the new school. You deserve it."

I flew home to Ohio for the summer with visions of teaching chubby-cheeked Eskimo children how to speak English and how to write their names.

ABC

When I returned to Tanana in the fall, the school still smelled new. The furnace ran robustly and without ceasing into the winter, a little café opened at the airport with hamburgers and pie, and there was talk of telephone service becoming available to connect Tanana with places outside the village. Life was very good in Tanana.

At the end of January, I'd read in the *Fairbanks Daily News-Miner* that the state legislature had approved appropriations for additional schools, with $90,000 designated for Anaktuvuk Pass.

Maybe my assessment had a part in that decision, I'd reasoned. *I wonder when that project will start.* I felt as impatient as Anna Hugo, a teenager who wrote me from Anaktuvuk Pass after I visited. "Well I wish you could come all right. Hope they build the school fast so you could come faster."

As much as I'd dreamed about teaching at Anaktuvuk and I cherished the field trip to the village, I was taken unaware when, in mid-February, I received a large packet of forms and a letter stating that if I wanted to open a school in Anaktuvuk, I should order the necessary supplies. I was speechless. I had just finished the Tanana school inventory and the requisitioning for the next school year.

The implications of choosing to go to this desolate outpost weren't only for me personally. Mr. Isaac informed me that if I took the assignment, there *would* be school. Otherwise, he doubted they'd find another teacher. No Miss Bortel, no school. Education for the Nunamiuts rested squarely and heavily on my shoulders. Simon Paneak's face flashed before me.

I replied in the affirmative. Anaktuvuk Pass would be the next venture in my Alaska experiences.

There were many obstacles and a plethora of details to work out. For one thing, the Anaktuvuk Pass school term would begin June 1, which would nearly overlap with the Tanana school year end. Another complication was the school building. The Anaktuvuk school would not be completed by the June 1 opening day. Mr. Isaac included a copy of the letter he'd sent to Rev. John Chambers to ask if the offer of the chapel for school purposes was still available. Obviously, all Pat O'Connell's talk of building me a school was just big-shot talk.

Letters flew back and forth among Mr. Isaac, John Chambers, and me; and then we added Bob Ahgook (AHH-gok), president of the Anaktuvuk Village Council, and Sig Wien to our frenetic correspondence. The later was one of several brothers who launched Wien Airlines and made the navy-blue-winged planes a common and welcome sight to Natives, hunters, missionaries, and all folk in the isolated villages. Transportation of educational and construction supplies posed a major difficulty. Anaktuvuk

Pass had no airstrip and, subsequently, no regular air service. Bush planes landed at the same lake where Doc had set down, which was a mile away. Distance wasn't the only issue. The lake thawed in July. This meant that a plane couldn't land on skis, yet there was too much ice for a plane to land with floats. Even so, the state department agreed to provide fuel oil for the church as a temporary school, but transporting 55-gallon drums would require more than a bush plane. Officials from Wien Airline informed us of good and bad news. There was a lake large enough for a DC-3, but that was sixteen miles away. This brought the discussion back to distance of any kind; no matter if it was one or sixteen miles: the village had no vehicles, only people power, dogs, and sleds to transport everything, of which the sleds were virtually useless unless there was snow on the ground.

Every time we figured out a creative solution, something else crept onto the horizon. Where would I live? Once again, John Chambers came up with an answer. A one-room, 10-by-12-foot log cabin awaited my arrival. This tiny dwelling would be 200 feet from the chapel-schoolhouse. John wondered if the Juneau office wanted him to run electricity from the church to my place. Throughout our feverish problem-solving, I realized that John Chambers and Sig Wien had deep personal interests in the inland Eskimos of Anaktuvuk Pass. What I didn't realize was that our initial concerns were only the tip of the iceberg in what I'd be facing.

ABC

Teaching in Tanana concluded with a farewell party at the community hall for all of us teachers. The evening was filled with cake and coffee, embraces, handshakes, and words of appreciation. I hung on to the poignant moments and then broke down in tears. Leaving was harder than I'd expected.

Herman had requested to stay at Tanana, and Harriet was assigned the school at Huslia (HOOS-lee-a), northwest of Tanana, on the Koyukuk River. Within days of completing the Tanana school year, my plane took off for Anaktuvuk Pass.

PART IV

1960

A WILLOW FIRE, CREEK
WATER, AND TWO-HOLER

I tore two sheets of three-by-five-inch paper from my note pad.

May 1960

Dear Folks,

Right now, I'm flying from Bettles Field to Anaktuvuk Pass. Andy,[3] the pilot, is my age, but already gray. Seems to really care about the Eskimos in this village.

It is beautiful here in the Brooks Range. The broad valleys are edged with steep wind-buffed sides and rising cliffs. We're past the tree line and the dense black spruce forests have slowly diminished into rare clumps of trees and finally given up to shrubby growth. I can hardly imagine that I won't see another tree until I come out in December! The John River bending below us is flowing, but it will be frozen by the time we reach our destination. In this expansive isolation, and in a four-mile wide valley, Anaktuvuk Pass (village) sits like an outpost …I expected my groceries to travel with me from Bettles, but they had not yet arrived from Fairbanks… I sent a message to Homer Mekiana at Anaktuvuk so he'd know I'd be on the mail plane. Homer, is the village post master and also the elder in charge of church programs while John Chambers, the itinerant minister, is away

Andy just nudged me. Better close so he can take this back with him.

I'M HERE!!!!

We circled to land. Bursts of bright parkas ran toward the frozen lake. The small plane skidded to a stop, and when the propeller stopped rotating, smiling faces pushed forward. Although the sun shone brightly, the wind tossed about parka fur ruffs. Shivers ran down my back when I opened the plane door. Anna Hugo, the soft-spoken teenager who had written to me after my visit with the medical team, edged through the small throng and shyly extended a pair of black rubber boots. The tundra was thawing, and rivulets of smelted snow dampened the ground. I appreciated her thoughtfulness, but there was one problem: the boots must have been a size five, and I wore a size ten. I was not the Cinderella she expected.

We'd landed on the still-frozen Eleanor Lake, also referred to as Summit Lake, where Doc Gaede and I had landed for our field trip. Notwithstanding the mile to the village, men and boys readily carried my boxes to the miniature sod-roofed log cabin I was to call home. This structure was a rarity. It took a forty mile dogsled ride to obtain such timber of any kind other than thin willows. Pat O'Connell had recently built the cabin and now rented it to me for $50 a month.

Homer Mekiana opened the door, stooped, stepped inside, and beckoned me to follow. The quiet and dignified man stood with hands folded, not saying a word, while I looked around. Linoleum covered the floor. The primary furniture, which had been shipped out by the State Department of Education, consisted of a dinette set with a pair of vinyl-seated metal chairs; a sofa bed; and a wall cupboard that rested on the floor, ready to be hung. Two low, plastic-covered windows let in muted light. The wood-burning stove, which was a 55-gallon barrel cut in half with a flat metal top, would serve for both cooking and heat. Since wood was scarce, Mr. Isaac was considering getting me a small oil cook stove with the dual purpose of furnace. For the time being, shoulder-height willows along the stream were my fuel source.

A stream of helpers placed my belongings on the floor and within the120-square-foot cabin, small piles started to grow. I paid my helpers for their work and felt embarrassed as they glanced around the room before leaving.

I wish I would have sold more of my belongings.

Anna Hugo remained behind the others.

Pat, my new landlord, poked his head in the cabin. His lined and weathered face reflected the wear and tear in these regions.

"Anna, why don't you and Anna Hugo come over for lunch?"

"Oh, Pat! I'd appreciate that so much. It's obvious that I'm not quite set up for meal-making yet." This was an understatement. It wasn't as though there was a café nearby, or a river for barge delivery. I needed to figure out quickly how to provide for my needs. "Give me a few minutes and I'll be over."

For starters, I wanted to chase the chill out of the cabin with a fire. The villagers had hospitably stacked willow twigs and branches outside my door, with which I commenced my first fire-making.

After sparks resulted only in puffs of smoke, Anna Hugo suggested softly, "Pull the coals up to the front of the stove, and then lay your willows on."

This simple act of kindness was the beginning of a deep relationship with the serious and intellectually inquiring girl.

Her instructions worked perfectly. The only trouble was that the twigs burned so quickly that I'd have to feed the fire every ten minutes if I wanted consistent heat.

"Let's go eat," I finally said.

Pat's house was near the bridge that crossed Contact (Kayuk) Creek, a perfect location for someone interested in everyone's comings and goings. It was like living in an intersection. Anyone who landed on the lake had to cross the bridge. Anyone who hunted or picked berries to the north crossed the bridge. The log house I rented from him was a stone's throw away from his. Both houses were down the hill from the chapel, about 200 to 250 feet away. He had built mine as a retirement house for an Eskimo who was working in the hospital in Anchorage. The Eskimos' sod house settlement was a short distance to the south and east.

Since I'd eaten stew at Pat's with Doc, I expected to walk into a one-room house. I didn't expect to walk in and find that he'd wallpapered his room and painted his support beams; nor did I anticipate finding three plates sitting on the floor.

"My floor is as clean as any table," he asserted, seeing my surprise.

At that moment, I didn't care. The room was filled with the smell of something delicious, and my stomach growled. It seemed incongruent that a man who could serve up a scrumptious meal of caribou and gravy with chunks of onion and potatoes, could appear so malnourished. Maybe he used up the nutrients just trying to stay warm.

Pat functioned as a combined realtor and visitor center in his information-giving, and the conversation flowed to what I'd need in this place devoid of what many people deemed necessities. He also revealed that in September, he would turn sixty-five and would leave the village. If that were true, except for numerous scientists who came and went, I'd be the only white person permanently living in the village of Nunamiut Eskimos.

When we left his place, he handed me a loaf of prune bread. I was grateful for anything that would help sustain me during this awkward transitional stage.

Anna's cache and outhouse, Anaktuvuk Pass, Alaska, 1960.

First, Pat showed me the outhouse he'd built to accompany my rental cabin. Lack of lumber prompted ingenuity. He had used poles for a frame, packing boxes for the enclosure, and a caribou skin for the door; a thoughtful act of generosity. Even with this convenience, I imagined there would be some days or nights when I wouldn't want to struggle against the wind and cold, so I'd brought along my *white elephant* chamber pot. Electricity did not come in the housing package either, unless we strung wire from the chapel. As in the shelter wells, *I* would be the running water. Fortunately, the creek flowed about sixty feet away.

Later in the day, my school janitor, Frank Rulland, wanted to show me how to fish for grayling in this same creek.

"Watch me," said the handsome older man. "Hold it like this."

Without waiting, I threw in my line just as he was starting to demonstrate and coach me on the proper technique. A second later, I felt a tug and pulled in a fish.

"Oh! I never expected that!" I said, pleased with my immediate victory.

His jaw tensed, and he frowned beneath his short, black moustache. Without saying another word, he turned aside and made an easy cast. I hadn't meant to disappointment him. I'd fished before, plus, a fish had been in the right spot at the right time, but apparently, I'd circumvented Frank's desire to impress me.

All in all, the day ended with a wonderment of success and information.

The following morning, I set out to reduce my pile of boxes. I was assessing my mountainous task when I heard a knock. I opened the door to three men with rough outdoor jackets and heavy boots. They ducked their heads in the crowded entryway. When I invited them in, they seemed to fill up half my little house. A quick introduction let me know the burly fellow was Sig Wien. The barrel-chested man with short hair beneath his cap silently surveyed the room. I felt embarrassed by such a surplus of belongings. Then he removed his cap, fingered it with both hands, and shifted his weight.

"I've heard about you," he said, and then paused.

The other men looked expectantly for him to continue. He didn't elaborate, but what he did say was brief and genuine.

"I hear that of any school teacher, you have the best chance of making it up here in this environment, and with the odds against you. I know these people. They will work hard for you. Thank you for making personal sacrifices. I wish you well."

That was it. Before I could engage him in more conversation, he turned and followed his companions out the door.

At that moment, I didn't realize how instrumental he had been in the struggle for education in Anaktuvuk. Fifteen years earlier, in 1945, bad weather had grounded Sig at Chandler Lake, forty miles east of what would become the village of Anaktuvuk Pass. A band of inland Eskimos, future Anaktuvuk people, were camped there. This chance meeting was the beginning of a deep alliance. Sig took it upon himself to connect the Eskimos with non-Natives, such as whalers, who would exchange rice, sugar, and ammunition for furs. The benevolent Norwegian's interests were more than a mercenary; consequently, he endeared himself to the Nunamiuts, who trusted him to assist in their goals. In particular, they expressed their desire for education for their children, knowing full well that speaking English was a necessary asset to successfully trading with non-Natives.

Sig had listened quietly and hadn't let them down. In May of 1948, he arrived at Anaktuvuk Pass with a bilingual Eskimo teacher from Barrow. For six weeks, she taught all the villagers. Following this, a young couple from Barrow was sent in. The rigorous living conditions interfered with their teaching efficiency, and the endeavor lasted only six weeks. Unsuccessful attempts at starting a school persisted.

Later, reflecting on Sig's determination to provide these people with consistent education, it dawned on me that Sig, on this impromptu visit, was not looking at my conglomeration of boxes but instead, he was inspecting *me* to see if I could fulfill his expectations as a teacher. He'd had a mission. Had he accomplished it with my arrival? Time would tell, with everyone being the judge.

Little about this experiment would be conventional. To accommodate the Nunamiut's survival and sustenance requirements, which included a traditional pattern of winter hunting and wood gathering, school would commence with a summer term and then be let out for *timber time* between November and February. Without vehicles, roads, or a waterway, the Nunamiut relied on dogs and sleds for trapping to the south and bringing in logs. These sustenance activities were only possible when there was adequate snow on the ground for sled runners. This was similar to that of 19th century America, when classroom time was adapted to the agrarian needs of planting in spring and harvesting in fall.

Here, that meant school would start in June. To meet this timetable, I needed to transform the log chapel into a classroom; even before that, I wanted to make sense of my new living situation. I turned around and around in the constricted space, trying new arrangements and angles to make my conglomeration of boxes, housekeeping supplies, and daily living provisions fit and still allow me room to move about. After a while, my creativity ebbed and my inquisitiveness got the best of me. I left to explore my unusual environment.

Approximately 105 people lived in Anaktuvuk Pass. The typical 18-by-20-foot, one-room dwellings sprawled over thirty acres. The 174 sled dogs outnumbered people.

Anaktuvuk Pass was the major passageway for the caribou's north-south migrations above the Arctic Circle. *Anaktuvuk*, literally translated, means "place of caribou feces." Everywhere I walked, there was evidence of caribou as the sustaining dynamic. Caribou hide with hair left on, is one of the best insulation against the cold since the hair is hollow, and traps insulating air not only between the hairs but also inside them. The skin is extraordinarily warm, lightweight, water repellent, and durable. These Eskimos lived in caribou tents, wore caribou fur, ate caribou (raw, frozen, dried, or cooked), used parts of caribou for dog harnesses, fed their dogs caribou, and made sewing thread from sinew and needles from caribou bone. Few edible wild plants braved the arctic terrain and could not be relied on to provide much nourishment. Grizzly bears, sheep, ptarmigan, and ground squirrels offered some variety.

Until the 1940s, separate bands of the Nunamiut had moved around the passes, acutely aware of caribou rutting, birthing, and migrating seasons. Their lives depended on this knowledge. During that time, Sig Wien had continued to make occasional contact with the various bands and served as a liaison for trading furs for guns, ammunition, and simple staples such as flour and tea. Prior to his services, the *inland* (Nunamiut) Eskimos had to journey long and arduous miles to the villages of their *coastal* (Taramiut) relatives. These people subsisted with resources from the sea, those of whale, seal, and polar bears. Trading with the whalers brought the Nunamiuts provisions such as guns and ammunition and metal pots and knives. In Point Hope, Barrow, and other villages, the Nunamiuts traded their caribou skins, wolf fur, and other caribou items for seal oil, fabric, and metal products. Alcohol was not a part of these transactions. Anaktuvuk was a dry village. This in itself would make living and teaching here different from my experience in Tanana.

The uniqueness of the Nunamiut was not that they were mobile; nearly all Alaska Natives have a history, or current practice, of moving around somewhat, whether for hunting or to set up a fish camp during the summer. The distinction of the Nunamiuts was two-fold: they had no single place for ever coming together, and, second, they had initially been a coastal group that had gone inland. Over time, the perpetual nomadic movement slowed and some permanency developed.

In 1949, Pat established a trading post with the people. In 1951, and primarily due to his urging, a post office was set up on the old hunting grounds of Anaktuvuk Pass. Homer Mekiana became the United States postmaster, and the post office followed him wherever he pitched his tent or lived in a sod house. Even though the people continued to follow the caribou for extended periods, at some point, they would all return to this location. Construction of the Presbyterian Church, Chapel of the Mountains, in 1958 tied the people even more closely to this area. Education and the construction of a schoolhouse would secure the knot. Although still moving freely for short-term hunting and trapping, they would claim this spot as their home. The mobile inland Eskimos would settle.

Simon Paneak and Homer Mekiana spoke and wrote English. This set them apart from the other Nunamiut. Both men had, at times, lived on the coast, around Barrow, where they were exposed to missionaries, traders, nurses, and doctors. Homer had completed grades one through six. As a result of their life encounters, they could more easily communicate with scientists and white visitors. Many oil officials, geologists, hunters, or government officials would seek out Simon or Pat, whereas the English-speaking missionaries found a kindred spirit in Homer, who embraced common values of faith. Of course, in these interactions, Simon and Homer experienced personal satisfaction, but neither assumed superiority over the others in the bands; they used their skills for the benefit of all. Both men wrote diaries that, in the future, would provide invaluable insights to Nunamiut history and traditions for their children and their children as well as for anthropologists.

ABC

Bridge across Kayuk/Contact Creek, Anaktuvuk Pass, Alaska, 1960.

I was flabbergasted and dismayed when just as I'd completed my move into my log cabin, the rest of the villagers, who I'd expected would be neighbors, moved out of their winter sod houses and into skin tents. The tents were set up approximately a quarter of a mile away, across Contact Creek. The creek flowed anywhere from 12 to 30 feet across, depending on the time of year, and a foot-bridge had been constructed of thin spruce. The rudimentary bridge was raised a short distance above the water with poles buried in the streambed and supported by rock piles. It reminded me of a bouncy gymnasts' balance beam, narrow with no handrails.

This custom allowed for sanitary cleanup after having dogs chained around their houses all winter. Furthermore, the sod houses were dark, and the Eskimos were eager to move into light, airy tents. The May weather with occasional snow squalls was still chilly to me but apparently warm enough for them. With only meager possessions, it required little effort for them to move. They took along wood stoves, caribou skin mattresses, blankets, trunks for clothing, food utensils, and, if so fortunate, a piece of plywood that served as a table. Their natural flexibility showed itself not only in their migration after the caribou, but also in this summer-winter shuffle.

ABC

Frank Rulland beating the "bell" for church services, which he'd constructed for the school children, Anaktuvuk Pass, Alaska, 1960.

On Sunday morning, the beating of a suspended oil drum announced the church service. The log chapel sat on the northwestern hills, beyond and about thirty feet higher than the village home, which were spread around a thirty or so acre area. Mount Sauqpak rose majestically behind it. The 5,883-foot mountain dwarfed the building even with the two-mile distance. I joined the Eskimos who filled the log chapel. Squirming babies, restless youngsters, and gap-toothed elders sat on the newly tiled floor for the hour-and-a-half service. I understood the songs and Bible reading, which were in English, but the prayers and devotional thoughts were spoken in Inupiaq (their Eskimo dialect). All the same, the attitude of worship transcended language differences.

The next day, everyone worked to transform the tiny, one-room church into a school. They had waited a long time for this day, and there were jokes, laughter, and singing as everyone engaged in a project. Some of the men dug and constructed a two-holer, three-sided outhouse that faced toward the mountains for some degree of privacy. Others put up blackboards. Ambitious volunteers carried books, desks, and supplies from the storage tent up the steep hill. A snow squall swept through but didn't deter a soul, not even an eager little fellow who showed up with nothing below his waist. Frank Rulland busied himself with bookshelf construction on both sides of the 6-by-8-foot arctic entry. He was capable and observant of what needed to be done.

During the industrious commotion, my cheerful, pleasant students-to-be curiously eyed the educational supplies that were as strange to them as their environment was to me.

Many hands made quick work and encouraged this first full-time teacher in Anaktuvuk Pass, who felt as though she was at the end of the earth.

The REGISTER, Santa Ana, Cal. Thurs, (e) Feb. 2, 1961

ALASKAN REPORT

"Education Faces Special Problems"

JUNEAU, Alaska (AP)

Size, climate, and isolation combine to give Alaska some educational headaches either unheard of or long-forgotten in the South 49.

They are the problems of a big, sparsely settled land, where winter shows its fiercest side and hamlets and village are the rule rather than the exception...most students are scattered over 586,400 square miles of largely uninhabited land, from the timberlands of the southeast to the barren tundra of the Arctic coast.

First and foremost among Alaska's school problems is transportation. "We can't haul our children to schools in consolidated districts because in more places, transportation just isn't available," says Dr. Theo J. Norby, the soft-spoken ex-Californian who is Alaska's commissioner of education. "That accounts for the great number of schools in the state, compared to the number of students. Most of our schools are tiny by South 49 standards, with 10, 12 or 14 students and one or two teachers."...Teachers are recruited from every state in the union. The 1,900 teachers employed last year represented all 50 states and Canada.

The teacher at Anaktuvuk Pass, high in the Endicott Mountains above the Arctic Circle...28 Eskimo students, is Miss Anna Bortel from Grand Rapids, Ohio. She has been teaching in Alaska for six years; doesn't mind that her home is made of sod.

FIRST SCHOOL IN ANAKTUVUK PASS

On June 1, 1960, church and state clasped hands as the chapel/school made the miracle of consistent education possible in Anaktuvuk Pass, Alaska. The entire community rejoiced on that opening day. They had been insistently vocal in their requests for a school and had made many sacrifices for what they believed was the survival tool for their children and culture.

In October, 1959, the village council had implored Howard A. Matthews, the Alaska commissioner of education:

> Dear Mr. Matthews:
>
> We are writing and asking you for a school in Anaktuvuk Pass, Alaska. We have quite a few kids here that are of school age and they are waiting for the schoolhouse at the Pass.
>
> We don't want our children to be like us who don't know how to write one word. We have two men here who do our writing for us when we want to do some writing, and we don't want our children to do the same. We are American citizens. When are we going to have a school? We will be expecting an answer from you, we will answer you if you write.
>
> Sincerely yours,
> The Village Council at Anaktuvuk Pass (Congressional record – Senate 1961, #13202.)

The determination of the people paid off—and continued. On that first day of school, twenty-six students, ages six to eighteen, crammed themselves into the make-shift classroom. The whiskered older boys conducted themselves in a mannerly fashion with none of the backtalk to me or ridicule among one another that I'd experienced with other teenagers. Teenage girls whispered and giggled in huddles. Children, who had sat on the willow-boughed dirt floors all their lives, slid into desks.

Anna with students in front of Chapel of the Mountains, Anaktuvuk Pass, Alaska where the first permanent education was conducted in 1960.

My textbooks were definitely not written for these children. The traditional A is for Apple would have to be changed to A is for Anaktuvuk, Alaska; B is for Baby, Bear; and C is for caribou. I'd need to make worksheets with

2 fox + 2 fox = 4 fox

1 ptarmigan + 4 ptarmigan = 5 ptarmigan

I'd seen and heard the need to educate these children, and my hand had gone up in response; but now that I was here, the exhilarating opportunity was twins with sobering responsibility. *What part will an education play in their lives, and how can I establish a good guidance program for them? They are reaching out for something better and different, and they want to advance. The elders are staking their lives on the education of their youth.* It was a humbling place to stand.

Prior to Anaktuvuk, I'd primarily taught lower grades. Now I had students of all ages. The three teenage girls who had attended up to three years at the boarding school were quite advanced and could speak English easily. Children age nine and younger had never attended school, and some of the first graders could not speak a word of English. I floundered with preparing lesson plans. Fortunately, a pattern emerged. I divided the sixteen beginners into three groups. Children younger than age nine comprised the first group. The second group, ages nine through eleven, could understand English fairly well, knew the alphabet, and completed the third pre-primer within a month. Three students (Anna Morry, Alice Aklook, Roosevelt Paneak) fit into grade four, and fifth grade had six students (Mabel Paneak, Anna Hugo, Roseanna Rulland, Mark Morry, Jack Morry and Danny Hugo.) One older boy, David, was educably handicapped but wanted to attend school.

To manage so many individual starting points and lessons created an impossible situation, so I had the younger children attend school in the morning and the older children in the afternoon. The teenagers were allowed to come in the morning if they wanted to do their homework. We were packed in like sardines. This schedule provided at least a smidgeon more breathing space.

ABC

Schoolboy learning about planting a garden, Anaktuvuk Pass, Alaska, 1960.

Even though I'd taught Native children in Tanana, teaching here brought experiences I'd never run into before. One day, I decided that planting a garden would be an excellent science project. We discussed this project, and I thought their faces registered understanding of the concept. Any questions? No. I passed out seed packets of carrots, turnips, radishes, and leaf lettuce. The children studied the orange, green, and red packets. We left the classroom, and they bounded cheerfully down a trail to a level spot at the edge of the village. I held out the shovel and expected a volunteer to grab it, press the cutting edge to the ground, step on the blade shoulder, and then use the weight of their foot to push it into the ground. No one moved. Finally, one boy reached forward. He looked puzzled.

"Turn over the dirt," I said, demonstrating with motions.

He pushed the shovel into the ground, lifted some of the sod growth, and then stopped. His big brown eyes asked, "What next?" I realized I'd made the assumption that he understood gardening. I proceeded to explain, again, about preparing the soil, planting the round and feathery seeds, and seeing little green knobs of growth probing through the dirt. The children stopped their chatter and listened intently. Each took a turn working the shovel through the thick, root-matted tundra. After the soil was tilled, they poked seeds into the soft furrows and patted down the dirt with flat palms. Then they shook the dirt from their hands.

"Miss Bortel, we will see tomorrow?" asked one of the boys.

Without waiting for an answer, he bent down and picked away the dirt blanket.

"No, no. Leave the seeds covered," I said and shook my head. "Nothing will come up for a week or more."

They really did not know about a planting and growing cycle. I hoped this lesson would produce tangible learning and a few turnip greens or radishes.

Several days later, I met some boys watering the garden, but not with a traditional watering can. They clutched chunks of green, lacy moss they'd carried to the creek, soaked, and squeezed to produce gentle showers. I smiled. They were doing their best to figure out this strange miracle they'd heard about.

ABC

School children learning about geology from Stephen Porter (Yale graduate student), Anaktuvuk Pass, Alaska, 1960.

Along with surprises came opportunities. Stephen Porter, a doctoral student from Yale, was spending time researching geology in the Brooks Range. I'd often see him stride about the village in tall, black rubber boots, appearing as if he were on a mission and occasionally picking up a rock or pebble along the way. One afternoon, he offered to take the students on a field trip. Our entourage followed him up a low hill that presented a superior view of the valley. He bent down and chose one of the stones and encouraged the children to search for similar rocks. They scrambled about, picking and choosing and comparing their finds.

"Look at your rocks," he said, signaling them to move closer.

Every eye was on him.

"Rocks are different ages, just like you have grandparents who are older and little brothers and sisters who are younger."

The erudite youth attempted to relate simply. He explained what to look for in the object and how to classify it. The little scholars ran their fingers around their specimens, and some wet their fingers to rub the grime off their specimen to see what color lay beneath. One by one, he took the time to help them assess their particular find.

Next, he directed our attention to a nearby pebbly outcrop and pointed out the stratification as well as the effects of weathering and glaciation in the area. No one groaned or sat down in boredom. These children, who were so attune to learning from the land and through their five senses, felt at home in this classroom without walls.

From the moment children followed their parents on a hunt or berry picking, they were learning to become very *natural* natural scientists and orienteers. They didn't need formal, sit-down education about weather patterns, snow accumulation, animals' favorite foraging areas, patches of the most plump berries, the variability of wind, or how to find their way back home after checking a trap line. All this was second nature. On top of the steep hill, the highly educated student with sandy hair and light skin who stood tall among them and looked different and talked differently from them was speaking their language.

ABC

School in this village couldn't be regulated by schedules, classroom walls, or calendar days. It wasn't uncommon for a student to break the stillness of the classroom by exclaiming, "*Tuttu* (Too-too)!" which means caribou. Their excitement of seeing the animals never waned. Even though this first-for-me migration was sparse, I was ecstatic to see several caribou mosey at the edge of the village.

Spectating had its thrill, but when Frank Rulland invited me to go hunting after school, I dropped everything for a hands-on experience. I pulled a wool scarf over my head and stuffed a wax-paper-wrapped peanut butter sandwich in my pocket. The straps of my large binocular case hung over my neck and under one shoulder. When I popped out my cabin entry, Frank had a little smile on his face.

The man's feet sped over the boggy tundra like a caribou himself. I followed like a faithful, panting dog in slick-bottomed brown loafers. I had never thought of buying hiking boots. He walked purposefully in the backyard of his world. He and the others knew the topography like the back of their hand, and I'd never seen anyone pull out a map before heading into the hills.

Steadily we climbed over hill and dale. Gray-white lichens formed on rocks submerged in the tundra, and stubby, white flowers lay against the moss and among the short stalks of grass. Frank seldom spoke a word, and he didn't seem to be breathing hard at all. I was grateful when he finally stopped and I could catch my breath.

"What do you see?" He pointed at my field glasses.

With no trees for cover, the views were endless. I scanned a distant range and caught sight of a statue-still figure sitting behind a stone blind. I passed the lens to Frank.

"That's old Hugo."

Apparently, this wasn't anything to elaborate on, and apparently, our rest break was over. Frank started off again. The cushioned tundra gave way to a field of boulders, perhaps the aftermath of a century-old slow glacier action.

When we'd started out, my adrenaline had spiked with the proposition of conquest. I'd imagined a magnificent caribou in front of us, Frank taking aim and shooting, and the animal crumpling. Now, after several hours, I realized that shooting a caribou was not to be a part of my day. Was I disappointed? Somewhat. But would I have wanted to stagger back with a slab of meat on my back? Perhaps the silent, panoramic views were reward enough. Frank had given me the gift of trailing after him, touching the land and learning firsthand the unceasing labor required by the Nunamiuts to sustain life.

By 7:00 p.m., the summer evening had no intention of ending the day, and the 50 degree breeze pleasantly cooled my face from the exertion. Frank had slowed his pace, and I didn't feel so frantic to keep up. After a while, we stopped to survey the ridge where Old Hugo Enualurak had sat earlier. The warrior hadn't moved. These were a patient people.

ABC

If it wasn't a caribou herd taking precedence over my lesson plan, it was an airplane. By the time I'd discern the sound of the engine, a student could name the type of aircraft. These distractions wove in and out of school and church.

Shortly after my arrival, Andy Anderson brought in my first mail, along with several Japanese men who spoke broken English. Their gear led me to believe they planned to take movies for television. Even though their fluency was limited, and so was the Eskimo's, somehow, everyone communicated satisfactorily. I learned that the Eskimos were being paid to do traditional dances for filming purposes. I reflected on this and wondered who would turn on their television set and be transported to Anaktuvuk Pass? What image of Alaska would be portrayed? How would a Japanese interpretation color the program? I would never know.

I'd had no idea that this little dot on the globe would be such a hot spot. One afternoon, the little log building nearly vibrated apart. My students looked at me.

"Okay," I answered their unspoken question.

Like a small herd, we moved toward the door. In front of us, a huge helicopter with an arched middle section and tandem rotors pulsated to a stop and dumped out four Air Force medics. The friendly young men introduced themselves and good-naturedly joked with the children.

"Would you mind if we take a few pictures of your students and your classroom?" one asked.

The students seemed pleased by the attention, and it was near the end of the school day.

"Certainly. Step inside," I said.

While one fellow was taking pictures, another shot-gunned questions at me. When he learned I was from Ohio, he got all excited.

"Hey! I'm from Toledo! Do you want me to call your folks when I get back?"

I was speechless and couldn't even remember my parents' phone number.

Two of the medics returned to the helicopter, and the remaining adventurers started on foot to Barrow. Their mission was to test clothing for arctic conditions. June and July were scarcely testing conditions in the Far North, but I was sure they'd have plenty of tales of other kinds of tests along the way.

One of many helicopters that landed by the chapel, Anaktuvuk Pass, Alaska, 1960.

The following days, Andy winged back and forth, returning with some geologists. Then, on Sunday, a helicopter landed on the flat area beside the church and *more* geologists tumbled out. Singing dwindled to a murmur as the congregation rose from the willow bough floor and poked their heads out the door. The passengers matter-of-factly exchanged introductions with Homer and headed straightway to find Pat.

"From an oil company from Umiat (OO-mee-at)," said Homer.

The small hill down from the chapel was as busy as a highway. The geologists, with no sense of humor or sociability, resolutely hiked *down* while the Japanese assembly with squints and grins on their faces, and dust churning around their feet, tromped up the knoll. The lay leader of the service waved his arms for the flock of worshippers to return to the chapel, and the relentless film makers jumbled into the parka-clad group with camera gear poking in all directions.

A hymn was announced and voices lifted. Elijah Kakinya, who I'd met in the Quonset when I'd assisted with medical exams, sang out lustily from his spot in one corner, and his jovial spirit rallied the others to join in. I'd recently learned that this older gentleman had been a medicine man. Without waiting for an invitation, and apparently feeling very much at ease, the film-makers set up tripods and shot pictures during the singing and preaching. People from a world apart tried to capture this world. Dark, slanted eyes met and embraced other dark, slanted eyes, thick, black hair everywhere. Broken English, English, Japanese, and Inupiaq filled the air. The biblical Tower of Babel was here in the middle of Alaska.

ABC

What seemed mundane to me was astonishing to the children. Even though I'd closed my cabin door, the little people would creep into my microcosm. Out of the corner of my eye, I'd discover bewildered eyes watching me rhythmically tap on my typewriter. Unbeknownst to them, I saw them and continued typing to my parents. Later that day, I heard soft chatter as I washed my hair with heated creek water. When I mopped the floor, I sensed the movement of pint-size elbows nudging one another. Their floors were dirt with willow boughs, so mopping was irrelevant. Even if unnerving, I came to understand that household privacy was not a part of their culture.

My personal *schooling* was through trial and error. When my food order arrived two weeks after I'd arrived, I found spoiled hot dogs. Such a let-down. I'd looked forward to charcoaled wieners covered with mustard and relish. That would not happen soon. I gave the *dogs* to the village dogs. The bacon, lettuce, and carrots fared a bit better. As disappointing as it was, my food selection would be better preserved if I stuck to canned goods.

I knew this place was remote, but head knowledge is not the same as experiential knowledge. Elsewhere, there were year-around dirt airstrips, nearby rivers, or handy ocean beaches, but in this valley, the basic requirements were at times nonexistent. Andy landed on the lake when it was either frozen or ice free. Now, near the middle of June, the ice was too soft and unstable for skis, yet the water was too clogged with frozen ice cubes for floats.

Andy did what he could. He flew low and threw out the mail bag near the church. On the other hand, *sending* mail was impossible and frustrating.

In the same way, letters and packages could get stuck on the ground, visitors in the village could get stranded indefinitely. This happened to the Japanese, who had finished their filming and were ready to move on, yet milled around in the village while airplanes flew overhead. One day, when I picked out my letters from the air-dropped mailbag, I recognized Andy's scrawl on the back of an envelope: "walk north to the biggest lake." I communicated the instructions to the Japanese. If they'd had the wherewithal to arrive at this Nunamiut village, they'd have to find their way back. The last I saw them, they were bobbing over the tundra in the distance, with tripods bouncing over their shoulders and eye glasses reflecting the glaring sun.

When the lake *did* thaw in July and the ice melted adequately for a float plane to land safely, more researchers dropped out of the sky. These scientists kept my mind stimulated and provided unexpected post-graduate education.

On a sunny evening, I had just settled down to work on lesson plans when Roosevelt, one of my students, announced, "Miss Bortel, here is a man to see you."

The tall, twentyish man stooped beneath my doorway. His thick, blond hair needed more than a trimming. He held a jar in one hand, and with the other, he clung to a heavy green army surplus backpack.

"I'm waiting for my plane to return. This boy said I could wait here."

"Sure. Come on in," I replied.

He didn't move but just stared at my cramped space. Finally he left his pack by the door and carried the jar to the table.

That broke the ice.

"What's that?" The funniest creatures swam gracefully in the jar, with eyes on stalks and feathery legs.

"Ferry shrimp."

This PhD-to-be and two other co-scholars had been studying algae all over the north slope of Alaska.

"We haven't found any organism that is harmful to a human being anywhere," he said earnestly, as if marveling at that fact.

Whether it was testing clothes, scrutinizing algae, or digging in dirt, common threads linked these people together, exploring questions of why and having the courage to go into the unknown and unvisited.

ABC

A short time after my arrival, I learned that the Fourth of July was a major Eskimo celebration. Prior to the big day, I'd walked into the Paneak tent where Susie was sitting on a mattress next to Simon. I often thought they looked like an Eskimo version of the Bible patriarch Abraham and his wife, Sarah. A pliable piece of sinew thread darted in and out of rich turquoise cotton fabric. We sat and sipped hot tea. She communicated through Simon that she was making the atiga for me to wear at the celebration. Already, she had taken me under her wing as my Eskimo mother, making sure I was dressed appropriately, and I felt honored by her efforts.

The sewing scene replicated itself in every summer tent, where women prepared for a kind of fashion show. At the same time, the men worked on their drums in preparation for the Eskimo dance at night.

When the Fourth had arrived, the women turned their attention to cooking for the feast. By 2:00 p.m., the festivities started with the bang of a shooting contest. These people were all crack shots, so competition was stiff. Simon won the contest. The villagers then carried the feast preparations to the large happy tent. I contributed a large pan of strawberry Jell-O and slipped it among plates of caribou meat and rice, sourdough biscuits, hot cakes, Eskimo doughnuts, cooked dried apples, coffee, and tea. No alcohol.

Teenage boys and girls, dressed in their very best, served everyone. Grins, jokes, and a kaleidoscope of atigas added to the festive spirit. The women complimented me on my new outfit, and Susie beamed when I credited her for the creation.

Eventually, the eating and drinking drifted into drumming and chanting. For a while, I watched this form of storytelling. Like other people without a written language, the Eskimos perpetuated their culture through storytelling and ceremonial dances. They loved the old dances with the beat of the drum and the rhythm of the singers. The women wore gloves when they danced and stood in one spot. Bodies swayed and hands moved from one side to another. The men depicted hunts with sweeping muscular movements. The event continued until after midnight, but I returned home well before the evening concluded.

ABC

Washing clothes became my next undertaking. I'd been forewarned that the only electricity in the village was produced from a generator at the church, so I'd brought along a tub and washboard for laundry purposes. During the summer, this would be easy, relatively speaking, because the nearby creek was conveniently located for hauling and heating water.

Drying clothes was another matter. No clothes dryer. No trees or post for a clothes line. I hung clothes on a wooden rack outdoors, but the odds were against me. Drying lingered since the eternal but feeble top-of-the-globe sun didn't produce much heat. Even in summertime, snow flurries could make a renegade appearance. The constant breeze, which in other latitudes would have aided the process, only rumpled clothes to the ground. Moreover, most of my clothes were made of cotton or wool, fabrics not inclined to let go of dampness.

One afternoon, when I was up to my elbows in water with strings of soap bubbles running down my arms, Nick Gubser stopped in. Nick, a Yale student, was working on a degree in ethnology (*The Nunamiut Eskimos: Hunters of Caribou*). He had chosen this ethnic group of Nunamiut Eskimos to live with and study. A director of the Naval Arctic Research laboratory had entrusted Nick to Simon Paneak. The quiet, baby-faced lad with brown, disheveled hair had been here the previous year and had stayed with Simon Paneak, attempting to live and eat like the Native people. This year, his determination eroded when he'd roamed by my place at suppertime. An enticing whiff of caribou roast and my special Mrs. Halbert's Cocoa Cake drew him closer. The villagers teased him about coming to my place for "white man food," and although easily embarrassed anyway, he never turned down an invitation.

At this particular moment, he stood and watched me rhythmically scrub a pair of slacks. I paused.

"So, what's new, Nick?"

His head was usually full of profound deep thoughts and theories. Now his voice rose and fell about the Nunamiut roles of relating within families. I swished clothes through clear water and wrung out socks. All at once, he remembered he was meeting Simon and walked toward the bridge.

I unfolded and straightened up a drying rack. A drone overhead caught my attention. Shielding my eyes from the sun, I recognized the navy blue with mustard yellow trim airplane as the Wien airline that flew tourists between Fairbanks and Barrow. Such aircraft could not land here since there was no suitable landing strip. All the same, some aspects of the village were visible from the sky, and the plane swooped down and circled. Hungry for contact with the outside world, I waved vigorously. The plane seemed to dip lower than usual. In my eagerness to see a friendly face or a responsive wave, I stepped on a log as if to stretch higher and closer.

Much to my mortification, the log rolled and tossed me down a small rise. I somersaulted backward. Landing on my knees, I felt like a circus performer, a silly one indeed. With my glasses still intact, I jumped up and continued gesturing. To my disappointment, the plane leveled out and gained altitude. No lively appearances of reciprocated sociability. A woman walked by and glanced at me curiously.

"I wonder what story the tourists will tell about the *Native* they saw while flying over Anaktuvuk Pass!" I said with a blush.

Following the strenuous clothes-washing, and after the clothes finally did dry, it was time to consider ironing. I had delayed this chore because it meant carrying my ironing board up the hill to the church generator. Truthfully, I felt like a criminal using up precious gas, which made the generator produce electricity. It didn't help that when I'd consulted with Pat, he'd been irritated and raised a finger in my face, "What will the others think? Like you're better than they are? Or they'll see you using up the money for the gas!"

At that early stage in Anaktuvuk, I hadn't caught on how he tried to control everyone's money, decisions, and life.

After considering that the many scientists and film-makers who came through never minded using the generator for their needs or projects, I decided to go ahead and make my move. A trail of small observers joined me. I struggled to tote my ironing board and a basket of wrinkled clothes.

"What's that?" a girl asked, pointing to the large, heavy iron in my basket.

How could I explain its function or this entire activity?

She nudged the girl skipping beside her.

"Look see?"

My reasons seemed trivial.

"You'll see."

Frank met us and started the generator. I plugged in the iron and set up the ironing board. Once again, I was a spectacle.

"Why do you put your finger in your mouth and touch that thing?" a grade-schooler asked.

"To see if it's hot enough."

The board teetered as a boy tried to crawl beneath it and tugged on the full skirt I planned to iron first.

"Where does it go?" he asked.

Just as they'd looked beneath their desks to see what might be hiding, now his concept of object relations and space was in question.

And so it went. Every day, my students learned reading, writing, and arithmetic in school and, outside the classroom, witnessed the strange and unusual customs I'd brought with me.

After completing four weeks of school, I walked home with children tagging beside me, singing and teasing in a mix of English and Eskimo. The air smelled crisp and pure. Splendid mountains rose on either side of the valley. *A* was for *Anaktuvuk* and *Alaska*. And, I, *Anna,* loved it here!

THE LORD'S DAY

Homer Mekiana outside Chapel of the Mountains, Anaktuvuk Pass, Alaska, 1960.

Outside the chapel entry, Homer Mekiana, the lay leader, and Frank Rulland stood solemnly in white shirts, ties, and black suit jackets. They could have been ushers wearing their Sunday best at any church in the Lower 48 States. I shook their hands.

Prior to John Chambers's current itinerant ministry at Anaktuvuk, Reverend William and Bonnie Wartes had pioneered the Presbyterian work at Anaktuvuk Pass. Just like the Chambers, they were based out of Barrow. Tom Brower, of the famous Brower family of Browerville, outside of Barrow, had donated half the money for the church. His father had been a whaler and his mother an Eskimo. Subsequently, his interest in the Anaktuvuk Eskimos developed. It was at the instigation of Bill Wartes that a chapel had been designed and built, and he had accompanied the Eskimos south to the timber section to fell logs for the church.

The villagers filled the compact log chapel whenever there was a worship service; however, there were no Sunday school classes.

ABC

As an adolescent, I remember one Sunday when my mother hung up the black wall phone and turned to me and said, "Anna, Helen is very ill. Would you be interested in teaching her primary-age Sunday school class tomorrow?"

Thus began my Sunday school teaching in the little white church in Bowling Green, where I dramatically told the stories of Noah's ark and the flood, Baby Moses in the bulrushes, and the boy David fighting the giant Goliath.

Both my parents honored God, and our entire family regularly attended Sunday School, morning and evening worship on Sundays, and Wednesday night prayer meeting. My father either taught a Sunday school class or served as Sunday school superintendent until in his seventies. My parents' social life centered around church, and their hospitality often extended to pastors' families and visiting missionaries. Whenever missionaries visited our church, my parents invited them for Sunday dinner and we children were treated to stories about other countries.

As is often the case, we imitated our parents' behavior. On Sunday afternoons when Daddy and Mother visited relatives or made calls on people shut in by illness, my friend Betty would meet with Millie and me in our living room to play church. Millie played the piano and we would gustily sing, "Tell me the Story of Jesus" and "Trust and Obey." On other occasions, we conducted prayer meetings in a friend's playhouse. Fervently we squeezed our eyes shut, clasped our hands, and prayed, "God we love you very much—we will do whatever you want us to." We weren't really sure what that might lead—maybe Africa.

One summer I attended vacation bible school. The cookies, lemonade, leather crafts, hammered tin foil pictures, and games were wonderful; but amidst all this fun, the lessons from the Bible spoke to my heart and I recognized my need for a personal relationship with Jesus Christ. Later on, a number of us teenagers were baptized in the Maumee River

As a child, I had no way of knowing that these decisions would eventually lead me to Alaska and that, just as my family had entertained missionaries, I would work alongside missionaries.

ABC

As enthusiastic as I was to launch a Sunday school program, I would not do so without conferring with John Chambers. In the interim, another opportunity arose.

"Will you play the organ for the service?" Homer asked one Sunday morning.

They'd seen me play my accordion. Most likely, they suspected that I also played the pump organ too. Happily I accepted the offer to pump the boxlike portable organ, not knowing that I would endure leg-strengthening exercises due to the leaky bellows. Fortunately, most of the songs were familiar, and it seemed that at every service we sang "Does Jesus Care?"

Much to my joy, the Eskimos were superb singers. Accordingly, it was a mutual pleasure when I organized a teenage choir to sing at the worship services. The teenagers showed up faithfully for practices and effortlessly learned to sing with harmony parts. The parents and adults beamed proudly when the choir performed its first number of "Isn't He Wonderful?" The following Sunday, they quoted the Twenty-Third Psalm and then sang "The Lord is my Shepherd."

Years after I'd left Anaktuvuk Pass, I received a cassette tape from these Eskimos. Tears flooded my eyes. The adults and young people had purposely created the tape when they'd been requested to sing for a Barrow radio station. They knew I'd share their joy of passing on the harmony-singing tradition to the next generation.

ABC

One morning during the reverie of worship, I heard something odd. It sounded like rain on a tin roof. Mystified, I looked around. There was a two-year-old tinkling into a lard can that his mother had brought with her. I'd seen parents walk outside with the youngsters and then quickly return. These were matter-of-fact, practical parents; the toddler's pants were all split for easy elimination, thus making potty training a no-stress procedure.

On another Sunday, the benediction and the simultaneous throb of a helicopter concluded the service. The helicopter landed in the usual spot on the knoll beside the church. People spilled out of the log building and encircled the chopper, waiting to see who might deplane or what items of interest might emerge. The door opened. Three men crouched below the whirligig propellers and moved toward us. Once out of danger, the men straightened up; two of them gawked wordlessly at the parka-covered congregation and then over at the assortment of tents and sod cabins in the valley. One would have thought they had just landed on the moon. Without uttering a word, they started down the gravel hill, glancing back at us as if we were aliens.

As if their dumbfounded expressions and cameras around their necks weren't clues enough, the pilot, who remained behind, shook his head in amusement and told us, "Shell Oil officials visiting different camps. New to Alaska."

ABC

Toward the end of July, John Chambers flew in for a pastoral visit in his four-passenger *Arctic Messenger*, a Cessna 170.[4] As usual, the adults and children ran to the lake to meet the plane. On their return, the small parade passed my house to the chapel. Children skipped. Men and boys carried his suitcase and boxes. Babies bobbed on the backs of their mothers. Bits of conversation and laughter floated in the breeze.

I pulled on my sweater and went up the hill.

"Why don't you and Frank Rulland come for supper?" I asked.

He accepted.

Nothing was urgent in this village, so while he walked around the village, visiting with people, I stirred up biscuits to bake in my wood stove. Egg noodles boiled on top of the stove and when done enough, I added a can of beef. Lima beans rounded out the meal.

A tap at the door announced my guests.

"Mmm! Smells good!" said John.

Although initially compelled to do missionary flying in Brazil, he and his bride, Barbara, had left East Glenville, New York, two years ago to take the Presbyterian church in Barrow. His zeal to reach the ends of this Alaskan world with God's message manifested itself through his kindness and friendship and willingness to fly in nearly every kind of weather.

Even though Sunday was the traditional day of worship, church in the village had to accommodate a minister's arrival. Thus, services were on Thursday and Friday nights. During this occasion, John Morry, the chief of the village, joined the church. His daughter, Anna, also joined and was baptized. These decisions and rituals were registered in an official chapel in the Mountains book. After the Thursday service, John Chambers asked if there was anything I would like to discuss with him.

"Yes!" I quickly replied. "Would it be possible for me to start Sunday school classes for the children?"

His face lit up, and his eyes shone behind his rimmed glasses. "Anna, I can't believe you want to help us with the church work besides all the regular school teaching you do."

He'd talk with Homer, and before I knew it, Homer was at my door with a plan. Homer would teach the adults; his son, Justus, would teach the children; and I would take the English-speaking teenagers. I couldn't wait.

John recommended that we teachers meet on Saturday nights to study the lesson to be taught the following day. I invited Homer and Justus to my home where there would not be so many children and other distractions. We sipped hot cocoa, and Homer set up the schedule. First, we would meet at the church and sing. Then, Justus would collect his youngsters in his tent. The teenagers would follow me to my home, and the adults would remain in the church with Homer. After the designated lesson time, Homer suggested that we return to church for closing exercises and the regular morning worship services. Each group would say their Bible memory verse as part of the transition time. Homer named these classes A, B, and C.

At the first session, seventeen attentive teens squeezed into my house. I didn't know the extent of their Bible background, so I quizzed them about stories, names, places, and parables. Even with sporadic ministerial visits by Reverend William Wartes and John Chambers, they could answer all the Bible questions. Like sponges, they soaked up every word I added to this foundation.

When I'd taken the students to plant the garden, a Bible application had unexpectedly sprung up, even though I *did not* teach Bible lessons at school.

As the students struggled to find an area free of rocks, Joseph had piped up, "This makes me think of a Bible story."

"Which one?" I asked.

"The one about seeds on rocky ground that couldn't grow. You know, some people hear Bible stories, but it doesn't do anything to them."

That situation in Matthew 13 was true not only in the land of Israel, but also in Anaktuvuk Pass. The exception was that in this village, the hearts were well tilled.

Following the vegetable planting, Joseph reported frequently, "I was down to the garden, and it isn't doing so good."

The soil had been sandy beneath the sod, so I didn't think it was a problem with rocks.

One day, he even showed me proof, "See how bad it is?" Gravely, he pulled some lettuce out of his pocket.

Centuries later, in this remote village, parables still could turn abstract concepts into applications for living.

ABC

As if leading the choir, teaching a Sunday school class, my regular classroom work, and dealing with the rigors of daily living were not enough, I wanted to start a story hour. I imagined that this once-a-week meeting would be for grade-schoolers, since children younger than five really couldn't understand English. My only hesitation was the prospect of more than the usual mukluked feet parading into my house. But then, I imagined those cute little kiddies sitting on their knees or cross-legged in a circle, parka hoods thrown back, wholeheartedly singing choruses and eyes wide, listening to Bible stories and watching, spellbound, as Joey, my hand puppet, made spiritual values applicable. I concluded that household tidiness didn't seem that important. I wrote my parents, "I can stand a dirty floor if it will help children have a clean heart."

Later, John Chambers sent me a newsletter that conveyed mission updates to his supporters in the States. Much to my surprise, I saw my name mentioned.

> Having Miss Bortel at Anaktuvuk is like having another missionary on staff. Thank God for her and pray that she may be of great help in the work of Christ there.

A SOD HOUSE
BECOMES A HOME

"Pat, I can't stay in the cabin this winter if it isn't winterized," I declared.

At this summer moment, the cabin was acceptable, even though sun rays squeezed between the unchinked logs and the children peered through the cracks in the door when they came to visit. But now, at the end of July, I needed to prepare for winter. I didn't want to awaken with a blanket of snow across my bed some morning.

The trader raised his cap to scratch his head and looked at the ground. "I can't do any more work on it or I'll lose money."

Winterizing was only one problem. Size was another. I felt as though I had to walk in and back up to get out of my dwarfed house. Finding a house was the clincher. I couldn't just call up a realtor and go house shopping. There were no unoccupied sod houses in Anaktuvuk Pass. I prayed for the impossible.

Few secrets hid in such a small community, and one day, I heard that Justus Mekiana had plans to build a new house. That would leave his current sod house available. The previous winter, he had transported logs by dog team from the Kivik area, approximately forty-five miles south of Anaktuvuk Pass, for his project and planned to have it completed by late summer when he and his family would rotate from their summer tent into a winter house. Not only would his current residence make a snug winter home for me, but it had been used as the common meeting place and was larger than the others in the village.

I walked to Justus and Ethel's summer tent, contemplating, *How much should I offer him for his house? I don't want to pay too little or too much.* I came up with the amount of $200, and hoped this wouldn't offend him or be awkwardly overgenerous.

I called out a hello and slipped through the tent door. Justus righted himself from lying on a caribou skin on the floor. He never seemed in a rush to talk, but mulled over his responses. Ethel, a young mother, smiled a welcome and then busied herself making tea and left the conversation to her husband. He and I talked about his latest litter of puppies, the status of meat availability in the village, and the weather. Then I brought up business.

"Justus, how much do you want for your sod house?"

He took another sip of tea. My heart beat anxiously. Ethel glanced at her husband and then stooped to tend the fire. I got the feeling they'd discussed this beforehand. Justus responded slowly, "Would $200 be too much?"

My eyes widened. *How could there be such a meeting of minds? Thank you, God, for your direction.*

I opened my checkbook and wrote out a check, even though I wasn't sure how he'd cash it. His eyebrows lifted when I handed it to him.

"All at once?" he asked.

I thought this was an odd response.

"Yes, Justus, all at once." I smiled.

Walking back to my cabin, I reflected on this brief conversation. To a person who depended on caribou for his livelihood, along with a small income from the sale of pelts to Pat, $200 was indeed an extravagant sum of money. I had no idea that the significance of this transaction went beyond the actual payment to Justus.

At one point, I was asked, "Did you know that you are the first person to have a real estate transaction in this village?"

Justus had been so proud that he had this fact written up as Anaktuvuk Pass news in the *Fairbanks Daily News-Miner.*

Sod house construction, Anaktuvuk Pass, Alaska, 1960.

Now I had to get busy making my new quarters suitable for my life-style before I moved in. Sod house construction consists of logs hewn to make a framework and additional logs placed vertically against the frame, creating an igloo shape. Two to four feet of sod are placed against this structure. In my house, there were three windows covered with a single layer of heavy plastic and deeply recessed in the sod layers.

The wood-burning stove sucked the moisture out of the air in my cabin. That would not be the case with the oil stove, which the State Department of Education had sent for the dual purpose of cooking and heating. The difference would not be noticeable or significant until the temperatures dropped and the moist air would condense on the single thickness of frigid window plastic, forming a sheet of ice. I'd learn to deal with this by gently grasping the lower edge of ice, lifting it toward me, and removing it. This process would be repeated all winter. The follow-ing year, I would use heavier plastic and add a second pane to create a thermopane effect. But at this initial stage, I'd never lived in a sod house in the wintertime. I had no idea of the long-term effects of the plastic, which I thought was appropriate. All I knew was that I'd have oil brought in and I wouldn't have to scrounge for twigs and willows to feed my bar-rel furnace.

Beyond the standard sod house features, Justus had used cardboard to cover the ceiling and walls. This kept the dirt from filtering out of the sod and also provided a base to tack up a wall covering. What a bonus. I imagined a number of decorating opportunities.

Although there was plenty of light outside at 10:00 p.m., inside my little cabin, I lit a candle to thumb through a Montgomery Ward's catalog. In the background, I heard drums beating. Sound carried easily, and oftentimes, I'd hear children laughing in their tents a quarter mile away.

I put in a decorating order.

Send Air freight to:
Anna M. Bortel
Anaktuvuk Pass, Alaska

2 Ceiling Blg. Paper gray-textured	2.8 lb.	$5.90
2 Enameled Tacks gray	.9	.90
3 Nails 11/4"	Gal. 16.4	.30
1 Terra Cotta Brown Paint quart	2.2	1.29
1 Brush	2 ½ in.	6.98
		$9.37
Air Freight		9.75
		$19.12

I placed an order to Sears, Roebuck, and Company for forty feet of Vinylthrift linoleum. At the hefty weight of 85 pounds, I still requested that it be shipped speeded parcel post. I expected it to cost $19.85. How surprised I was when I was billed for only $3.00! Otherwise, who knew when it would arrive?

Andy flew in my order in a rainstorm. The village men trudged over the sodden tundra to the lake and carried my wares back through the pouring rain. I gladly paid for this, literally, last leg of transportation. The money would be used wisely on food, ammunition, and maybe fabric.

As the makeover gained momentum, I wanted to spend every second pushing even harder toward completion. I spread glossy terracotta paint on the support posts in the middle of my abode and then painted the trim around the windows and door. Big thumb tacks held the printed, off-white building paper to the cardboard walls. Next, I went to Justus and Ethel's tent to use her sewing machine. In the same way as the other women's machines, hers was operated by turning a side handle. Unbleached muslin curtains to string over my plastic windows took shape, along with a floral, ceiling-to-floor curtain to partition off a large storage area for my food supplies, clothes, and the chamber pot.

I didn't need anything extra to keep food cold. A chilly corner on the kitchen floor made do as a refrigerator. Frozen items were placed in the entry way or on the cache outdoors. Kitchen plumbing consisted of a water pail and a wash basin.

Nothing changed in regards to my light source: a candle on the table, kerosene lamp hung from the ceiling, and a flashlight beside my bed.

Anna in front of her sod house, wearing the atiga made by
Susie Paneak, Anaktuvuk Pass, Alaska, 1960.

ABC

The kerosene lamp transported me back to my childhood when my aunt Elnora made lantern lighting seem like an evening ceremony. She and my uncle Newman lived on a farm where my great-great grandfather Crosby had homesteaded the land. On their Kalamozoo wood stove, Aunt Elnora fried bacon or chicken in a large, black, cast-iron skillet. I'd huddle nearby, taking in the pleasant aromas and sounds, and feel the wood heat chase the morning chill out of my body. Not realizing the work it took to carry the wood and stoke the fire, I'd thought dreamily, *Someday, I'll have a stove like this.* Here in Alaska, I'd taken a step-back-in time, and it wasn't quite as dreamy.

ABC

A lively procession of youngsters and teenagers lent many hands to transported bedding, suitcases, boxes, books, and food supplies to my new house. The younger ones sang the "Bow Wow" song they'd learned at school, although they couldn't finish a verse without a spasm of giggling. I'd never met such a group of people so uniformly and consistently characterized by good humor and affability.

"Here you go," I said, digging into my wallet.

I paid each a shiny dime, except for the bigger fellows who had lifted heavier items. To them, I proffered two dollar bills each. "Thank you, thank you!" rang out everywhere, and the little ones jumped up and down. The teen guys held up their bills, quietly folded them, and carefully pushed them into their pockets. Grins from ear to ear said more than words.

Before running off, the little inspectors nosed about with *oohs* and *ahhs*, fingering the curtains, running their hands on the posts, and peeking behind the divider curtain.

Just making a structure comfortable and attractive wouldn't make it a home; that would require simmering good times into memories. One evening, a group of teenagers stopped in. I introduced them to popcorn, Kool-Aid, and accordion playing—as strange to them as sheep heads and caribou kidneys were to me. The popcorn seemed like magic. They stood around the stove, startled by the sudden pops; otherwise, they didn't say much, but just looked bashfully at one another. I carried on with refilling cups and playing songs. Eventually, they relaxed and sang along.

A few evenings later, several other young people showed up with a chunk of caribou. I invited them in and fried the meat in bacon drippings. They crowded around, and when the meat sizzled, they sniffed the unknown aroma that steamed up from the skillet. The hot meat was layered onto a plate, and they licked their lips at the unfamiliar flavor. Now I laughed.

After dinner, while we were singing, two village council members dropped in. The kids started to leave, but then one of the members spoke to his daughter in Eskimo. She translated, "He wants a floor like yours." This started a series of business transactions with me ordering first linoleum and then building paper and also some lumber. Selecting materials for interiors turned into entertainment for the villagers and a fascinating pastime for me.

ABC

The village kids dropped in frequently. Sometimes, they'd talk to me; other times, they'd just be there. One day, Joe Mekiana, a teenager, stopped by. Usually, the children traveled around in a small pack, but he was alone.

"How are you doing?" I asked, bending down to meet his eyes.

His shoulders slumped, and he just stared down at the floor.

"I don't feel so good," he replied.

The skinny, downtrodden child had come over before, looking just as sad and lonely as today. I'd offer whatever I had on hand, and he'd devoured anything I put in front of him, even if it was untested by his taste buds. Now, I heated up water and found some gingerbread. Over the tasty treat and some cocoa, we talked. His family's tent overflowed with children, so he stayed in another tent without a fire. Even in August, temperatures dropped low and snow dusted the ground. I couldn't change anything about his life, but I could listen and put something warm in his tummy.

I had letters to type, but he was in no hurry to leave.

"Joe, here is some paper and some crayons. Could you draw a picture for Naomi Gaede? She is always writing me letters and sending me pictures."

He settled onto the floor and started drawing. I refilled his cup. Except for the clicking of the typewriter, the room was contentedly quiet.

ABC

Before my home improvements were complete, I had one more to-do. Fortunately, the same morning I intended to do this project, Jane Rulland, Frank's daughter and a frequent guest, stopped to watch me hang out my laundry. Earlier in the week, she'd brought by a sheep heart, which made me feel accepted. Dried blood and grease stains discolored her jacket, and runaway strands of hair had pulled out of her scarf.

"Hey, do you want to help fix my entry?" I asked. "Then we'll get something to eat inside."

A smile spread across her angular face.

I hadn't attempted anything like this before. The sod entry was about 5-by-6-feet and only 5 1/2-feet tall, which was typical of the other houses. The ceilings were purposefully short to trap any cold air before the door to the interior was opened. Everyone automatically ducked going in and out of house entries. The sod was dried out and had pulled apart at the seams, creating more of a breezeway than a barrier. I didn't need breezes in the summer, much less in the forthcoming winter.

Jane dug in with her fingers and pulled off the heavy, stale sod squares in front of my house. I grunted alongside and let her take the lead in the how-to of this endeavor. She leaned into the job and was strong as any man I'd seen. Bits of conversation mixed between our struggles to lift our loads and catch our breath. During one of the lulls, I started singing one of the songs I'd taught my students. She quickly picked up the tune.

Removing the dried-out turf blocks was much easier than digging fresh ones. Fortunately, tundra building supplies were only a few yards away. Jane ran back to her tent and returned with a long, narrow shovel. She pointed it to the ground and jumped on its shoulders. The narrower cutting edge bit into the ground easier than my garden shovel.

"How large do we cut these?" I asked.

"So we can carry them," Jane replied.

We laughed. Without a wheelbarrow or wagon, whatever needed to be carried would be with the assistance of our two arms. Sometimes we nearly tipped over with our armfuls.

"You are such good help!" I said, pausing for a moment.

She beamed.

"Let's get lunch."

When we returned to our job, a cluster of passersby had stopped to stare.

"Not woman's work," said one man, shaking his head and dramatically folding his arms over his chest.

Frank was among the group. I expected a kind comment, but he didn't say a word. Jane and I resumed cutting and lugging the tufted squares. All of a sudden, I heard laughter. It started as a kind of snort and then turned into a full-blown bellow. Frank was laughing at us. Not only that, but tears edged out the corners of his eyes. I stared with my mouth open. He batted his hand in the air, as if to push me away, and ambled down the trail.

I wasn't sure what to make of his behavior. First, he'd wanted to impress me with his fishing ability, and that had failed. He *had* worked tirelessly turning the chapel into a classroom, after which he'd put hours and skill into fashioning my new sod house into a cozy and attractive home. Perhaps now I'd denied him the chance to show off his manliness by constructing a new entry. Conceivably, this was his way to deal with the disappointment of thwarted courtship.

But at that moment, Jane gave no interpretation of the incident and worked tirelessly. When the last piece was wedged into place, we stood back to admire our work.

"Not bad for women, eh?" I said.

We chuckled.

Now all I needed was a caribou skin for the door.

ABC

The villagers begged me to visit their homes. The homes consisted of one room with thickly spread willow boughs on the floor and caribou skin mattresses rolled up against the wall for the day. I'd walk in to find the family sitting on the floor around a large metal pan of boiled caribou with cups of steaming, strong tea. The loose tea sometimes floated to the top, and I'd strain it through my teeth or pick a speck off my tongue. They'd beckon for me to join them, and I'd sit straight-legged and pick hair or tundra grass off the meat. The first time I'd heard a cracking sound, I looked at the stove, thinking it was the characteristic pop and hiss of wood burning. But then the crisp sound became a chorus around the room, accompanied with, *Mmm*. The children were cracking small bones and digging out the marrow, a delicacy. From the very start of these visits, I savored the delicious meat and fine company.

These people could not live without caribou, but I wondered if they could live without tea either. The Nunamiut drank tea to warm the body, comfort the soul, celebrate an occasion, and most likely to fill the mourning moments of a funeral as well as pass the time.

Other than caribou, they consumed sourdough hot cakes for breakfast when they could afford flour. They loved eating these pan-sized delights and usually devoured them plain and rolled up. Whenever they had the luxury of a bit more sugar, they'd sprinkle that on top.

I supplemented my caribou or sheep meat with egg noodles, rice, or potatoes; canned fruit and vegetables; dried beans; and Jell-O. Whereas the Eskimos usually boiled their meat or, if out on a hunt, ate it raw, I needed variety. I experimented with grinding caribou for meat loaf, frying pieces in oil, and, of course, baking chunks in my oven. How jubilant I was when, in spite of the adverse conditions, my garden produced a few radishes, leaf lettuce that had not been pulled up by students, and turnip greens. Oh how I missed fresh, green things.

One evening, I invited Simon Paneak; his wife, Susie; Nick, and some others for supper. Simon's receding hairline pushed his straight hair back on his head, yet dark, bushy eyebrows crouched over his glasses. I found myself awed by his wisdom and knowledge. This fact, along with his undisguised curiosity, always made for out-of-the-ordinary conversations. I'd brought in extra chairs and tried to accommodate everyone. Susie spoke very little English, so when she hung back from the table, I pointed to a chair. She shook her head, nudged her son toward it, and squatted her compact body on the floor with a smile.

My menu consisted of baked moose heart, gravy, rice, canned corn, and lemon pudding. Nick knew exactly what to do with the tasty array and heaped his plate with all but the pudding, which I held back for dessert. My other guests took one item and sampled it and, before adding anything else to their plates, would finish that single selection.

One time, I served canned peas. Their natural conclusion? Green blueberries.

ABC

After I got settled into my house, I was ready to get out of town, wherever *out* might be. In anticipation of finding some walking companions, I packed cheese sandwiches, Fizzies, graham crackers, and gum—enough for a nice afternoon walk. The people here had never seen the small fruit-flavored tablets that fizzed and dissolved when dropped into a glass of water, and it was fun to watch their faces. I wandered around the village and ended up at the Paneaks' tent.

The boys told me the teenage girls had just left for Come Out Creek, "Over there." They moved to the side of their tent and pointed north. I could see Mabel Paneak (eighteen) and Anna Hugo (fifteen) in the distance. The girls waved from the rise of a hill and sat down to wait. The teenage girls in the village included me, and I got such a kick out of their girl talk, questions, and silliness. At the same time, I was wonderstruck by how they chopped caribou ribs for a meal and deftly mended a fur parka with caribou sinew thread. Anna Hugo was extra special to me. Her mind ran deep, which came out in questions about faith, and she worked hard in school, always wanting to know more.

When I caught up, Mabel explained that her parents, Simon and Susie Paneak, were camped beyond Come Out Creek. She identified a landmark some distance away. It was a beautiful day, but I had no intention of walking all the way over there.

"I'll go with you for a while," I agreed.

We chatted about school, my interior decorating, their caribou skin sewing projects, and hair rollers. The girls, who had gone out to school, had learned how to curl their hair with rollers and had brought to the village a shorter, wavier style than the long, straight Native style. My lunch sack swung alongside me, and Anna Hugo's gun jostled against her shoulder. An hour flew by.

"I guess I'd better go back now." I said with a sigh.

"But what will you do if you meet a hungry bear?" asked Mabel.

The girls had told me that *they* were prepared if *they* encountered such trouble. Anna's gun had one shell *just in case.* I doubted one shell would do the job, but she seemed confident in her ability to protect all of us.

"Let's have lunch, and I'll think about it."

I was glad to sit down on the cushy tundra and enjoy the ample picnic, which provided plenty for our trio. My loafers inside my rubber boots had not provided sufficient ankle support, and my feet and legs ached from tromping over the uneven ground.

"It's not too much farther, Miss Bortel."

Both girls had a reason why I should continue.

Back on our trek, I enjoyed the serenity of rolling hills and majestic mountain peaks, but I wondered what I'd gotten myself into. It was certainly a much longer walk than I'd expected, and it became more arduous as we traveled farther.

"How are we going to get across here?" I asked.

The Anaktuvuk River,[5] which had been in the distance, now flowed in front of us.

"Roll up your slacks," suggested Mabel.

I followed my guides into the river with my pants rolled above my boots. We edged in gingerly. The clear water created an illusion of shallowness, and it only took one step into a low spot before frigid water poured over our boots. With a chorus of wild yelling, we scrambled over the slippery rocks, through the swift current, and up the creek bank.

Once on dry ground, we pulled off our boots and wrung out our socks, but we had no choice but to put back on the only slightly dried-out footwear. Our feet squished and boots squeaked as we continued onward. An accumulated four hours and ten to eleven miles later, we walked into the Paneaks' campsite. My companions didn't seem to be any more worn out than if they'd been out for a Sunday afternoon stroll, but I was ready to sit down for more than a short break.

Triumph was written on the faces of the hunters: Simon Paneak; his father-in-law, Elijah Kakinya; and Nick. Chunks of freshly killed bear cooked over the fire. The fat dripped down and made little sparks. Remains of marmot and squirrels lay scattered around, small bits of meat separated from tufts of fur and skin. Susie welcomed us with a beaming face; then she returned to meal-making with Mae, Elijah's wife. I cozied up to the fire to thaw my still-frozen feet and pulled off my useless boots. My soggy socks hung down over my shoes.

"Oh look!" I exclaimed when I peeled off another wet layer.

The brown dye from my loafers had stained my socks and toenails a dirty orange. The girls laughed as though it was funniest thing they'd ever seen.

Two tents sheltered the fire. I stayed inside this comfortable circle and warmed my colored toes. Susie stirred a large, cut-down Blazo fuel can of tea water. Since she could only say a word or two in English, and I did not know Inupiaq, so we shared one another's presence.

When she considered that the meat was ready, she presented me with broiled bear rib and bear claw along with a cup of very strong, hot tea. I knew what to do with the rib and the tea, but the claw was perplexing. I gingerly picked at it with my fingers.

Elijah teased, "You not like Eskimo food? We teach you."

His eyes twinkled beneath craggy eyebrows, and his long, pointed chin dropped down when he laughed.

The taste reminded me of whale blubber or muktuk. *What if my friends could see me with this bear claw?*

Simon and Susie had brought along several of their huskies as pack animals. After the meal and while the men dressed out more of the bear, we women folks walked with the dogs to the site of the recent caribou kill approximately three-fourths of a mile away. My, could those girls cut meat quickly! They made chunks into sizes that could be dropped into caribou hide packs on the dogs' backs. Each dog carried between twenty and thirty pounds of meat, a hefty load by any account. In this culture, where it appeared the wheel had not yet been invented, man and woman's best friend, the dog, had work that was never done.

Mabel laughed behind me as we returned to camp. "You look just like an Eskimo."

I suppose I did. I carried a caribou skin over my shoulders, and a dog walked slowly by my side. I took her words as a lovely compliment.

That night, I was bedded as a royal guest with a sleeping bag on three caribou skins. The long journey, full stomach, and toasty bed eased me into slumber. Even though I thought back over the unusual bear claw meal, I didn't have nightmares.

I felt as though I'd just closed my eyes when I realized there was gray daylight and people awake outside my tent. I found my glasses, ran my fingers through my mussed hair, and pulled aside the tent flap. Ground fog hovered around the campsite and made it feel like as though we were in a soft-sided pavilion. Simon and Elijah sat before a quiet fire that pushed away the morning's frost from their feet. No jokes. No conversation. Just a lazy motion of bringing cup to lips with barely audible sips. Nothing broke the silence except hot cakes sizzling.

Susie flipped the enormous pancakes into the air and adeptly caught them on their reverse sides. She'd probably done this a million times and could have done it in her sleep. When she saw me, she poured batter into the skillet and pointed to me to flip it. I waited for bubbles to form and then tossed the semi-gooey circle into the air. The sphere turned over and started back down. I caught it, most likely by accident.

Eventually, the sun ate away the curtain of fog and the girls, dogs, and I started back. The dogs were burdened heavily, and I felt badly for them.

"We will rest them now," said Anna.

It seemed to take us longer getting back, and I was glad for rest stops, for them and for myself.

The village could be easily spotted at this time of year when the canvas tents reminded me of sailboats on a green, wavy sea. In winter, it would be obscured and a hide-and-seek for pilots.

ABC

By the end of August, I felt settled into my home, my community, and the valley. Each morning, I awoke to a *National Geographic* setting. Frost painted the mountainsides with splotches of red, and nearby, the blueberry leaves had turned to a red violet. I couldn't believe I lived in a sod house. What I did know was that this was feeling more and more like home.

NEW WAYS AND OLD TRADITIONS

Students in the classroom-chapel, Anaktuvuk Pass, Alaska, 1960.

Every inch of the log chapel showed evidence of its dual function: an array of bookcases, chalkboard, and desks; a jumble of flash cards; boxes of pencils and scissors; children's artwork; and a large map of Alaska. The pulpit was pushed against a wall with hymn books stacked nearby. No other place in the village could have served these two purposes.

For Anaktuvuk to have a real school facility, the State Department of Education would need to fly in a prefabricated school and teacherage. An airplane massive enough to accomplish this would require an authentic runway, not a lake. Sig Wien and Wien airlines agreed to assist in this major undertaking, which would take place a half mile east, in the old, dry creek bed.

The first step appeared impossible: bringing in an earth-moving Caterpillar tractor (Cat) from Umiat, somewhere around 100 miles north of Anaktuvuk. The terrain between that military station and Anaktuvuk consisted of permafrost bogs and tundra, rivers, tussocks, and other unknown and unstable surprises—not exactly a highway. Scientists protested the endeavor with arguments that the tundra would be damaged irreparably. Withstanding these obstacles, Wien sent employees to Umiat for the incredible journey. Three weeks later, the Cat could be heard rumbling in the distance, shaking the ground as it approached.

The wheel had arrived. Ironically, the brawny machine did not have a blade or scoop; therefore, even with this contemporary piece of equipment, old-fashioned sweat equity was still required to start the project. Were the villagers disappointed that this contraption did not live up to other-world expectations? Perhaps not. They knew nothing different. Their traditional hand labor was a proven resource and, as it turned out, the means to providing financial resources.

By mid-August, a number of village men were hired to carry rocks by hand, one-by-one, and then follow up with shovels to cut out a landing strip. Even seventy-five-year-old Hugo Enualurak had a job. Each morning, the old-timer gathered a bundle of willow twigs and started a fire at the edge of the worksite where he brewed coffee. He wasn't one to retire to his tent or sod house. Instead, he created a niche and stayed close to the activity.

The temperate days of summer had slid by, and hints of seasonal change caught my eye. After a few nights of frost, berry bushes were edged with red violet and dwarf birch bushes turned yellow. Crimson blotches of stubby vegetation stood out against the gray mountainsides. Small herds of caribou, harbingers of what the Natives hoped would increase in numbers, migrated through from the north. I reveled in the glorious colors yet felt a twinge of sadness, knowing the vibrant hues would bid farewell before I was ready to let them go.

A trail of frosty footprints led to Hugo's cheerful blaze. Cloudy steam rose above coffee mugs cupped in work-worn hands as men clustered around and warmed themselves before reaching for picks and shovels. The tundra sod was obstinate enough when thawed by summer's temperatures; but when touched by the deep chill of below-freezing nights, the effort was even more labor intense. Urgency hung on the worker's shoulders. Beating winter's opposition would demand hasty labor. Even so, the men knew the ground, the weather, the seasons, their endurance, and the opportunity for work. They walked to the worksite, joking and in good spirits.

Completing an airstrip would be a mammoth footstep toward constructing the school; however, actual assembly could not take place during the winter or even spring. In August, I wrote home:

> I don't think they will build the school before next May or June. It will only take about 3 days when they do erect it. They are bringing it in during the winter month. It will come in three sections.

As demanding as the work was, the airstrip construction pumped energy to the village. Conversations, which had previously revolved around dogs, tent repairs, moving back into sod houses, and the dried-up creek, now expanded to curiosity about how the Cat worked and speculation on how large the plane would be to bring in a school. Along with this was verbal list-making of what to purchase with dollars they were promised.

After school, children hastened to watch the workers and the lumbering, exhaust-snorting, yellow Cat as it dragged and leveled the uncovered tundra. Women took breaks from fire-tending and hauling water—which was now a mile's walk to the lake—to examine the progress. For everyone, the backdrop they had known forever was changing.

Fairbanks, Alaska, Monday,
November 6, 1961—15¢ per copy

"Primitive Methods"

The most primitive methods of construction were used at Anaktuvuk Pass because a large ship could not bring in equipment and supplies. A tractor was taken in overland last spring from Umiat. It required three weeks to travel around 100 miles.

Because there was no blade for the rig, the Natives—some 12 of them hired on the spot—carried rocks one by one and worked with shovel until enough strip was roughed out to allow entry of a CD-3. The ship brought small equipment, including a "tumble bug," which was hitched to the tractor. It was a slow, time-consuming job but it was finally completed.

The Natives were paid a total of $7,500, which was more than they had ever seen before, being isolated as they are from a place called civilization. Few have ever been to Fairbanks. Their average monthly cash income, mostly from trapping, is said to be around $10.

Rayburn said a great deal of credit should be given to the Natives for the work they did on the strip with tools strange to them…Natives who worked on the strip were Ben, Jonas, Robert and Noah Ahgook, John and Zacharrias Hugo, Homer and Justus Mekiana, Amos and Riley Morry, Raymond ad Robert Paneak and Frank and Johnnie Rulland.

ABC

"Look! A plane is circling the village," exclaimed Roseanna Rulland in the middle of arithmetic class. Roseanna was Jane's younger sister. She had a winsome smile and dimples when she laughed.

We all knew that the runway area was extremely rough and not ready for use. The navy-bellied plane announced it was one of Wien's fleet. The Cessna 180 completed another go-around and started the downwind leg of the landing pattern. By this time, the children had left their desks and stood with faces pressed to the windows. Long division and subtraction had taken a backseat. The girls squealed as the plane descended and extended its flaps for landing.

"It gonna [flip] over!" shouted one of the boys.

The tail-dragger's[6] main wheels touched down with an awkward bounce. The students sucked in their breath, and I held mine. The aircraft settled to the ground again and, with wings rocking wildly, came to a halt. A chorus of sighs filled the room.

On August 24, 1960, and with the runway nearing completion, Ed Parsons, assistant to the Wien president, had landed on the Anaktuvuk Pass airfield. One of the older teenage boys who had been at the airstrip when he landed told me what happened. After the historical touchdown, Ed had climbed out of his plane with a big grin, raised his arms in the air, and yelled, "Good work!"

He was not a man to stand around and make small talk. Energetically, he waved for his employees to come, including Bob Sutton, who was the field superintendent, and the Nunamiuts. He conferred with his crew about the field project, talking quickly, asking questions, and gesturing here and there.

When he arrived at my classroom, his cheeks were ruddy and he was panting as if he'd run all the way.

"Anna, we'll get you a real school yet!" Without waiting for a response, he continued. "Gotta talk to Pat and get a cup of coffee."

If anyone would see that the undertaking was accomplished, it would be Ed Parsons cracking the whip, in a kind way.

Two and a-half weeks later, on September 18, with initial construction completed, the first large airplane, a Wien DC-3,[7] approached the village. As it slowly circled, checked out the runway, and made a final approach, villagers flocked to greet it. The aircraft rumbled down the 4,000-foot runway. No longer would air transportation be dependent on a nearby lake's frozen or thawed conditions.

Men and women hung around the aircraft, which had a fat fuselage, tail solidly on the ground, and nose pointed into the air. Unlike the bush planes, which adults could walk up to and peer in the windows, they looked up at an unreachable door and small square windows. Wien employees tugged open the large cargo doors and prepared to lower ramps. Villagers moved forward to assist. Over several hours, two tons of heavy equipment was expelled with which to extend the airfield to 4,500 feet. Among the machinery emerged two large unlabeled brown cardboard boxes. Bob Sutton pulled open a corner of one with his leather gloves and looked up with a crooked smile.

"Hey! Look at this," he called to several women nearby.

They moved toward him hesitantly and reached inside. "Oh!" they said as they lifted out wool jackets, cotton shirts, and leather boots. Someone had sent used clothing. Chattering happily, they filled their arms with as much as they could carry, summoned their children to help, and went off to sort their prizes for distribution among one another.

I stood with several of the teen girls. The plane dominated the simple panorama. Rachel Mekiana brushed a strand of wind-tugged hair out of her eyes and away from her heart-shaped face.

"I never thought we'd see such a big plane land here," she whispered in wonder.

That sentiment echoed throughout the entire community.

The New Airport

(student paper)

Ed Parson is the first man to land an airplane on the Anaktuvuk Pass Airport. He brought a little boy whose name was Don. We were screaming when the plane was trying to land. When it landed Miss Bortel rang the bell. We went down to Pat's to the see Ed and the boy. Ed sure was smiling. He came up to see the school. He said that he was going to take Anna Bortel down to Barrow, Alaska sometime.

Anchorage Daily Times

"Wien Alaska Anaktuvuk Pass Strip Opens"

Anaktuvuk Pass, the small Eskimo settlement high in the Brooks Range some 200 miles northwest of Fairbanks, is going to have year around amulet-engined air service.

Wien Alaska Airlines announced it has just completed a 4,000-foot-long strip at that village high above the Arctic Circle in a treeless terrain

Completion of the strip marks another step in the company's program of providing its own facilities wherever necessary and possible. The new facility will accommodate the larger ships of the Wien fleet. Also, the field has brought the first radio communication with the village.

Prior to this time there was no strip and small planes landed at the nearby lake on floats in the summer and on skis in the winter. Necessarily, there were long periods during breakup and freeze-up which prevented landings.

George Rayburn, executive vice president of Wien, said construction of the field is part of a five-year program of such improvements…for all intents and purposes, the cost has been out of the Wien treasury.

ABC

Life changed. Modern airplanes could now land in Anaktuvuk Pass, Alaska. At the same time, life remained the same and revolved around the caribou.

Over Labor Day weekend and between the two historical landings, I was walking toward the creek when two men approached.

"The caribou come through pass by foothills," whispered Zaccharias Hugo.

Zaccharias was an adroit hunter. In the spring, he would go wolf hunting to bring in much-needed cash. One pelt would bring him $50.

"We keep kids and dogs quiet so herd leaders go through," continued Jack Ahgook. "We shoot too soon, they scared. They turn, go back, and find another valley. They go south now to timber for winter."

Sound carried easily in this open space, and concern about frightening the caribou subdued movement and communication. Word that the caribou were approaching flew across the spaces in silent signals and hushed tones. No one chopped twigs. Running stopped. Children ceased their rambunctious running and ball throwing. Dogs were silenced. Only the sound of restless wind filled in the background and rustled door flaps.

Teamwork was imperative; accordingly, the village decided as a community when to hunt the caribou.[8] Unlike some years when 65,000 to 75,000 caribou migrated through Anaktuvuk Pass, caribou had been scarce for several years, and a sense of desperation could be overheard in conversations. Caribou can run at speeds up to 35 and even 50 mph. Covering twelve to twenty-four miles in a day could be typical for the caribou and exhausting for a human. All in all, this opportunity for subsistence could not be sabotaged. The men slowly and cautiously stationed themselves at strategic posts. Each one knew his position and role. One hunter crouched, ready to herald the herd's movement. The remainder hid in readiness behind previously erected stone blinds close to the foot of the moraine hills. They would hold their fire until a section of the herd had migrated through.

I crawled stealthily on top my tundra house to view the dramatic spectacle. Resting my elbows on the prickly sod, I scanned the treeless region and then settled my sight on hundreds, maybe a thousand caribou. Females weigh between 130 and 370 pounds, and the males range from 220 to 700.

Many nonchalantly fed while older ones bedded down peacefully and rested. Younger ones gamboled carefree. Bulls shook racks, bloody from rubbing off their velvet or from fighting each other. Calves nuzzled their mothers or frolicked with one another. I lay on my stomach, mesmerized.

While the caribou grazed in tranquility, adrenaline coursed through my veins, as I expected it did through the male villagers.

Who will kill the most caribou? Which young man will make his debut as a hunter of great promise? Will they down enough caribou?

Regardless who shot a caribou, the meat would be shared with all.

Time passed. Brisk autumn wind ruffled my hair, and I pulled my jacket collar more tightly around my neck. Then shots rang out. Frantic caribou sped safely on their way south, but some did not. Through the successful aim of a hunter, they became life-givers. They would not make it to the timber but instead would contribute to the sustenance of the Nunamiut and their dogs.

Women followed the rhythm of tradition and made their way to the scarce willow groves to gather twigs for fire building. It was time to make tea. Soon, the ulus would be cutting the meat in round motions.

ABC

Men weren't the only hunters. Women set and checked trap lines. One Saturday, I had just finished breakfast and was about to mop my floor when Ethel Mekiana appeared in my doorway and asked if I'd like to go check her traps for ground squirrels.

We crossed the now-dry Contact Creek and headed toward the verdant green hills about two miles away. Patches of wild cotton bobbed in the breeze and looked like cotton balls stuck on stems. Blueberries were ripe, and we picked and ate as we walked along. In this far north, all vegetation lay close to the ground to protect itself from the harsh elements. The blueberries themselves were miniature. Hiding in the tundra, they teased berry-pickers to find them in a kind of hide-and-seek. A schoolboy traipsed behind us, lingering at the berry patches we'd discovered before him.

When we arrived at our destination, the boy ran ahead and set a trap of his own while we checked Ethel's. To our disappointment, one after another held nothing.

"Hey! Look here!" the boy called out.

He'd wandered over to Ethel's line and then darted over to check his before we started back.

The little critter was still alive. I pulled my camera from my pocket and took shots of the proud boy and his catch. The boy laughed. His tongue was purple from berry-eating. After the amusement, Ethel reached for the squirrel, bopped it on the head with a rock, held its head down with a stick, and pulled out its heart. I grimaced at the irony of the soft-spoken woman with a brutal touch. Until that moment, I'd thought I'd like to go hunting, but after seeing the killing demonstration, I decided I was too chicken-hearted.

ABC

Caribou continued to appear regularly. The tenor of the village was light and more relaxed than it had been in months. This was to be a good year. A week later, the children excitedly ran in at recess.

"Miss Bortel, the tuttu are coming!"

Their eyes had already detected hunters camouflaged across the ravine. Sure enough, soon, there was a great rush of caribou. Hoof beats thundered as they answered the innate urge to hurry south.

"Come children! Let's go inside now!" I shouted. "The caribou are coming between us and the hunters!"

The children practically dived into the classroom. After some time, the firecracker sounds tapered off. I took my binoculars and peeked around the schoolhouse. All was safe.

How can a teacher and students keep their minds on book work when the caribou are staging such a magnificent challenge?

In a perfunctory manner, we eventually completed worksheets and the children sprinted out the door for the day. I would have liked to follow, but instead, I sharpened a red pencil and graded papers until Cyrus Mekiana burst in the door, his mop of black hair flying in all directions.

"Teacher, nine caribou were killed between the village and the lake!"

I laid down my red pencil, scooped up my papers, tapped them into a neat pile, and then walked down the hill for my 8-mm movie camera. A half-mile later, I stood at the snowy site. Blood and entrails covered the ground in a red-and-white mess. It was hard to look beyond the carnage and imagine that what wasn't eaten would be used for parkas, boots, mittens, mattresses, and sewing thread.

"Here. You milk," offered one of the men, handing me a cup.

I bent down to a still-warm caribou cow. Tentatively, I reached out to her udder and squeezed streams of milk until my cup was half-full. Glancing around to see if anyone was watching, I took a sip and then another. I hadn't had any kind of fresh milk for long, and this was delicious, so much better than the thin, blue, powdered milk I'd grown accustomed to in Alaska.

"Teacher, you take home," said George Paneak, handing me a caribou liver.

I'd been presented with a prized portion. Later, the heart and ribs showed up at my house. (The dogs would receive meat from the hind quarters.) I returned the favor with a can of pears.

"Quinak tamn tuttu nike," I replied. "Thank you for the caribou meat."

ABC

At the end of September, amidst landing strip construction and caribou hunting, two men from the Land Management Office flew in to inquire if the people wanted to make their settlement into a town site. If they agreed, someone would survey the area and divide it into lots. All kinds of enthusiasm abounded for this proposal, and the chapel bubbled with Eskimo-English discussion. Having lived with these nomadic people for even a short time, I questioned how this would actually play out. They were so used to living in their sod houses during the winter and then, in the summer, pitching their tents across the creek in random, squatters' rights fashion.

A few days after this meeting, there was another gathering to elect three advisory school board members. Explaining the concept of this position was challenging enough without searching for simple English words. I wrote my parents:

> You can imagine trying to give that term out to these folks... We had a warm south wind today and all the snow is rapidly melting...when I tried to go up the hill to the school I'd just slide back. I decided I'd have to find some bare ground to go up, but that proved too steep and I went tumbling down...Everyone came in their joyous way as they always love meetings of every type. I asked Doris if she would interpret for me.

The following night was yet another assembly, this time to actually vote on the town site issue. But that first of many firsts in 1960 was not all. They also wanted to discuss the presidential election of John F. Kennedy or Richard Nixon. Pat did not attend any of the meetings, especially not one with politics. He hated Nixon, and someone had told him that I was related to that man. I thought the idea was hilarious and didn't tell Pat any differently.

At first glance, these people were radically isolated. In reality, however, they made the most of erratic radio contact with the outside world and conversations with anyone entering their simple society. In previous decades, when their migrations had taken them to Barrow, they gleaned information about world events from their coastal cousins who interacted with whalers, school teachers, nurses, and missionaries.

Simon Paneak's brilliant mind assimilated any bit of news, which he would disseminate to the others. He, Homer Mekiana, and a few other adults who could read benefited from a rare newspaper, *National Geographic, Alaska Sportsman,* or *Time Magazine* that found its way in through a bush pilot, visiting researcher, John Chambers, or an actual subscription.

ABC

My primary role was to teach the children, but when I realized there were adults who could not write their names on petitions and forms, I gladly took on the prospect to teach them such a fundamental skill.

The first week in October, I sent out verbal invitations to the adults.

"Boys and girls, would you please tell any adult in your family who cannot write their names that I will be happy to teach them if they come to the school on Friday at four p.m.?"

The students nodded solemnly.

That first Friday, I placed long sticks of white chalk in the blackboard trays and waited. I didn't know what to expect. Hugo Enualurak shuffled slowly through the door and sat down at a desk. This was as unfamiliar to the elderly grandfather as it had been to many of my younger students. Susie Paneak arrived next, and then a woman with school-aged children. Several young women with babies on their backs followed. The new students tittered as they tentatively made marks on the wide-lined paper with the freshly sharpened pencils. All in all, seven self-conscious but determined and hopeful adults ventured through the door: Hugo Enualurak, Susie Paneak, Molly Ahgook, Jane Rulland, Ellen Hugo, Olive Morry, Dora Hugo.

To begin with, I wrote their names on the chalkboard. After demonstrating some basic handwriting techniques, I gave each student a sheet of paper with his or her name written on top as an example to follow. I had no idea how to spell Hugo's last name and had to ask Frank Rulland for help. Wordlessly, they struggled with positioning pencils, holding paper at an angle, and shaping letters. Beads of perspiration formed on their foreheads. Several concentrated so intently that they held their breath, letting it out in a big rush when they completed a letter or two.

"It's warm in here, and you're working hard. You might want to take your parkas off," I suggested, hoping they might relax and become more comfortable.

One young mother loosened the tie around her parka waist and dropped her baby down from his snuggly cocoon on her back. The naked-from-the-waist-down toddler explored the classroom while her mother practiced writing on the blackboard.

Susie scarcely spoke a word of English, and now she was trying to write her name. I got so tickled when she'd write, "Susie Susie," instead of "Susie Paneak." When I tried to correct her, she'd write, "Paneak Paneak."

Then there was old Hugo. In all his long life, he had never written his name. To help him feel the flow of the letters, I put my hand over his massive, weather-worn, arthritic hand. I thought of how this gnarled hand had dressed out many caribou to provide food and skins for his loved ones. He laughed with delight as we ascended to the L in his last name.[9] When he stood at the blackboard and used the chalk, he burst out with, "Oh," followed by a louder, "Oh," and finally a crescendo on the third, "Oh!" Then he looked at me, startled. Pointing at his name, he realized he'd left out the "n" and now didn't know what to do. I patted his shoulder and handed him the eraser.

"It's okay, Hugo. You can try again."

At the end of the first class, I asked each student to line up on either side of the names written on the board, and then I took a picture of the landmark event.

After several more classes, Hugo and the others hit their new target, not the usual one of wild game, but that of writing their names, along with, "Anaktuvuk Pass," and other words meaningful to them. Hugo carefully wrote his name on a piece of cardboard that he put in a little box with the rest of his prized possessions.

Teaching the adults to write their names (Ellen Hugo, Hugo Enualurak, Jane Rulland, Molly Ahgook and baby Esther Ahgook, Susie Paneak, Dora Hugo).

ABC

In mid-October, I received a packet from Wien Airlines requesting that I assist in filling out applications for Social Security and withholding tax statements for the men who worked for a combined $7,500. Even when divided among them, it was an enormous amount in their near-cashless economy. I lugged my typewriter to John Morry's house to type in the required information. He had a passion for maintaining the traditional language and understood how learning to write would help perpetuate this ability.

Men filed in to answer my questions and to sign their names. Old Hugo was among them. After I completed the form, I handed it to Hugo for his signature. He squinted and rubbed his tired eyes, straining to see in the dim light. I reached out and moved the candle nearer. A smile spread slowly across his wrinkled face.

"Now I write name. No more put X," he said.

Tears welled up in my eyes. To write one's name gave identity and dignity. New skills for people of old traditions. Adult education was not an added burden, but an unforeseen reward.

IS THERE A DOCTOR IN THE HOUSE?

Shortly after I'd arrived in Anaktuvuk Pass, I was down by Contact Creek, learning a new skill: chopping willows for my wood stove. Since the creek provided two basic necessities, water and willows, it was common to meet other people. On this occasion, I bumped into the mother of Danny, a student who had not been able to attend the opening of school because he was ill. Ellen Hugo, the mother of a half dozen children, worked extra hard and assumed additional responsibilities because her husband, Clyde, was often in poor health. She spoke only Inupiaq, but when she saw me, she tugged on the coat a nearby man who could speak both Eskimo and English.

"She wants you to see Danny. Danny sick," he said.

That was all. No details. In a previous conversation with Pat, I'd learned that he'd recently taken the fifteen-year-old boy to Hunt's Fork, where they had hunted and trapped. Danny had taken on some of the responsibility of providing meat for the family.

"Danny was healthy when we got home. Don't know what happened." Pat said with a shrug of his shoulders.

That introductory incident in June started my unlikely medical involvement in Anaktuvuk Pass. Throughout summer, health issues had threaded through my responsibilities and activities of school teaching, leading Sunday school classes, teaching adults to write their names, picking tundra grass off caribou dinners, picking berries, following along to check trap lines, hauling water from the creek, and discovering scientists or pilots in my doorway.

On that initiation day, I stacked my willows outside my cabin door.

What might I need for this house call?

I located a thermometer and tongue depressor, very bare essentials, but those and my own hand to take a pulse were about all I had. Since the villagers had moved across the creek into tents, I had to practice my balancing skills on the narrow, unsteady bridge. Focusing on the creek bank ahead helped. In the settlement, little children swarmed around me, calling out "Miss Bortel! Miss Bortel!" and led me to Danny's family's tent.

Susie Paneak and Anna , in front of a typical Nunamiut
summer tent, Anaktuvuk Pass, Alaska, 1960.

The boy lay motionless. Thin and gaunt, he huddled beside the stove. His flushed face indicated a fever. I shook him gently to tell him about the thermometer. For a moment, he lifted his head and complied and then shut his eyes, and curled more tightly with his arms tucked between his legs. The red marker crept up to 102 degrees. I did not know what else to examine. Ellen spoke to one of the older children in the room. I couldn't understand her words, but I could hear her concern.

"Tell her I'll come back two times a day," I said softly.

Several days later, the fever had not broken. Danny lay as listless as ever.

Dr. Stanley Hadley, one of the physicians who had replaced Dr. Gaede at the Tanana Hospital, had previously instructed me to send critically ill villagers in with Andy. I didn't mention to Ellen, or anyone else in the village, but I suspected that Danny might have tuberculosis. Calling the ambulance in the sky was not that simple. Several of the men had radios that could be used to contact Andy or the Tanana hospital, but these were only effective when weather conditions were conducive. Even when contact was made, transmitting and receiving was patchy, and garbled communication confounded what did come through. Fortunately, this time, it only required a few attempts to reached Andy regarding Danny.

Shortly before Andy could schedule a run into Anaktuvuk, I got a message from Ellen Hugo saying she had a toothache. Thinking there was no hurry, I finished washing my dishes. What a surprise when I entered the tent to find a group of people *and* a just-born infant. Her husband had delivered the rosy-brown, squalling child and held it in his large hands.

It was only after more time living in the village that I figured out the Inupiat Eskimos didn't name the specific body part or area of the distress; instead, they identified some unrelated place. Perhaps evasive communication stemmed back to some superstition. I expected that in the future, I'd have to look for other clues when called in for health care.

At this moment, my mouth dropped open at the unusual birthing scene.

I whispered to Jane, "Do you weigh the baby?"

Her brow wrinkled. "Weigh?" she said.

I tried to explain and illustrate but got nowhere. At my house, I had a postal scale for mailing. "I'll be right back."

When I returned with the scale and placed the baby on it, the enthusiastic crowd circled around me. I thought it was curiosity about the scale until I learned that Ellen didn't have a name for her son.

"What about Elmer?" I suggested.

The villagers knew Doc Gaede from his medical trip the year before. She nodded her head and smiled, but when she tried to pronounce the name, it came out, "Hammer." I chuckled and pronounced it again. At some point, I discovered that she'd designated Gaede as his middle name.[10]

After I weighed the newborn, Ellen swaddled him in a soiled man's sweatshirt. This bothered me. I hurried home and found a baby gown and large piece of soft fabric. These I pressed under my armpit and beneath my coat to warm on my return. There were more babies on the way, so I wrote my mother to collect and send baby clothes.

A few days later, Andy arrived to transport Danny to Tanana, where the young man was diagnosed with tuberculosis and subsequently transferred to the Anchorage Native Services Hospital. Before long, letters arrived telling us how homesick he was. He pleaded for dried caribou meat rather than the eggs, green beans, and other strange food he was served.

More pregnancies culminated in quick succession. In July, shortly after I'd introduced the great mystery of ironing to the school children, another baby came due.

"Would you pray for one who is about to have baby?" requested Homer when he stood up to lead a church service.

I knew it must be his married daughter, Doris Mekiana Hugo. After church, when I carried my bucket to the creek for water, I observed that many of the congregation had gone to her tent door and were peering in. I set down my running water and joined the group, who drew me inside where the baby lay at the mother's feet. The baby's bawling face was ruffed in a thatch of black hair distinct to the Natives' babies. I was a bit caught off guard by the lack of privacy for what I considered a personal experience.

Simon Paneak, a skilled midwife, had delivered the child, and now, Jane Rulland rigorously bathed the squirming red infant with rough lava soap. I cringed. When I revisited newborns later, I recognized the rashes they all sustained for at least a week.

"Where are the baby clothes?" I asked the father, Zaccharias Hugo, who was putting cold cloths on his wife's head.

He walked over to a suitcase and pulled out some much-used garments. I took the shirt he handed me, held it against me to warm, and positioned the scales. Jane handed me the bawling child, who most likely wanted to return desperately to the warm womb he'd departed from.

Simon and Jane motioned for me to help move Doris. I didn't know why we needed to disturb her until I saw that the caribou skin used for the delivery now contained the afterbirth. This mess, along with her dress which had been cut off, was taken out and destroyed.

The hustle and bustle continued, and a party spirit ensued. I'd never seen the like. Rachel made coffee, and someone ran out to buy peanut butter and Pilot Boy crackers from the store.

"What will you name the baby?" I asked.

Simon and Doris looked at each other and then requested that I select a name. I thought for a moment, then asked, "How would you like Paul, after the Apostle Paul in the Bible?"

There were no Pauls in the village. Doris nodded.

"That will be an easy name to say when I get after him," she said.

Most likely easier than *Elmer* would be for Danny's mother.

Doris Hugo and baby Paul, Anaktuvuk Pass, Alaska, 1960.

ABC

Mothers and babies weren't my only patients. Another time, Mark Morry, one of my students, cut his leg quite badly on a sheep hunt. I removed the crude bandage and studied the deep wound. The gash needed stitches.

This, however, was not an option. I'd just read how to make a butterfly bandage, so putting my knowledge to use, I pulled the wound together.

"He really needs some crutches," I told his father. "I don't want him putting weight on this leg and pulling everything apart."

The next day, the boy hobbled to school with homemade crutches, whittled and smoothly finished. The Anaktuvuk Eskimos were fine craftsmen, regardless of the project.

ABC

"Did you know that Rhoda Ahgook had her baby?" announced Ethel Mekiana, who had appeared in my doorway.

It was the end of August, and I was papering the cardboard walls of my sod house. "What did she have?" I asked.

Ethel didn't know, but she was on her way to find out. I put down my brush, pulled on a heavy sweater, and joined her. Ethel's pregnant tummy pooched against her jacket. A baby epidemic must have hit the village, a highly contagious epidemic at that.

Roosevelt Paneak, one of my older students, saw us coming and called out, "Bring the weighty thing."

The "weighty thing" referred to the small scale. I surmised that I must have become an official part of the delivery team.

We pulled aside the tent door flap. As usual, the tent was full of people. What was not usual was the silence. No customary merriment. No baby crying. No one made eye contact, but focused exclusively on his or her duty. Simon massaged Rhoda's abdomen "to put the womb back in place and to stop bleeding." Dora twisted thread to tie the umbilical cord. Bob Ahgook, the baby's father, stood mutely, his eyes darting from Rhoda to Simon to the baby. He was a kind, caring man and esteemed in the community. Jane diligently soaped and scrubbed the baby, who didn't respond in any way to her roughness.

Bob had reason to be concerned. His baby was blue with extremely white hands and feet. Jane handed the tiny child to me. He lay limply in my hands.

What if he dies in my hands while I weigh him?

Surprisingly, the little guy weighed in at a respectable seven pounds. I wrapped him in flannel baby clothes I'd brought and handed him to Rhoda, who tried to nurse him. People left slowly, letting bursts of cold air into the tent.

Bob, Simon, and I sat down on the floor and sipped hot tea. The only sound was an occasional pop of wood in the stove.

"I'm not sure the baby will live," I said in a low voice. My chest felt tight, and I drew in a sharp breath before standing to leave. *Dear Lord, help this family.*

The next evening, I walked over to see how the blue baby was doing. I felt like a physician, albeit an untrained one, making rounds and checking on my patients. Through the tent walls, I could hear Rhoda sweetly singing a hymn, which made my heart even heavier. I found her and her newborn cuddling on a caribou skin.

She turned to me with a hopeful smile, "His name is Peter."

I tried to act cheerful, but felt so sad. I suspected that this fond mother-child bonding would come to a heartbreaking end.

ABC

By the end of August, school had assumed some routine and I had completed most of my sod home improvements. My orange toes had recovered their normal pinkness after the Come Out Creek adventure. Not much else was normal, unless normal was people streaming in and out of my house and babies being born at a steady pace. In rapid-fire succession, I had guests for coffee, meals, and night's lodging. I'd met many geologists, a limnologist, ethnologist, and "oligists" I could not pronounce or remember. Hunters showed up, but spent their time at Pat's or Simon's.

John Melville from the State Health Department arrived for several days. He checked the classroom and wrote down the names of all the students, and then he met with the village council.

Two eighteen-year-old girls came sobbing into my house.

"He makes 9 p.m. curfew!"

Somewhere, there had been a misunderstanding and John thought I wanted the students in bed earlier. I enjoyed the long summer daylight and reading after midnight myself. I could understand how they hated to go to bed early, even if it meant dragging into class the next day. On the other hand, I knew that the chief was annoyed by their late-night giggling that drifted a quarter mile away through the tent walls that even the wind could not drown out.

"I suppose they will put us in stocks next," one girl wailed.

"Just like the Puritans in Massachusetts," the other moaned, collapsing in a heap on the floor.

"Well, let's see what happens," I said, suppressing a giggle.

I'd have to give them an *A* for retention of Early American history, which apparently they'd learned at boarding school.

"By the way, have you tried the grape-flavored fizzie pops?"

Eyes were wiped, and they gathered themselves from the floor. Now they wanted to know how many flavors there were of the effervescent tablets that foamed magically when dropped into a glass of water.

ABC

John Chambers; his wife, Barbara; and two little girls flew in from Barrow. I'd anticipated meeting John's family and welcomed them into my home. The well-behaved girls were so dainty, and even in this rugged country and bush flying, Barbara had them dressed to the nines. They had heads of ringlets and were so cute in their pink frills. "Please," and, "Thank you, Miss Bortel," endeared me even more. Barbara had packed along fresh, homemade bread and chocolate chip cookies. It was so nice to eat someone else's cooking. The sweet family slept on my floor, and what a pleasure to listen to their prayers after I turned down the gasoline lantern. The weather had been terrible and their flight frightening and long. The toddler had thrown up en route. Grown-up and children's voices took turns thanking God for safety.

Miss Lois Morey, my dynamic supervisor, arrived hot on their heels. I put on my best northern hospitality and took her artifact-digging, introduced her to the families, and cooked caribou for her. She poked around in my house, wanted to explore every cranny of the village, and censored none of her comments. What nearly pushed me over the edge was when she insisted on starting the gasoline lamp herself. When she didn't have success, she stuck her finger in the mantle and broke it. No mantle, no flame, no light. I had several extras, but it wasn't as though I could run to a store and readily buy another. I'd have to put it on an order list.

Just as I we were saying good-byes and I was about to breathe a sigh of relief, she enthusiastically blurted out, "I can't wait to return in November!"

I didn't say a word, just let her talk. She only stayed two days. I was thankful when she left.

In all fairness, she was a perfect fit for her job. She thrived on jumping in and out of bush planes flying all around Alaska, and lack of conveniences didn't faze her, nor unpredictable, weather-troubled schedules.

The evening before she left, two men approached us as we were walking down the hill from school. "Ben Ahgook say baby come."

Ben Ahgook's wife, Elizabeth, was in labor.

I thought Miss Morey would be displeased that I was using my time in this way, but she assured me that it was okay and that she'd just wait in my house. I gathered up the weighty thing and some baby clothes. Instead of feeling overjoyed for Elizabeth, I kept thinking about Rhoda and Baby Peter, and ached for those parents. I wrestled with my unrequested role on the delivery team. If I'd been allowed to walk away when circumstances felt uncomfortable or disturbing, I would have felt differently about the baby announcements.

As before, Simon served as midwife.

"His shoes are coming first," he said matter-of-factly.

I stared at him. Even when the villagers spoke English, I had to learn *their* English. In this case, I figured out that the concern was about a footling breech birth, or feet coming first.

Nothing was happening at the moment, so I sat cross-legged on a caribou skin, off to the side, and drank tea that Ben offered me. As it turned out, this first summons was only false labor. That was fine with me. I returned home thinking, *How did I get involved in this? I am educated in education, not medicine.*

The respite was short-lived. The next week, with my arms full of books and papers, I was intercepted again. This time the men informed me the false labor had actually been Elizabeth's water breaking and she was now feeling very bad. I figured that if this baby was going to come with its *shoes on* rather than a *hat on*, we needed to get Elizabeth to the hospital.

Radio contact and battling through nasty weather were not the only obstacles. As much as Andy would go out of his way or find his way to help anyone in the Bush, he'd been caught between the needs of people and the bureaucracy of the government. Now he was wary.

Things had changed since Doc Gaede left Tanana. In recent months, the quiet-spoken, seldom complaining Good Samaritan bush pilot had done his job; he'd filled his airplane with gas and rushed a prospective patient from Anaktuvuk to Tanana. Instead of receiving appreciation for a job well done, the doctor had assessed the health concern as not critical. As a result, papers weren't signed that allowed Andy to be paid for fuel and time.

Just lately, Alice, one of my students, had been out chopping wood when her ax missed the wood and severely cut her foot. A number of us had worked together anxiously to stop the bleeding and bandage the foot. Everyone knew that she required immediate medical attention. After much wrangling with the Tanana hospital and persistence in contacting Andy, she'd been flown in. The doctor had to admit that it was serious.

"We must call Andy!" I said. "She needs stitches."

"He won't come," said one man.

I expected a rebuttal, but the next response was the same.

"Will doctor say it bad enough?"

The question implied that the physician might think we actually could have managed it ourselves.

Given this background and the uncomfortable tension between Andy and the doctor, no one wanted to be blamed for an impulsive decision. Even Simon, who was highly regarded by the Natives, Sig Wien, Andy and other bush pilots, and every scientist who sat at his feet, turned to me and deferred.

"You decide."

I shook my head in disbelief. I was a short-time resident and a newcomer to the Nunamiuts, only a school teacher, not a wise King Solomon. On the other hand, Dr. Hadley had told me to send in critically ill patients.

No one moved.

"Let's go find Bob," I said with resignation.

Bob Sutton, the construction engineer, had an upgraded and more dependable radio than the others in the village. He didn't think twice about making it available for the community's needs. First, he dug around in his coat pocket and pulled out a print handkerchief to wipe grease off his fingers from a current repair on the Cat. Between the two of us, we contacted Andy regarding Elizabeth. I prepared a memo for Dr. Hadley that explained the urgency of the situation and why we in the village were not qualified to handle a potentially complicated delivery.

"Bob, I hope he can get in soon. I don't think Andy wants to deliver a baby with or without shoes, boots, or mukluks on or in an airplane!"

ABC

My house smelled of barbeque sauce, and I couldn't wait to sit down to a quiet super with a new recipe for caribou. Canned corn bubbled in a small pot. I loved these people, but sometimes just needed a moment for myself. A tap on the door interrupted my plans. Jane walked in without waiting for me to respond.

"Elizabeth Hugo has chicken pox," she informed me.

For a moment, I was confused and thought it was Elizabeth Ahgook, the mother of the baby with shoes on, and then I realized that it was a different Elizabeth *and* a new health predicament.

"Am I on call?" I asked.

Jane didn't understand what I meant, and I didn't feel like explaining.

Illness didn't naturally reside in the village. Only when an outsider returned with a cold or other ailment was anyone sick. But when this did happen, the malady ran from home to home. The simple cold was often not a culprit as much as the resulting complications. Or, in this case, a common childhood disease, such as chicken pox, could be life-threatening to these people who did not have any naturally immunity from so-called *white man* diseases, which were not inherent in the Native population.

I turned off the gas burner and set the oven to low. In mid-September, the temperatures had dropped and glittering frost paved my way to school. My parka hung near the door, and I stuck my arms in the sleeves as I moved through the dark entry and out into the daylight.

The seasonal drop in temperatures had urged the Eskimos out of their airy canvas tents and back to their thick, sod-insulated houses. They'd accomplished their fall house-cleaning by bringing in fresh willow branches for the floor, rebuilding entries, and disposing of dog excrement around their winter tie-downs. I liked having neighbors back on my side of the creek.

The creek itself was pretty much dry. The last time I'd gone down with my pail, I'd searched and searched for a spot low enough to dip my cupped ladle. Everyone headed upstream to another area for water. The longer walk curtailed my water use, and I rationed every ounce.

I examined Elizabeth. Red welts covered her body—not chicken pox. "She has hives."

Her two sisters looked at me, not knowing if this was better or worse.

"I'm going to give her a soda water bath."

I hurried back to my house for baking soda. My, how good my house smelled, and I salivated like Pavlov's dog. I left reluctantly.

This soda bath alleviated the itching, and Elizabeth relaxed. I got up off my knees and shrugged my tight shoulders. Suddenly, she turned deathly white and opened her eyes as if startled. I thought she'd speak, but she just stared into space. My heart raced.

Oh dear. Maybe she's dying.

Then she started crying out and moaning.

"Let's pray!" I gasped.

I grabbed the sisters' hands, and we crumpled around Elizabeth on her caribou mat. The short prayer gave me a moment to think.

"Amen. Get a cold, wet cloth for her head."

They did as I advised, and I started to sing "Only Trust Him." God was our only hope, and I did trust Him. The singing made me feel as though I was at least doing something.

Gradually, the tears stopped and groaning subsided. She lay still and quiet. Rather than feel at peace, my fear escalated. I checked her pulse. Nothing. I tried again, desperately. I could feel my own heart pounding wildly, but nothing of hers. Finally, my fingertips found a racing one hundred beats per minute on *her* wrist. I sat stunned.

"Change the cloth!"

"Oh God! Help us!" I prayed out loud, and then started singing again.

I felt so distressed and alone. *Oh, where can I get some medical training?* Saving lives wasn't in my job description, but if I'd know what to do, I'd do it.

Within the day, Pat found out that he hadn't been informed of this issue. The pounding at my door was not that of the Eskimos' gentle rap—when they remembered.

"She has chicken pox, not hives," he growled.

I disagreed. He turned abruptly and left. Before I'd finished changing the sheets on my bed, he was back, puffed up as tall as he could stand in the middle of my house.

"Okay. I looked again and thought again. It's not chicken pox. Her blood is just too hot."

His temper was too hot too. He would not be convinced that my diagnosis might be accurate. I bit my tongue.

After two long days, my prayers for healing were answered and Elizabeth was walking around and back to her daily tasks. Or course, I was glad she'd returned to health, but the feeling of overwhelming helplessness mounted with her near-death, the bloody foot that could barely be suppressed, and babies headed the wrong direction.

ABC

"Would you please pass your music books in?" I asked my afternoon class of students.

The children shared my fondness for music, and I found myself running overtime in that subject.

Just then, we heard a knock on my school room door. Bob Sutton stood there in his heavy work overalls, completely out of breath not only from his run up the hill, but with the urgency of his message. He struggled for breath.

"Bob Ahgook's baby...sick last night...hasn't awakened...yet." He paused a second. "We think we should contact Tanana Hospital...I'll call the hospital on my radio. Everyone would appreciate if you'd do the talking."

I gave instructions to my trustworthy older students and hastened down the hill on my mercy mission. Baby Peter had made it six weeks, longer than I'd expected when I'd placed him on the weighty thing.

When I entered Bob's cabin, he sat hunched over his radio, his heavy coat still zipped, working with settings and dials.

"I'm not sure I can get through," he said grimly. He pulled off his cap and ran the back of his hand across his forehead.

Communication with the Tanana hospital was snarled.

"Would it make any difference if we'd try the FAA station at Tanana instead of the hospital?" I asked.

The static and screeching made me wince, but Bob wouldn't give up. Then we heard an actual voice.

"That's Jo Myberg! The Wien agent's wife," I exclaimed.

Jo was from the Netherlands and spoke with a Dutch accent, which complicated matters even more. Somehow, we managed to piece together a system of communication. I talked to her on the radio. She called the doctor on one of the few Tanana telephone lines and then she relayed information between the two of us. Dr. Hadley authorized hiring a charter for the baby.

Bob threw off his coat and immediately called Andy at Bettles Field. I trudged back up the hill to resume my trained-for, paid-for job of teaching fractions and vocabulary. My hard work, combined with their attentiveness and motivation, was showing up on worksheets that confirmed that teaching *was* the right job for me.

After school, Andy flew in with a stocky Beaver airplane.[11] In round, elementary-school-teacher handwriting, I wrote a note describing Peter's condition and folded it into my pocket. Then, bucking the ever-present wind, I pushed toward the airstrip. The customary mile walk had been reduced with the semi-completion of the airstrip construction. It wasn't ideal, but it was good enough for Andy to land with his big, shock-absorbing tundra tires. Andy walked toward me, his body also bent in the wind and his parka hood flapping. Men, women, and non-school-age children moved in small clumps between us, their small-print-and-flowered atigas ballooning in the wind. No matter the weather, a welcoming delegation would always be present.

"Bad news," shouted Andy. "Tanana is socked in. Nothing coming or going."

Rhoda moved near us and sat on her heels in the mid-September squall. She appeared even frailer in that position and as if a single gust could topple her at any moment. Beneath her parka, she clung to Peter. I waved to a bilingual woman, and we met by Rhoda. Together, we leaned down and I put my arm around Rhoda's slight shoulders.

"We will have to wait until morning," I spoke close to the interpreter's ear.

A gust snatched the words from the bystanders, but they comprehended the disappointing conclusion. Once again, we needed the Great Physician who was not limited by airplanes, radios, and weather.

Andy inquired about getting a cup of coffee after unloading supplies Bob had ordered.

"I don't want to stick around here much longer. Gotta get back before that storm really bears down."

He and Bob hustled back to the plane. Several women surrounded Rhoda. The rest of the group dissipated. I felt torn between staying with Rhoda and returning to my students. I couldn't be everywhere at once, and my first responsibility was to my students. I braced myself against the gusts and left for my classroom. My several-at-once lesson plans were difficult enough to follow with the various grades, and now with the upsetting interruption, I felt like a fish jerked out of water, released, and trying to swim once again.

Shortly after I dismissed my students for the day, I checked on Peter. The newborn's breathing was irregular with long pauses. Whenever he'd stop breathing, his father would shake him. Peter would struggle and temporarily start breathing again.

"What do you think about Peter?" Bob asked me.

His voice was dull and hopeless, and his shoulders slumped in weariness.

I really didn't want to say what I thought.

"Bob, I'm sorry." I brushed a tear from the corner of my eye. "I don't think Peter will make it until morning."

I sat with Rhoda and Bob awhile longer. The pitiful breathing process persisted. Long minutes filled the room. As excruciating as that was, I would have stayed longer; however, Danny had regained his health and had just returned home from the hospital. In celebration, the village teenagers were coming to my house for a welcome-home party within the hour. I left little Peter, trying to find a party spirit.

ABC

Danny poked his head through my door. His face beamed. What a changed young man this was. No longer was he skinny and disheveled. There was flesh on his bones, and he'd carefully slicked back his hair. Teens kept crowding into my one room and sprawled onto the floor or my day bed or sat at the table. The untroubled banter was such a contrast from the distressing event at the Ahgook's.

I'd asked several teenagers to bring their guitars, and everyone robustly joined into the songfest. Dominoes and Cootie were pulled from my game box, and Anna Hugo requested Spill and Spell. In between the day's teaching and healthcare, I'd managed to make cherry Jell-O with fruit cocktail as well as oatmeal cookies. The kids poked at the Jell-O and giggled when it jiggled. Danny soaked in all the attention, which was later written about by several students and read on KFAR radio. [12]

"Guess what the beds were like." Danny gave his version of hospital beds and laughed so hard that he tumbled out of his chair. This was only the beginning of descriptions from his adventures outside the village: sleeping with sheets, using a flush toilet, watching cars go by beneath his window, and hearing a telephone ring.

I sat back and took in the scene around me. My tiny home was filled to its cardboard edges with gladness and pleasure brought by renewed life and the return of a much-loved community member. Danny had written me consistently from his hospital bed, and I felt a special attachment to him. His letters touched my heart, as did the Eskimo name he bestowed upon me, *Napikuk* (NUGH-pee-kuk). I humbly accepted this honor.

I expected a long night and finally shooed the teenagers out the door. The wind carried jagged bits of singing and joking back to my cabin. That evening, our little village rejoiced with Danny's transformed life and, at the same time, prepared for a funeral. Peter had passed away at 6:20 p.m.

ABC

Cups and plates covered my table, but I didn't have time to heat water and wash them. They could wait. Bob and Rhoda could not.

Outside the Ahgooks' house, men cut wood and pounded nails for a small casket. The long daylight hours of summer had disappeared, and early darkness personified the solemn circumstances; heavy snowflakes made all efforts more difficult. Inside, the women cut and pinned fabric for a small bunny-looking suit. Each person had a task to accomplish and did so with purpose and resignation. Little Peter no longer struggled to breathe, but lay peacefully on a caribou skin with his brother and sister sleeping nearby. Rachel Mekiana started the chorus I'd taught in Sunday school, "The Lord is my Shepherd, I'll live for Him forever." Other voices joined in.

"Pretty," said Rhoda, using one of the several words she knew of English. She stooped near the wood stove and poked at the willows, all the while chewing hard on a piece of gum.

How can I comfort these people? I pondered what would have the most meaning for them.

I was about to quote scripture verses when Rachel burst out, "Let's sing about the foolish man and the house on the sand!" She pounded her fists on top of one another.

I was speechless. That robust and animated song seemed out of context. She waved her hands in the air and spread her fingers like the rain coming down on the house on the sand.

"Sing! Sing!" she insisted.

After singing it through one time, I tried to change the subject.

"Let's talk about heaven."

I spoke about God loving the little children, angels, and Peter going to a happy place where he would be dearly loved. Although Rhoda couldn't grasp what I said, she nodded her head.

My impromptu devotional ended when the men shuffled in with the casket. Rhoda tucked Peter's pathetic tiny body into the bunny suit and wrapped him in a blue blanket. The group stood silently. I waited. Everyone looked at me. I looked at them. What was the agenda? At length, Bob Ahgook asked me to put the baby into the casket.

"Oh!" I said, caught off guard.

I'd expected that ritual to be assigned to one of a family member. Gently, I laid Peter in the casket. Zaccharias Hugo positioned him so none of his body touched the edges of the box, and then the men placed layers of blankets over him and carried the casket matter-of-factly out the door, into the shrieking storm. None of the women followed.

"Where did they take him?" I asked Jane.

"They put him on cache for night."

I didn't see that anything else could be done, so I gathered my parka, mittens, and flashlight and stumbled home through the drifting snow. I couldn't believe that within a mere twelve hours, I'd taught classes, run out to the airstrip, hosted a party, and put a baby into a casket. My wind-up clock beside my bed showed midnight. I fell asleep instantly.

The next morning when I awoke, my first thought was that Andy would fly all the way over here and expect to take Peter to Tanana. I tried to see the weather through my plastic-covered window. The storm had worn itself out and left in its wake arbitrary drifts and snow that sparkled like diamonds. Every footprint from last night's party and burial preparations had been swept away. I dressed in preparedness to run out at the noise-of-a-motor's notice.

Near noon, I put on my mukluks and sought out Bob Sutton to see if he'd heard from Andy. The wind had packed the snow hard against the hill to the school, and children shouted with glee as they slipped and slid on their backs and tummies. Red, green, orange, and blue parkas stood out against the colorless background. The chopping sound of a helicopter overhead subdued the lively commotion. Bob and I talked to the pilot and learned that another snowstorm was blowing in from the north. Andy's departure would be from the south, but in all likelihood, the storm would barricade him out before he made it here. As it turned out, Bob had been unable to make contact with him, which was just as well.

My day was broken into pieces. I tried to do housework, but didn't want to miss out on anything. In Tanana, there had been funerals, usually at the Episcopal church, with a service at a set time and a casket, procession to the cemetery, and other formalities. I figured out slowly that customs here were different. No church service, no flowers, no formalities for babies—only burials. My curiosity and sympathy kept me rubbing on my frosted windows and glancing out to see if anyone was leaving for the cemetery.

I'd just swept my floor when Ethel Mekiana showed up.

"Going now."

I pulled my parka ruff tightly around my face and fought against the north wind as we started toward the cemetery, which was by the lake. Halfway there, we met Rhoda, on her way back in a dogsled. She and Ethel exchanged a few words. After standing around, watching the men start the digging process, the poor young mother was chilled to the bone and needed to warm up before taking little Peter out for burial. Ethel and I turned around and followed the sled. Walking south, with the wind at our back, was a welcome relief, even when it knocked us off balance.

Sometime later, the men accomplished their laborious undertaking and returned. I couldn't imagine that they'd been able to make any sort of indentation in the frozen sod, much less dig a hole deep enough for the casket. The burial group gathered at John Morry's house where Rhoda's nieces had fixed tuttu and hot tea. People of all ages filled the room to its sod edges. All at once, Bob Ahgook stood up, tightened his parka hood around his face until only his eyes peered between the whiskery ruff, and pulled on long caribou gloves. He stooped beneath the doorframe and left. Everyone followed suit, zipping parkas, tightening boots, and covering any opening that might allow in the determined frigid air. I trundled along after the procession.

Bob and several men climbed to the top of the cache and lifted down the small casket. In bunches of four and five, the villagers, including Nick and Bob Sutton, began the funeral march. Ethel walked beside me. The wind limited our conversation, and we invested our energy in forward motion.

ABC

Large picks lay on the ground around the funeral site. The men had fashioned a canvas to break the wind. A raised gravesite functioned as a table for a Coleman stove, which was lit immediately, and a pot of tea water set on top. In readiness for caribou, guns lay nearby. Just that morning, forty animals had migrated south, and hunters would be prepared if more migrated through now. Their life was not bracketed by single events, but flowed together in a continuous stream. For this moment, the project at their feet consumed their attention. The grave was still not deep enough, and the men resumed chipping notches in the icy sides of the intractable earth.

My fur ruff tickled my face, but I didn't laugh. I flexed my fingers in my mittens, ready to hold a cup of warm liquid. More and more, I appreciated their tea tradition.

Once the notches were satisfactorily cut, poles were fit into the indentations to create a platform for the casket. Then poles were added on top and like a little tent, caribou draped over the casket.

They are born on caribou skins and buried beneath caribou skins, I thought.

"It's ready now," Bob told me.

He looked at me expectantly. I didn't know what he wanted, unless it was to pray. I thought Homer would be there to pray since he was the current lay pastor at church. I assumed I was only there to lend support. No one said a word.

"Do you want me to pray?" I eventually asked.

Bob nodded his head forlornly.

I began, "Lord, we come to you today knowing that little Peter is with you in heaven. We trust we will see Peter again someday. Thank you for letting us have Peter here for a short while. Please comfort Bob and Rhoda. Amen."

I opened my eyes. Rhoda pressed close to her husband, who, for a second, had covered his face with his thick mittens. The kind and well-respected leader in the village was brokenhearted.

It had been a long, emotional journey, and now the little blue baby lay at rest. The men filled in the grave amid swirling snowflakes that heralded another storm. Everyone helped pack the tools, guns, and tea-fixings into the sleds. The sled dogs uncurled and stretched in their harnesses. Their tails unfurled like flags.

"Would you like to ride in sled?" asked Bob.

Ethel and I joined his family in their large work sled and returned to the village.

ABC

I pulled frozen caribou ribs from my cache and proceeded to chop them with an ax. In their current condition, they were much too large to bake in my oven. The night before, temperatures had dipped to 7 degrees; already, at the end of September, winter was nearby. Several children saw me hacking the ribs on the hard-packed snow and came running. Breathlessly, they broadcast the latest news.

"Miss Bortel, Elizabeth Ahgook is back!"

"What is the baby's name?" I wondered if her baby had actually arrived with boots.

They shrugged.

"Cute baby," said one of the girls.

"But you don't know if it is a boy or girl?"

"No."

With that teaser, they ran off, tripping in the drifts. I carried a small chunk of ribs into the house and placed it in a pan to thaw. Typing letters home would have to wait while I went to catch up on baby news.

I stepped out my entry, and Justus Mekiana swerved past me with a team of huskies.

"Checking traps?" I hollered.

He nodded.

His wife, Ethel, had added a baby girl to their pack of boys. Judy was a cutie. I'd been asked to name her too.

The snow brilliantly reflected the sun and left me blinded when I crouched into the dark entry of Elizabeth and Ben's sod house. I felt my way to the interior door and knocked.

"Come in, Anna," Elizabeth called out.

She knew it was me. Anyone else would have just walked in.

I laughed. Elizabeth and Ben laughed too.

"So, what did you have?"

"It's a boy," said Ben proudly.

Elizabeth handed the little bundle to me. The child gurgled and cooed. I snuggled him closer and pressed my cheek to his. "What's his name?"

"No name."

The carriers of Anaktuvuk morning news had been correct. Ben looked at me and then the baby. Once again, I was to be the name-giver. Once again, I chose a Bible name.

"What about Phillip?"

That settled it.

ABC

"Miss Bortel, *Tundra Topics* says public health nurse will be here tomorrow, if the weather is good." Roosevelt arrived at my door with radio news.

Tundra Topics, broadcast on a Fairbank's radio station, was a personal message broadcast that people tuned in to and could hear when someone was flying into their village, had a request for fish, knew where the caribou had just migrated through, or had a medical emergency and needed a bush pilot to come, and so on. Whenever someone overheard a message for another villager, he or she would contact that person.

Noting the late hour, I knew I'd have to get up early and rearrange my house so she could hold clinic the next day. I was a night owl and looked forward to lazing around on Saturday mornings, but no sleeping in this Saturday.

Ann Bergen arrived as scheduled, and my small quarters became an examining and waiting room. Ann pushed back her thick, strawberry-blonde waves and hooked them behind each ear, and then she rolled up the sleeves of her navy-and-white-striped knit pullover. She was ready. Saturday and Sunday filled quickly with TB skin tests and checkups for individuals with a variety of physical complaints. One woman told us that she had too much air in her stomach, and another was concerned because her stomach wouldn't cough. This tickled me to no end, but the two of us never batted an eye at these descriptions, until that evening, when we laughed like girls at a slumber party.

The proficient nurse demonstrated how to give penicillin shots. She'd brought along oranges on which to practice. I would have preferred just eating the oranges and really hoped I wouldn't have to jab anyone with a needle. Aside from that lesson, I enjoyed preparing patients for their exams and assisting with paperwork. In addition to the actual examinations and treatment, she taught the women how to bathe their babies. I was relieved to see her demonstrate with a *soft* soap.

Before Ann left on Monday, I plied her with questions and took notes. After the harrowing experiences I'd had in only five months, I didn't even want to imagine what I might encounter next in my village medical practice. One question she couldn't answer was why the villagers relied on me for medical assistance.

ABC

"Scientists know everything," a teenager told her friend one night when they were studying at my house.

Then it dawned on me, except for traders and pilots, the only other contact with white people had been with scientists. I'd acquired the status of health care expert because I was white. If only it were that easy. Regardless of my *Merck's Manual* and a soon-to-arrive Dr. Spock book, I knew I was much better qualified to teach school than to treat broken bones, stomachs that wouldn't cough, and babies born with shoes on.

TIMBER TIME

Alaska is an enormous state, and daylight hours vary considerably. Above the Arctic Circle, there are months between mid-May and August when the sun does not set at all. Playing by the same rules, there are months in winter when the sun does not show its face, much less the top of its head; only a rosy halo reflected above the horizon. The Native people think little of the darkness, which closes them in like a winter box; and in Barrow, there are actual celebrations when the sun shuts the door and hibernates from November 18 through January 24. Not me. I found myself hungry for light. I'd look at my calendar and calculate when the shiny globe would pull itself out of its dark grave; rise again; and then, in full glory, fill the sky with life-giving brightness.

The decreased daylight hours squeezed tightly the parameters for Andy to fly in during the less darkness at midday with the always anticipated mail or luxuries of Dream Whip, real potatoes or carrots, or frozen chicken. My mother sent baby clothes, and Ruby Gaede sent books, all of which spent time at Bettles Field, waiting.

My "running water" was no longer relatively convenient—it was now at the lake. I staggered against the wind and walked on top of wind-crusted snow until I unexpectedly broke through. At home, I measured out water for each task and made as few trips as possible to the lake. I didn't dare forget an ax to chop the ice.

The ruggedness manifested itself in beauty as well as unforgiving reminders that survival required everyday vigilance. In the dim light, I could see the snow-draped fortresses of mountains on either side of the valley. Occasionally, I'd see smudges of a pink sunrise followed shortly after by glimpses of a blushing sunset even though the sun itself remained hidden. The pass didn't get the snow accumulation that some parts of Alaska did, such as Valdez, but the wind packed down what did fall, making a firm foundation for dog sled travel.

Already, in mid-October, I'd stuck my toes deep into the caribou socks Susie Paneak had sewn especially for me. The fur against my ankle socks kept my toes toasty, and the additional padding inside my mukluks cushioned the walk on the frozen tundra. It seemed that if one's feet were comfortable, the rest of the body warmed more easily.

Icy fingers of cold reached into my sod hut and chapel classroom, but multiple bodies helped. On any given night, teenagers and children gathered near the glow of my gasoline lantern to do their homework rather than struggling at home with dim candlelight. When the Eskimos didn't have a candle, they would dip a piece of cloth in caribou fat and strike a match to it; that small, flickering flame would be the only light in their house. My lantern could not chase shadows out of the corners, but it was faithful in providing a liberal circle for reading and writing.

While I worked on lesson plans or wrote letters at my table, scholars sat on the floor or an extra kitchen chair. The older students read quietly or helped with dishwashing, but the younger ones hovered at my elbow or begged me to play Cootie. Sometimes I felt like I was in possession of a very large family. After they'd leave, I'd find Cootie legs or eyes beneath my bed or under my feet in the middle of the night when I used my honey pot behind the privacy curtain.

Rachel Mekiana, Anna Bortel, Anna Hugo, Rhoda Ahgook,
Alice Aklook, Anaktuvuk Pass, Alaska, 1960.

With the constant visitors, I wrote my sister Millie, "I am never lonely." I was fortunate.

I thought I'd made progress in adapting to the no-knock policy of my village visitors. I was wrong. One afternoon, I returned home from an intense day of teaching. My flashlight led me through the arctic entry and into the dark house. Typically, as soon as I entered, I'd pump up and light my lantern, but on that day it seemed like too much effort. I didn't have the energy to even take off my parka, and I collapsed flat on my back, on my bed, and then drifted in the twilight between wakefulness and sleep.

Somewhere in my drowsy state, I sensed a presence in the unlit room. I strained my eyes. Suddenly, a light shone in my face. I bolted upright.

"There you are!" It was Jack, a schoolboy.

I felt relieved, but my heart still thumped. He moved the light from my face, and I stood up with *my* flashlight and shone it at him.

He sprang back. "Miss Bortel, what is wrong?"

He explained that the kids hadn't seen a light at the classroom *or* in my house, which they expected after school let out in the afternoons, so he'd volunteered to investigate.

"You okay now." He was genuinely relieved that nothing was amiss and ran out to spread the glad tidings that I'd been found.

Completely exasperated, on Friday, I stretched a rope across the two entry posts as a sign of *no visiting* hours. I didn't want anyone disturbing my lazy sleep-in on Saturday.

ABC

I'd expected new experiences in Anaktuvuk, but not all were met with laughter or satisfaction. One night, I awoke to a weird, high-pitched vibrating sound. It reverberated like the string section of an orchestra warming up before a concert. I'd become accustomed to the howl of the constant wind as it chased around my sod house, but this reverberation made sleeping impossible. I lay awake trying to discern its exact whereabouts. I visualized the outdoor thermometer and groaned as I mentally saw the mercury sunk well below zero. I did not relish leaving my cocoon of comforters. The cacophony continued. I tossed and turned, trying to muffle the racket by pressing my pillow around my ears. At last, I relinquished all hopes of sleep and crawled out of bed to find my caribou parka and boots.

The bitter wind smacked me in the face and pinched my lungs. Now I was fully awake. I stopped to orient myself in the darkness. Moonlight slipped through the ice fog and cast an eerie glow on the clump of sod houses and skeletal caches. The view intrigued me, but my warm bed enticed me more. I had a job to do. After digging around in the snow, I found my step ladder and leaned it against the sod. Up I crawled to the top of my house.

In the fall, when Gladys Main and Ida Mae Merrill, my Fairbanks friends, had spent a week with me, they had attached wires to secure my stovepipe and steady it against the wind. Gladys, also a school teacher, was tall and could ably stretch to connect the wires. Ida Mae, a cook at the University of Alaska, was fittingly plump. She could find something funny in any situation. For one second, I contemplated what she'd be joking about now.

The original concept was worthy, but at this time of the year, with the frigid temperatures, hoarfrost encased the wires. The combination of frost and wind set up vibrations that caused the high-pitched screeching sound. I rubbed on the wires with my mittens. The nerve-jangling racket subsided. The quiet was momentary. Howling huskies signaled to one another that something was amiss in the middle of the night, which perhaps they should all know about. That was music compared to the untuned orchestra on my roof. I edged back down and hoped for some rest. Eventually, the dogs' sad wails were replaced by the familiar sound of wind.

ABC

Baby Phillip wailed. He'd been born in Tanana, after he'd tried to arrive in Anaktuvuk with his shoes on. The three-week-old child looked like a Korean orphan with arms and legs mere skin and bones. Most Eskimo babies were plump, like baby Elmer, who had cheeks like chipmunks. I found out that Elizabeth didn't have enough milk to breast-feed him, so she'd been giving him a mix of water and canned milk. Further questions revealed that Pat had run out of canned milk in his trading post, so Philip's bottles were filled mostly with water.

I held the distraught little boy and examined him further. His little bottom looked terribly burned, like an unchecked rash.

"Elizabeth, do you mind if I give the baby a bath?"

In short order, I cleaned him up and covered him with soothing oil. He seemed comfortable and fell asleep—with another bottle of warm water.

I doted on the tykes around me. Now with my role on the delivery team, I felt an even closer bond to the little newcomers. I wrote my sister Millie, "Phillip looks better. I found a formula in a little pamphlet—1/2 + 1/2 (ratio of water to canned milk) with a little sugar, so I think that will help my anxiety over him."

ABC

Winter curtailed prospects for a change of daily or weekly pace; the darkness and cold restricted the distance we could travel safely or warmly. In the summer, we could fish for grayling or pack a picnic lunch and hike the nearby hills. But in the winter, where could one roam besides neighborly visits, church, or a ptarmigan hunt?

"Miss Bortel, we walked to the end of the runway last night," Roseanna Rulland told me after class on Friday.

Aha! I'd never thought of the runway as a get-away.

"Let's go have a marshmallow roast tonight!" I exclaimed, surprised by my desperation.

Roseanna and her friend looked at me without understanding what I was talking about.

"You'll see," I said. "You find some firewood, and I'll get the rest."

It was unquestionably a party night. By the time we'd trooped through the village, our gang of older teenage girls had grown to six. Above us, the splendid moon illuminated the black sky and the Northern Lights arched from the mountains to the east across to those on the west. Swaying strands of curtains in blue, green, and red danced, and excitement stirred in the enchanted environment. Instead of dogs breaking the hush, the girls and I broke out in songs. We started with choruses, which changed to Christmas carols. A silent night and deep slumber surrounded us.

The twigs and tidbits of wood didn't want to spoil the darkness and sputtered about rather than bursting into flames. I poked marshmallows onto sticks and showed the girls how to toast, not blacken, them. I wished for a camera to capture the look on their fur-fringed faces. In the low glow of the fire, their slanted eyes rounded as the puffy white balls slowly expanded into golden puffs. They pulled off the sticky blobs and stuck them in their mouths. Glossy edges smooshed out the sides of their mouths.

The tiny fire refused to hold its own in the frigid blackness, and the girls who hadn't worn their mukluks complained of cold feet. Our party ended abruptly, and we sought refuge inside our thick sod houses.

I'd enjoyed the diversion very much, and near the end of October, I had another chance for fun. It started with trying to explain the concept of Halloween, costumes, pumpkins, and special treats.

"Be sure and make a mask to go with your costume," I said. "We'll have a parade before we eat treats."

"E-e-e-e," ("Yes, yes.") resounded throughout the classroom as the little ones squealed with excitement.

As usual, special school events expanded into special village events. Parents assisted by making masks, and the children twittered all week when they talked about their costumes. From what I could tell, mothers were using their sewing skills with skins and fur. The Halloween party finally arrived, and children donned their costumes. Some had full head disguises. Some masks had ears like an animal, and one mask had actual caribou ears. Other masks were silly faces. I expected glee and gaiety, but instead, an unexpected hush enveloped the room.

What is wrong? I wondered. I snapped pictures and tried to encourage lightheartedness, but the students moved away from one another, and one child started crying.

Finally, it dawned on me. *They can't distinguish between fantasy and reality. They are frightened by each other.*

Once they removed their masks, laughter resumed and treats of corn candy and cupcakes disappeared.

The school term of June to November sped to an end. I wasn't used to such an early break prior to the holidays, and before I knew it, I was completing the semester-end details and recording grades. I was pleased with the progress of this first school session, which had been measured by standardized test. I wrote home:

> The fourth graders had lagged in arithmetic, but in reading and language, they did fine. One boy who could only print at the beginning of school, rated up to seventh grade in language. Even my little non-English speaking students did real well on the readiness tests. I drilled them and drilled and it really bore fruits.

I was on the last lap of this race when there was a knock on my sod house door.

"Here, Miss Bortel," said Joe Mekiana. He thrust a section of sheep ribs toward me, "Dad got five sheep. We have lots."

I was happy to hear this news since, at various intervals, he'd shown up at my house when hunger prevailed in his home. The Nunamiuts rated sheep meat as the most desirable, and ribs ranked as the prime cut. His parents had honored me with a gourmet offering. I thanked him profusely. He walked toward the door and then turned around.

"John Hugo and other men go to Kivik and Ihyanituk to hunt.[13] They get cabins fixed for winter. Wish I could go. Dad wants me to take care of mail for him."

In part, I could understand his dejected look. I'd listen to narratives about the dogsled trips to the tree sections. Like Joe, I longed for the thrill of Eskimo travel and to turn these tales into personal experiences. Joe's comment heightened my curiosity.

When Anna Hugo dropped in, she stirred my desire further.

"My parents are going to Kivik at school break."

The entire village was preparing for timber time.

"Would there be a possibility that I could go too?" I inquired boldly. I realized that sled space was limited and that everyone who went along must make some contribution. I'd accept a *no* but hoped for a *yes.*

"I'll ask," replied Anna.

"I can take food and help with the cooking," I offered.

In a while, she returned with a message of acceptance from her parents.

"When do we leave?" I asked excitedly.

"Maybe Tuesday. Maybe not." She lifted a shoulder indifferently.

This conversation repeated itself for another week. I'd managed to schedule flying connections to Ohio for the winter break, which included a series of five segments, but dogsled travel defied such precision. After several more days, I told myself, *You must learn to go on Eskimo standard time.* From what I'd learned about these people, weather and family health were the determining requisites. Who knew when these factors would come together? Regardless, I prepared to leave at a moment's notice, and in one corner of my home, I stashed supplies I would need for the sled trip. Among the items were tomato paste and seasonings for a spaghetti supper, along with powdered chocolate mix for cocoa and peanut butter for sandwiches. Simultaneously, I packed my suitcases for the three-month break outside. Then I waited.

ABC

At 8:45 a.m. on November 4, Anna Hugo came over and announced our imminent departure. In the morning darkness, I hastily took medicine to a woman who was sick, emptied my chamber pot, and scurried to Pat's to purchase a pound of coffee and a pound of loose tea. The total payment was $3.75.

In the gray of morning, John Hugo placed a large canvas over the entire dogsled and steadily arranged our supplies. I watched in horror as the sled filled up.

"But, Anna, where will we sit?" I whispered nervously.

"We will sit on top of everything," she said casually.

The heap grew. "But how will we hang on?" I asked. I couldn't believe my eyes as John lashed down the huge mound. I had a foreboding feeling that this would be like riding a bucking bronco without a saddle. *How could I stay on for the ride?* My prospects looked grim.

John positioned his team in their harnesses. Ten dogs leaped forward, eager to pull and yelping in anticipation.

Then it was my turn.

"Come, Anna." Anna Hugo motioned me to sit in front of her as she climbed toward the back of the sled.

John took his position behind the sled on the runners, ready to release the brake and yell, "Go!"

I looked around for some anchor and finally dug my caribou-skin-mittened thumb under a rope. The dogs lunged forward before I could brace my legs around the supplies, and I lurched against Anna behind me. The wild ride began.

I knew immediately that this would not be a comfortable ride on a plush seat of caribou skins. I'd brought along two cameras and had planned to alternately take still slide photos and 8mm movie sequences. But now, I wondered if I'd miss all the scenery as we traveled down the John River. Hanging on by my thumb and thighs demanded all my attention, much less any chances of filming.

The omnipresent wind tossed our ruffs around our faces. We'd only just begun, and already, I was grateful for the caribou socks, mittens, and the mukluks.

I'd overheard the village mothers tell their children, "White people don't know how to dress for cold."

It was probably true. Susie didn't want the school teacher freezing to death.

Mile after mile the super-charged dogs raced over the frozen Anaktuvuk River without any indication of tiring. I clung to the raring sled bareback until I thought my tense legs would break. No wonder that when I returned home and undressed, I found that my thighs and calves were black and purple.

I just need to rest my legs for a few minutes, played like a broken record in my mind. After a while, a new message was added: *I just need to wipe my nose.*

Then, I took the chance. I let go of the rope to find a tissue in my parka pocket. At that instant, a strong gust overpowered the sled, pushing it sideways on the glare ice. It skidded out of control until we slammed into a pressure ridge. I sailed off the sled. John yelled at the dogs to stop. Anna clung to my parka and managed not to topple off after me as she dragged me alongside the sled until her father was able to stop the raring dogs. We looked at each other and, in comic relief, burst out laughing at the unexpected derailment. At least I'd managed to stretch my legs and blow my nose.

"We'll soon be there," Anna encouraged me.

Even with that hope, I reluctantly crawled back on the sled, stuck my thumb under the lashing, and braced my numb legs for the remainder of the trip. Three hours after leaving Anaktuvuk Pass, and none too soon for me, we arrived at our first day's destination: Ihyanituk (I-YON-uh-took), twenty-five miles south of Anaktuvuk and where the Anaktuvuk River joined the John River.

David, my learning-disabled student, stood beaming at the door of the sod hunting cabin. His hair was tugged in all directions and looked as though he'd just pulled off his parka hood. "I see you coming," he said.

Sod hunting cabin at Ihyanituk, twenty-five miles south of Anaktuvuk, Alaska, where the Anaktuvuk River joins the John River, 1960.

I was happy to see him, elated to get off a whale of a ride, and in seventh heaven to go inside a shelter.

I shivered and shook as we sipped his welcoming feast of hot tea and coffee and chewed on caribou meat.

Mabel Paneak and her brother, Raymond, arrived after us, followed by the Rulland siblings, Tommy, Roseanna, and Johnnie. Danny and his father, Clyde Hugo, joined our indoor campout too. We sat on the willow-bough floor, and bursts of laughter filled the air as we recounted the near catastrophes *en route*. Just like me, Mabel had flown off her perch and landed in a rock pile. Johnnie's dogs had careened about and dislodged him from his sled runners. Roseanna had given up trying to balance on top the sled over the bumpy terrain and attempted to run alongside. She'd tripped and fallen in a heap with the sled passing her by. The hilarity prodded the chill away. Tea steeped, tuttu simmered, and tales grew.

"Maybe we take out stove," Tommy remarked later when conversation lulled and the kerosene lamp dimmed.

I looked at him incredulously. *How will we stay warm?*

"Too many people," he said.

He had assessed the sleeping situation. If eleven people crawled into sleeping bags and stretched out, there might not be room for the stove in these tight quarters. We shifted about and, like a puzzle, arranged our sleeping accommodations until we succeeded to squeeze ourselves together on the floor. The stove remained.

The next morning, someone tossed more grounds into the coffee pot, and I prepared breakfast with my offerings of homemade bread, butter, and peanut butter. When I gingerly climbed atop the sled for our next segment of travel, I felt warm and satisfied, but the twinges in my stomach reminded me of yesterday's sled-riding anxiety.

We had traveled southwesterly to Ihyanituk. Now the mushers turned the dogs northwesterly up the Ihyanituk Creek. The trek grew increasingly difficult. Mushers struggled to guide the sleds over the frozen waterfalls. Dog's feet, cracked by running through the ice overflows, left red prints in the snow. Empty wolf traps left disappointment on faces. Swampland frozen with knobby hummocks increased the bumpy starts and stops of the sled as the dogs labored on the uneven surface.

At one point, the postcard view of spruce trees and snow-covered mountains drew my attention away from the hazards. Trees! I hadn't realized how visually starved I was for trees, with their color and their dimension against the flat landscape. I hadn't seen trees for five months. I'd missed them so much in the barren pass.

A moment later, a tree branch ran up my leg, shredding my heavy wool pants. I felt a numbing scratch, but couldn't risk examining the damage. After straining to go up a long, steep hill, the dogs quickened their pace as they started down the other side. We descended the hill, hitting every bump with gigantic force.

I cherished this trip with my friends and appreciated them including me; just the same, if I survived reaching Kivik, I would be happy to pay

Andy to come get me and fly me back to Anaktuvuk Pass. Unfortunately, like a desert mirage, this was only wishful thinking. No landing strip existed anywhere in this obscure and untarnished back country. I could adapt to sporadic mail service, outhouses, and eating sheep brains, but I wasn't sure I could withstand trips on top a dogsled. My admiration and esteem for the Native people rose to an all-time high.

Just when I thought I could *not* survive another jounce, Anna suggested, "Let's walk."

Finally, I could forget merely surviving and attend to the inspiring environment. We continued the arduous journey on foot. About 1:30 p.m., a log cabin nestled in spruce trees appeared. The dogs veered toward it. I'd made it.

Except for a small wood stove and one wide board, the cabin was completely empty. John built a lively fire in the stove with *real* wood, not puny twigs like we used in Anaktuvuk. Raymond chopped additional wood. Water heated up quickly, and we took the edge off our hunger with Pilot Boy crackers and tea. Mabel cut up meat, and I found the noodles I'd brought along. Our one-course meal, cooked in a clean, five-gallon aviation gasoline can, consisted of one-third of a can of water and plenty of caribou with noodles. We placed cups and plates on the board on the floor.

Anna cooking in a Blazo can at Kivik, Alaska (Mabel Paneak, Anna Bortel, Anna Hugo, Roseanna Rulland), 1960.

"I think I have the chicken pox," commented Anna as she stirred the contents. She pulled the hair back from her neck and I could see vesicles.

Then Mabel said quietly, "I think I have the pox, too." She rubbed her face.

Stifling a sigh, I thought with disappointment, *I won't get to explore, or hike, or go caribou hunting now.* Just the same, I said, "It's important that you remain inside and take care of yourself. I'll stay with you."

A number of children had passed around chicken pox before we'd left the village, and now the incubation period had ended for Anna. The villagers had not learned to care for themselves, which exacerbated the effects of what many people consider a common childhood illness. During a previous year, women, although sick, had continued to gather twigs and tend household chores. Many of them contracted pneumonia and died. Now, it was critical that Anna remain indoors, where it was warm, and she did not exert herself.

Following our afternoon meal, John left to check traps before the early winter darkness reined in outdoor activities. The girls attended to mending. Mabel patched Raymond's torn mukluks and shared some sinew with me so I could mend my wool pants. I asked that they teach me to sing "Jesus Loves Me" in Inupiaq. Mabel showed me how to use the sinew, and we passed the time singing and sewing.

Mabel Paneak scraping a sheep skin at Kivik, Alaska, 1960.

When John returned, his grin spread ear to ear and a dead wolf lay in the sled. This meant a $50 bounty and a parka ruff. Parka ruffs exemplified the success of the hunter and reflected the craftsmanship of the seamstress. A ruff that had small sections of fur expertly sewn together with the guard hairs evenly displayed at the outer edge was a piece of art.

The day ended with only mukluks removed; otherwise, our night clothes and day clothes remained the same. Conversation had slowed, and the fire crackled less. A lone wolf howled in the distance. A wolf pack answered back.

"A good sign," remarked Danny. "Maybe there is wolf in trap."

Tomorrow, we would know. Tonight, the dying embers fizzled and went out. I snuggled deep into my sleeping bag. The night would be cold.

The next morning, Raymond and David left their comfy nests and made a roaring fire in the sub-zero cabin. Ice covered the water pail. The rest of us emerged tentatively from our nighttime insulation. Mabel started coffee, and I searched for pancake ingredients.

"Coffee *tugok'pick*? (Do you want coffee?)," asked David.

"I coffee *tugok'tunga* (Yes, I want coffee)," I answered.

John and the other men left to set and check traps. Clyde and Danny took off for Hunt's Fork. Poor Roseanna was now breaking out with chicken pox. She itched everywhere. I figured she'd be okay for a short time, so I ventured outdoors anyway with my camera. In this arctic midnight of winter, diffused shadows covered the snow. I shot a few pictures, but too soon, complete darkness drove me back inside the cabin, along with the hunters.

I noticed how they paid careful attention to the barks of the dogs. A dog would bark and someone would cock an ear and then interpret the message of the bark. They could distinguish between typical dog talk, and the announcement of intruders, such as a wolf. In addition to getting wood, they'd come here specifically for wolf pelts; of course, that meant that wolves were in the area. This would have been more fascinating to me if I hadn't needed to go outside for bathroom needs. I didn't want to be out there when a big, bad critter sauntered into our area. I delayed the urge.

Finally, I could wait no longer and went out into the starry darkness. On my return, I saw the shadow of an animal between the cabin and me. *Was it a loose dog? Was it a wolf pup?* My indecision kept me rooted to the spot. I stood still. *Should I yell? Would anyone in the cabin hear me?* All at once, the tethered dogs sent an emergency call to the cabin.

The door flew open, and John looked out.

"Wolf?" I yelled.

"Dog!" he shouted.

I shuddered and stumbled through the snow to the cabin.

ABC

"Tomorrow, you will go back to Anaktuvuk," said Anna Hugo. "Roseanna, Mabel, and I will not go back until our chicken pox are gone."

They did not want to spread their illness to anyone else.

I blinked back regret at the thought of riding atop the sled for that distance. That would be a long haul, longer than when we'd come out here since the forty miles had been divided into two days. Anna read my mind.

"You will sit *in* the sled and even in a sleeping bag."

Sure enough, John put the wolf and fox skins he'd trapped below my seating section.

In comparison to the trip to Kivik, the jostling sled ride back to Anaktuvuk felt like a cradle. A big disappointment was to find that the sod house we had stayed our first night had burned to the ground. We stood in disbelief. But, in Nunamiut tradition, no one complained or expressed any futility about the situation. They dug away snow, gathered wood, and started a fire for tea. I shivered and waited for the water to boil. After I pressed the cup to my lips and the hot liquid ran down my throat, I still trembled. How could anyone really get warm in 30 degrees or more below zero? Someone on another sled hauled out a hind quarter of caribou and cut slices of the frozen raw meat. I pulled out peanut butter sandwiches I'd made before leaving that morning. I'd kept them near me for body warmth, but still they were as stiff as a piece of crusted snow—although they *did* have more flavor.

The hint of daylight diminished as we continued up the John River, and the cold intensified. John was riding the sled runners, and I turned to look up at his face in the last glimmers of light. The raw polar wind and cold had transformed his breath, moist from exertion, into an artist's brush. His parka ruff was covered with frost, as were strands of his hair, which hung down on his forehead. Even his eyebrows, eyelashes, and whiskers were silvered. I wanted to remember it forever. I reached for my movie camera but couldn't get it to snap a picture. I turned back to John's face and etched it in my memory.

We arrived in Anaktuvuk at 4:00 p.m. Dora, John's wife, had coffee and tuttu waiting for us. After the six-day absence, my outlook had changed and I saw Anaktuvuk like a city in comparison to the wilderness where I'd traveled.

The Anaktuvuk people had embraced me before, but now I felt like they'd flung open their hearts to me. This journey had been a sort of initiation; now, I truly belonged to them.

When I left for the winter break, several men carried my bags to the plane.

"We miss you play organ," said one man.

"Thank you. You teach our children," chimed in others.

"I'll only be gone until school starts in March," I promised them.

"You come back?" they kept asking, even when I assured them that except for what I needed for my trip back to Ohio, I'd left all my belongings right there in my cabin.

Before I left, I counted seventeen cases of chicken pox.

"You take care of yourselves," I urged, feeling my heart strings pulled with the good-byes. I didn't want anyone missing when I returned.

PART V

....

1961

GRAND CENTRAL STATION

···

Oh how I'd enjoyed fresh fruits and vegetables, *real* milk, sidewalks, indoor plumbing, and dinner with friends and family. Recent statehood increased the Alaska mystique, and my vacation was crammed with invitations to speak at school assemblies, parent-teacher meetings, and church groups.

By and large, I'd take the audience on an imaginary trip with my slides. "Buckle your seatbelts," I'd say, and away we'd go to Valdez, Tanana, and Anaktuvuk Pass. I included plenty of props: an Eskimo parka, mukluks, caribou socks, ulu, and so on. Question-and-answer time flowed into extended sharing over frothy punch and an assortment of homemade cookies and frosted bars. As much as I explained to them, and as many pictures as I showed, I still wondered if I was conveying more than a hint of the wilderness world in which I taught and lived. Even though I was on vacation for nearly three months, I'd stayed in contact with Anaktuvuk. I relayed to Ruby what I'd heard.

Eddie wrote that in *Alaska Ed. News*, it stated that "The school at A.P. in the Brooks Range will receive four new pre-fabricated building late in the spring of this year. The new structures will house 2 classrooms, quarters for teachers and power equipment....A number of Eskimos wrote and said that one couple had lost a baby. I guess it must have been a blue baby... They say that Pat O'Connell is gone for good...Homer has his own store now.

At the end of February, I prepared for my return, laden with long johns, scene-o-felts of Bible stories, books, and wonderful memories of time spent with family and friends. I could hardly wait to return to my sod house, located in a blank square on Alaska maps.

The return trip was long and arduous. I boarded a train at Toledo, Ohio, which took me to Chicago. During the extended layover, I discovered a Harvey Restaurant,[14] where I ordered a delicious toasted ham sandwich. St. Paul, Minnesota, was the next stop, and I found the most interesting machine for coffee. When I inserted a dime, a paper cup dropped down and I could select a button for "Black," "Sugar," "Cream," or "Both." I had never seen anything like it. Chugging through a blizzard, I made it to Seattle.

At this juncture, I switched to air travel and flew to Anchorage and then to Fairbanks. A stopover with Ida Mae and Gladys allowed me to catch up with the five-hour time change as well as do some grocery shopping before heading back into the Bush.

During one of our late-night slumber party girl talks, I'd casually brought up Eddie Hooley's name, a teacher in Kobuk. I'd first heard about Eddie from Ruby and Doc, a few years earlier. He and his friends, Mahlon and Hilda Stolfuz's family, had traveled down the Yukon, stopping in Tanana to visit before continuing downward to Russian Mission, where Eddie would teach school and his friends would operate a trading post. Presently, however, he was teaching at Kobuk, above the Arctic Circle and approximately 175 miles southeast of Anaktuvuk Pass.

Gladys looked at me knowingly, but Ida Mae launched into, "What if he just drops in on you sometime?" We'd see. They didn't know that I was already corresponding with him.

My full circle of travel expenses would amount to $500. Now the hops got shorter and took me through Tanana and Hughes before I arrived in Bettles. Nevertheless, I was not flying in a little, single-engine bush plane. Wien Airlines had upgraded to a modern 727-A Fairchild prop-jet complete with an aisle between seats and a stewardess. Between Tanana and Hughes, I was the only passenger, so I asked the stewardess, "Will you be flying into Anaktuvuk Pass next?"

"Yes. Next summer."

Our little private village would become a tourist attraction.

ABC

I spent the night at the Bettles's Lodge. In the morning, I carried my bags downstairs, where Andy was fixing breakfast for his family and the other borders. Bacon sizzled. Eggs hissed as they hit the hot grease. Andy stood with his back to me and worked over the stove in the kitchen. When he wasn't in the air, delivering scientists or hunters to a remote site or dropping off supplies and mail to villages, Andy called this place home. Not only could he crawl under fog blankets and uncover villages camouflaged on the tundra terrain, but he could find fresh bacon and real eggs in this remote country. I was in good hands.

Switching roles from cook to pilot, he untied his apron and put on heavy outdoor gear. Leaving behind the smell of wood stove and fried bacon, I climbed into Andy's Cessna 180. When I'd left in November, the sun had taken leave. Now, its cheerful face brightened the snowy pass. What bold beauty, a brilliant blue sky and air so clear that the mountains rose off the valley in sharp majesty. Five time zones from where I'd started, I was near my destination. I stared in sleepy reverie.

The plane banked, startling me. *What is Andy up to? Perhaps he's sighted a caribou herd.* I shielded my eyes and looked down to see not brown animal shapes, but crayon-colored dots moving on the undulating white landscape. I was already home! It seemed the entire village was heading toward the runway, the *new* runway. The aircraft glided on the snowy strip, and then the friction of skis on hard-packed, uneven drifts brought it to a stop.

I climbed out. My exuberant greetings tangled into bursts of ice fog. Children pressed against me. "Teacher! Teacher!" I was so thrilled to be back that initially I saw only happy faces. Then the adults spoke of the difficult times.

"Here." A man I didn't recognize thrust a letter at me. He'd heard Andy was flying me in and had mushed his dog team from Publatook

(POO-bla-took), thirty miles south of Anaktuvuk.[15] I unfolded it with thick gloved fingers. The letter stated that Jonas was gravely ill and the Natives would clear a runway so Andy could transport him to the hospital. I showed Andy the letter.

"Okay. Let's unload your gear, and I'll get over there. Gotta keep the oil warm."

It was 42 degrees below zero.

Word came back later that Andy had managed to land on the makeshift strip and take Jonas to the Tanana hospital for treatment.

"Nearly everyone here is sick," Nick told me. Worry lines creased the bit of forehead that wasn't hidden behind his parka ruff.

A young mother nudged my arm. "My girl don't eat."

"More got chicken pox after you left," said a schoolboy.

"Little Judy died on Monday," continued Nick. "Something about a weak heart."

My throat constricted and my heart ached. "Poor Justus and Ethel," I said.

I remembered when Judy had been born to the Mekianas. The delivery had been easy, and she appeared healthy, not blue like an infant with heart problems. Ironically, her father had turned into my patient. All day, Justus had worked on the airstrip, and then, the dutiful father of a new baby had gotten up in the wee hours to feed wood into the fire. He'd sat on a stool next to the stove to make sure it would burn properly, but as exhausted as he was, he'd toppled off his stool and cut his head deeply on the sharp, hot metal.

As usual, I'd been paged. I'd cleaned up the wound and urged him not to go outside. He'd slept all day. Even though he wasn't dizzy and his pupils appeared normal, I was uneasy. I finally concluded that he was exhausted and well deserving of extended rest.

My elation at being home was diminished by the numerous reports of illnesses. Amidst children's tugs and questions, I walked slowly toward my sod house, tuning out their chatter and trying to collect my thoughts and reorient myself. I'd sent a message over *Tundra Topics* to alert Frank when I'd be arriving. I'd requested that he start the oil stove to thaw out the frozen sod.

The wind had welcomed me in its typically blustery way, and the cold penetrated even more deeply. I could see my house ahead, and my preoccupation with the community health concerns ceased momentarily. I was ready for my comfortable home. Then I did a double-take. No smoke puffed out the stove pipe, not even a wisp.

Jack broke the news. "Frank go to Barrow to look for wife. He not start stove. Maybe he take key with him."

My mind flashed back to the intended fishing lesson, the mocking at my efforts to rebuild my cabin entry, and the Fourth of July. I'd learned later he'd anticipated showing me how he excelled in beating the drum and leading the singing for the dancing. He'd wanted to impress me. I'd had no idea that I'd been a candidate for courtship, but apparently, I'd hurt his feelings by leaving before he could perform. Now, since I'd failed to comply with his many efforts, he was indifferent to my return home.

If I wanted courtship, it would have been from Eddie. I hoped he wouldn't become indifferent to my return to Alaska, and, at moments, I even boldly hoped he'd move beyond that of pen pal to finding a reason to come to Anaktuvuk.

Jack went to find a hacksaw to sever the door chain so we could get in. The potatoes, celery, and lettuce I'd carried in my suitcase from my stopover in Fairbanks had frozen. If that wasn't disappointing enough, when I *was* able to break into my house, I discovered that the canned goods I'd left in my storage area were also frozen and that some of the cans had ruptured. I stood inside what I'd expected to be a warm, welcoming home with my teeth chattering. This was too much to deal with in the extreme cold. I deposited my bags, lit the stove, and went to visit village friends in their well-heated homes while my house defrosted.

My return wasn't entirely frustrating. When I *did* return to my semi-warm house, Elijah presented me with two frozen fish, entrails and all. Then Susie Paneak came with caribou ribs. To top it off, Simon declared that I was the *real* Napikuk now since the old Eskimo Napikuk had died at Kobuk. Danny had given me my Eskimo name earlier, but the significance had increased dramatically with this proclamation. I wasn't sure how the meaning, "vertebrate," fit. Perhaps it had to do with stability, like a backbone.

The next day, Nick appeared in late afternoon, and we traded information about Anaktuvuk's winter months and his study of the Eskimos for news outside of Alaska's Interior. He confirmed that Pat had left for good and that Homer was moving the store to his place, which he called "Mekiana Trading Post." I enjoyed the evening's lively exchange and was settling back in.

ABC

The odds were against starting school on time. Many students were sick at home or still in Publatook, where sickness prevailed as well. Even if the children *were* healthy, they had no way of getting back since their fathers were hunting. These nomadic people had survived because they followed the caribou or found other sources of meat; and right now, the meat shortage in Anaktuvuk had pulled them down to the timber line. When I'd recently visited Ellen Hugo, there was not a scrap of food anywhere. I'd heard her children were eating at other homes. That troubled me greatly, and when I got home, I dug into my pantry boxes to find rice to share. Regardless of their hunger, no one complained.

Whenever a hunter *did* return to the village, he brought me messages scribbled on the inside of Foremost canned milk wrappers or on a paper sack. The Eskimos were proud of their writing skills and practiced them whenever possible and on whatever surface.

Ethel Mekiana wrote me a most touching letter.

> Dear Anna Bortel,
> I just received your nice letter today, and thanks for talking to us about Judy. I sure miss her. But that o.k. I know she go to heaven to wait for us. I always get lonesome some time but I try to be happy. So please pray for me and Justus. God bless you and keep on praying.

The students' illnesses were only one thing with which to reckon. I struggled daily with starting the stove in the chapel-school, all too reminiscent of my battles in the Tanana shelter wells. Since Frank was in Barrow, his adult son, Johnnie, was left to assist me. We worked together, but he didn't understand the physics of fuel combustion. On such unbearably frigid days, the fuel burned more rapidly, which emptied the small tank quickly, and the tanks either gulped down the oil or the starter flame refused to ignite. When we did win against this contrariness, the wind showed no courtesy and the drafts won out against the fragile heat. I tried to reduce the room area that sucked up heat, and at one point, we draped a canvas behind the pulpit to partition off an unused open area.

Snow that tracked in on the floor never melted all day. Outside, the thermometer read minus 30 degrees. I layered myself with snuggies (waffle-weave long-sleeved shirts), long johns, wool slacks, and a Dacron thermal jacket and pant set. Fortunately, my *mukluks* allowed for two pair of socks *and* moccasins. *I can really enjoy* all *my clothing here*, I mused. Even at night, the layers remained. I just couldn't get warm.

Something that did let some welcoming light in to the long, dark winter days were the letters from Eddie. He'd tell me about his experiences in Kobuk, and I'd respond with teaching incidences, amusing conversations with villagers, and questions about what he liked about Alaska. I'd been down relational roads with other men, which had hit bumps and slowed to a halt because of differences in spiritual values, and early on, I asked Eddie about his faith. From all indications, we traveled a similar path in life, professionally and spiritually.

At long last, the stiff wind took a break. I warmed up. The families returned from Publatook and school resumed in full force.

One morning I told the students I had a surprise. The following day, I entered the classroom with a box and removed flute-o-phones, ten-inch-long, cream-colored plastic instruments.

"What is it, Miss Bortel?"

Every child squirmed on the edge of his or her seat, waiting in anticipation. I demonstrated. Fingers on both hands were used to cover the holes as the child blew on the mouthpiece, thus producing musical tones. After I showed how to generate different sounds, they cautiously placed their fingers over the holes and blew on the mouthpieces. Every time they "tooted," they threw back their heads and belly-laughed.

What this beginning band lacked in ability they made up in merriment. Their enthusiastic responses touched me, and I wished Bob Spackey, the Ohio music teacher who had given me these instruments, could share in the experience. Accordingly, during language class, the children practiced their writing skills penning thank-you letters.

I thought about the other songs I'd written about Alaska and thought that if lyrics were in their own language, songs would be more relevant. One evening, Jane and Rachel sat reading in my lantern light.

"Could you help translate my 'Wind Song' into Inupiaq?"

I sang the refrain: "The wind blows in the morning. It blows all through the day...

Outside, we could hear the wind whistling around the sod house, seeking an entry point.

"That's like Anaktuvuk," exclaimed Rachel.

Indeed, it was like Anaktuvuk, although I had the Valdez Blows in mind when I'd written it in a minor key. We worked with semantics and spelling, and finally, we celebrated our success by singing the words in Eskimo:

The wind blows in the morning
Ovlami anokoliksuk

It blows all through the day
Ovluknatluyo ilokanun innixalugo

And when the day is over
Taverasi ovluk natpun

I can hear it say,
Tusagiga okakmun
O-o-oo-oo-o-o

Just like the wind, this song spread among others in the community, and I was pleased when I heard other students singing what Jane and Rachel had taught them.

Whether it was music or writing, the students couldn't learn quickly enough. In short order, they went through all the storybooks I'd brought on my initial arrival. To provide for their intellectual quest, curiosity, and sheer entertainment, I wanted to set up a village library, just as I'd done in Tanana. When I'd been in Ohio, I'd solicited donated books, which I brought back with me. Already, four or five children had spied *The Terry Twins in Alaska* and, after reading it, begged for more adventure stories.

Before a library could be established, I needed to inventory and catalog what I had and make a list of others to order. The next decision was where to put them. The chapel, serving double duty, was crowded with school desks, chalkboards, and a pulpit; and my home was already an after-school study hall. After brainstorming options and not coming up with much, I decided to situate the library near the entryway of my sod house. After all, what was a little more traffic flow added to the already-steady stream of visitors? I measured. I could fit three-foot-wide shelves at about four feet high. Now I just needed to find boards. When I did get organized, I insisted that library visitors not come until after 6:00 p.m. I really did need time after school to relax, clear my mind, and eat supper.

ABC

During the summer months, the geologists, physiologist, limnologists, and ethnologists had stopped by to chat when they were in the area. I usually put on the coffee pot and listened to them share news about their projects. Now, March of 1961, brought more scientists to the village.

"Dr. Irving and a couple are coming out from Anchorage for a week," Simon drawled out in his slow, deep voice. He explained that Dr. Lawrence Irving was a well-respected scientist who had carefully collected zoological information about the birds of the Brooks Range and adjacent areas.[16] "They stay with us. I don't know if woman will take life here."

This was typical. From what I'd seen, scientists climbed out of bush planes, asked for Simon Paneak, and made a beeline to his place. Scientists were typically men. I smiled in amusement at his words of concern about this woman's comfort.

As it turned out, Simon worried needlessly. Dr. Keith Miller and his wife adjusted well, as did Dr. Irving, and they all enjoyed their stay with Simon and Susie in the one-room house with eight family members. Mrs. Miller's only request was that she come to my place for a sponge bath.

One of the studies had to do with tolerance to the cold. In other parts of the United States, March equaled robins with red breasts, yellow daffodils, and the smells of moist earth coming out of hibernation; but here, in the 49th state, winter still prevailed. Songwriters Tillman Franks and Johnny Horton were not that far off with their "North to Alaska" lyrics: "When it's springtime in Alaska, it's 40 below." We weren't having 40 degrees below, but snow flurries frequented the valley, and the tundra was weeks away from being squishy. Ironically, it *did* feel like springtime, with the temperatures up to zero.

Dr. Miller inquired about the use of my house for a cold weather laboratory and set up all kinds of wares to do testing. The couple administered tests on the villagers. The subjects would stand outside until they couldn't bear the pain of the cold, or they'd put their hands in ice water. Dr. Miller attached wires to the individuals, watched the indicators on his machine, and every minute dictated the figures to his wife. After examining a number of the Eskimos, he decided to include me. Potentiometer wires were taped to my forehead, neck, and fingertips. I sat outside on a wide sod windowsill for about thirty minutes with my parka on but no gloves. When the analysis concluded, Dr. Miller announced that I tested like the Eskimos. He concluded that I was acclimated to this arctic living and thanked me for participating in the program. No wonder I felt so at ease here.

During this same time, Dr. Irving clung like a shadow to Simon and discovered him to be a self-taught orthinologist. This surprised neither Nick nor me.

TUNDRA TIMES

Monday, Feb. 18, 1963
"Scientist Gives Fine Tribute to Native People of Alaska"
By Professor Laurence Irving, Laboratory of Zoophysiology,
University of Alaska, College, Alaska

It has been my good fortune to visit as a scientist in villages of Eskimo and Indian people in northern Alaska and Canada. I enjoyed the good company and hospitality of these people, but beyond that, I have come to depend upon their precise knowledge of their country and its animals and plants as a most important source of scientific information...I hope that Alaska native students will cultivate the kind of knowledge of nature possessed by their elders...In the course of improving education for native people let us not forget how much more interesting and valuable Alaskan education is becoming by the development of serious programs of studies of the arts, skills, knowledge, and ways of the original people of Alaska...

ABC

Deadlines loomed. I needed to requisition the next year's school supplies, which meant inventorying what I already had here. Then, Uncle Sam demanded that I fill out my income tax forms. No one seemed to be aware of these time-consuming obligations or that I might have daily lessons to teach.

Dr. Bill James, a new doctor at the Tanana Hospital, wrote that he had scheduled a clinic in Anaktuvuk within the next week. He instructed me to set up an area and have the patients organized into groups including pregnant women, school children, and preschoolers. He also requested that I test the school children for visual acuity before his arrival, in order to expedite refractions for glasses. I sent back a prompt reply with comments and a recommendation.

> I do not have an eye chart to test the children's vision. I did test them last October when the nurse was here. I have those results recorded. I have requisitioned an eye chart for next year.
>
> I wrote to the Anchorage Hospital last fall for vitamins, and they stated they were sending some, but we never received any. Caribou is scare now. The children have lost weight. Perhaps vitamins would help.
>
> Their continual struggle for existence—hunting caribou, daily cutting willow boughs for fuel, and hauling in ice and snow for water, does not help for a speedy recovery. Several started out on hunting trips too soon after being ill and suffered relapses.

I also told Dr. James that the Aeromedic shelter well, which Arctic Research had brought in and which Dr. Gaede had used several years before, might be available for lodging, or perhaps the cabin in which I'd stayed when I initially moved to Anaktuvuk. Wherever he ended up, one of the school boys would take over a bucket of snow to melt for water and bring in twigs for the stove. He was new to Alaska, so I reminded him to bring a sleeping bag and to be sure to wear heavy clothing.

I had to decide if clinic would be held in my house or at the school. In weighing the pros and cons of each, I took into consideration meal-making. I wondered if Dr. James would bring his own food or expect me to furnish meals. Since this would be his first time in the village, I reckoned he'd be caught unawares by the lack of amenities. I wanted his introduction to this wilderness to be positive, so I chose to free up my home for meals. Clinic would be held in the chapel-schoolhouse.

The night before his arrival, I worked in the schoolhouse to turn it into a suitable clinic. Dr. James had requested an examining table. I stacked books out of the way and cleaned off my desk. Then I pulled my desk over to the small, collapsible pump organ and placed a school desk beside it. I intended to stretch sheets up for privacy the next day and make a school desk available for filling out patient charts.

The following morning, I entered the classroom. There on my desk and table were all the books I'd removed. Jane, who was serving as the interim janitor, along with her brother, Johnnie, had put them all back where they belonged. I chuckled at her diligence and once again rearranged the clinic.

Dr. James, a young blond physician, arrived with two large metal cases filed with medical instruments, charts, and bandages. He didn't engage the villagers in conversation, but seemed irritated by the wind and was impatient to get to the chapel, where he went about arranging his examining room. At 4:30 p.m., he opened the clinic. When the children trailed in for their group appointments, I noticed a distinct smell of soap. I'd instructed them to be sure and bathe before their checkups. Sure enough, they were squeaky clean. They'd done their best, but even with the wafting fresh odor, I still detected the slightly musty smell of missionary box clothes that had been donated by a church group. The shirts, dresses, and slacks could have used a bit of airing after storage.

We took time out for dinner and then kept patients filing through until 10:00 p.m. Clinic resumed the next morning and lasted until 3:30

p.m. Some of the villagers didn't volunteer any medical information or history, so if Dr. James didn't run across a condition from his own observations, it was overlooked. For example, he'd forgotten to ask two women if they were pregnant. After their examinations, I mentioned their pregnancies, and he called them back. To his credit, in most cases, he didn't miss a thing. In the end, I requested that he check two of my students who had moles and watched as he removed a blue-black mole on one of them. He insisted that two young women fly back to Tanana for further examinations and treatments.

Just before Mark Stella, a bush pilot who flew frequently in Interior Alaska, arrived, the unseasoned arctic doctor asked me, "What do you eat in this village?" I knew he couldn't imagine how I fared so well and perhaps thought I'd brought along a secret stash of food from Ohio. When I informed him that I ate caribou meat supplemented by groceries I ordered from Fairbanks, he tightened his lips and shook his head. "I don't know how you stand living here." From some of the over-dinner conversations we had, I wasn't sure how he would stand living in any Alaska bush village either.

Eating here was not a big problem for me, but keeping up with a constant flurry of non-teaching activity was a bit much. Ann Bergen, the Alaska Department of Health nurse, sent word that she'd be flying in to administer smallpox vaccinations. She requested that clinic be held in my house and that she stay with me. I appreciated her visits to the village, but at this time of the year, her arrival would mean more snow-melting for water. New, fluffy snow was usually dry. If one dug under it, the old snow would produce more water. Even at that, ten inches of snow converted into only one inch of water. Water was consumed quickly with tea water, washing dishes, clothes washing, and bathing. It was depressing to watch an entire pail of snow placed on the stove melt down to a mere bit of water.

Ann was worth the effort. She invited Dora and Jane to come over for instructions on using the umbilical cord tie and silver nitrate drops. Prior to this, the delivery team had always used thread. I convinced Ann that if I fixed my little sock monkey with an umbilical cord and the women tried the tie, they would see that it really did work.

"This is not difficult. Just try it," prompted Ann.

Dora and Jane looked out the corners of their eyes at each other and didn't budge.

Ann's manner was patient but firm. I knew from her instructions to me about shot-giving that she would not brush off anyone's objections. Dora reluctantly tugged on the cord tie and found it to be strong, but protested to Jane, in Eskimo, to tell the nurse that "Maybe mother and father won't let her use it on new baby." Jane told the nurse. Unperturbed, Ann went on to show how to put silver nitrate into a baby's eyes. Once again, the two begrudgingly treated the monkey. It would take time for both the delivery team and parents to become comfortable with procedures so different from ones that had become standard to them. Despite that fact, Anne stated, optimistically, that she'd leave the supplies with me.

ABC

My Grand Central Station didn't shut down for strikes, spring breaks, maintenance, or overbooking. At the same time health education and care were going on at my house, two research men dropped into the village. I was teaching school and Ann was holding clinic when a seventy-three-year-old vertebrate paleontologist, Otto Geist, arrived at my house.

"I need to stay here," he informed Ann.

Perhaps he had been misled or unaware that scientists and researchers stayed with Simon. Between the medical supplies and Ann already sleeping on the floor, I obviously could not accommodate another soul. Ann clearly explained this to him. The following day over my lunch break, Ann and I heard a knock on the door. There stood the scientist, his muddy-gray whickers straggled onto his chest. His eyebrows went every which way, as if in alarm. I figured if I could not provide lodging, I could at least offer him lunch.

"No thank you. Just some coffee," he said curtly.

I thought I'd offended him, but he pulled out a chair and sat down as if he planned to stay indefinitely. Ann and I ate our sandwiches. He started a monologue. The eccentric storyteller spoke from a rich archive of experiences gathered from years of exploring Alaska's isolated areas and digging for artifacts. He was affiliated with the University of Alaska, and I remembered hearing about him when I'd attended classes there.

When he finally paused to take a breath, I interjected, "Otto, I understand that you possess a prized item from abroad."

His gruffness softened. I poured him another cup of coffee, and he settled back in his chair with an even longer story.

"Yes, indeed," he began. "I have the ring of Marie Antoinette."

Apparently, this priceless treasure had been handed down from generation to generation in his family, most likely originating from one of Marie Antoinette's servants who held it when Marie was led to the guillotine.

After a while, he drained his coffee cup, but I didn't move to refill it. Ann and I sat enthralled.

"And that's the way it happened," Otto concluded.

There I was in my one-room sod house, melting snow water on the stove, hearing Eskimo voices outside my door while at the same time listening to a true account from a living history book. It seemed that each day in my life was more than a page in a book; it was as full as a chapter.

"I'd better get back to my students," I said, shaking myself out of mesmerism.

Otto followed me through the door and picked up his gun that leaned against my house. "Think I'll go shoot two birds."

A few days later, the village council got together to discuss the wild scientist's behavior.

"What we do with drunk white man?" they asked me.

That amused me to no end, and of course, it was material for letter-writing to Eddie, but I kept a straight face and assured them that the oddly mannered white man really was not drunk. They had no idea how famous this man was and would become and that his name would be recognized on Geist Road in Fairbanks as well as a building on the University of Alaska in Fairbanks. Not the least, the many artifacts he found in his explorations would be in the museum on the campus.

Not all the researchers were mad scientists; some appeared more normal than others. In succession with the stream of others, Andy dropped in with Bob Rausch, whose purpose was to obtain animal carcasses from the hunters to ship back to Anchorage for study purposes.

Given the need for bush pilot chauffeuring and fairly consistent good weather, Andy was kept busy flying his favorite route. He was content yet challenged.

"Anna, I think I could stay happy just flying scientists in and out of Anaktuvuk," he said, grinning.

ABC

The Nunamiuts recognized the sound and sight of John Chamber's Cessna 170 and raced to the airstrip. As much as I really needed to catch up on homemaking chores, I wiped my hands on a kitchen towel and followed the rest of the welcoming committee. At least I'd finished my income tax forms and only had to pay $198 Federal and $18 Alaska.

John Chambers climbed out along with Reverend William Wartes and his wife, Bonnie. I had never met the Warteses, but standing on the sidelines, I could feel the dynamic personalities of this couple through the arms flung open for hugs, pats on shoulders, and big-hearted smiles. The history that had built the log chapel and forged lifelong friendships echoed in the, "Remember when you…," and, "That was when we all…"

The Warteses had preceded the Chambers as missionaries at the Presbyterian church in Barrow in 1951. Bill had been an Air Force pilot in World War II and had used his flying ability for mission work. In 1952, he'd flown over the pass on his way back from Fairbanks and stopped to inquire about any needs. This started an ongoing relationship that evolved into first-ever marriage ceremonies for the Nunamiuts, baby baptism, and general worship services. There was no building that could host the entire village, but those who could, squeezed into Homer Mekiana's dwelling, which, although the largest sod house, had a portioned area for the post office and, all in all, was not adequate.

Jack Ahgook had raised the question to Bill Wartes about bringing in timber and building a chapel. This would require arduous work and relinquishing costly hunting time. Bill drew up preliminary plans, and before he knew it, the men had departed the village with dog teams headed down to the tree line. Having a place to study God's Word, sing praises, and grow in their faith was of high value. The people were willing to make the sacrifice.[17]

Rev. Wartes's energy never subsided throughout the afternoon of visiting or the evening service. Preschoolers snuggled onto Bonnie Wartes's lap while her husband preached fervently. It reminded me of an inspirational campfire meeting where souls are touched deeply, participants carry away encouragement, and kinship is strengthened.

I invited the guests to my house for cake and coffee. Children followed behind and poked their faces through the doorway. I wished my cake could have multiplied like the Bible parable of fish and bread.

ABC

Frank returned from Barrow without a wife. I wasn't sure if he'd attempt to court me again, but I *was* relieved to once again have his capable janitorial services.

A SCHOOLHOUSE FLIES

Spring was in the air, and long-johns were still on my legs. By mid-April, daylight hours stretched into the middle of night and winter no longer hurried me between warm destinations. I'd put caribou ribs into my oven that morning and savored a tasty supper before covering my table with textbooks and lesson plans. At 6:00 p.m., I heard commotion outside my door.

"Miss Bortel, is it time for library?"

Impatient children stood in a group.

This started the cycle. Children entered, sat on the floor, examined books, wrote their names on library cards, and left just in time for other students to occupy the same spot. Jane hovered near me, watching me grade papers. Then, three teenage boys entered the room. Two requested permission to strum my ukulele, and the other offered to help grade workbooks. The happy hum of contentment prevented me from shooing everyone outside.

Actually, the entire village hummed with anticipation. For one thing, hope of an actual school building, which had stalled out during the winter months, had risen again. In fact, I'd recently received a letter from Mr. Isaac that included a map of the Anaktuvuk village. He requested that I mark the tracts claimed by Wien Airlines and by the Presbyterian church and then select an area for the school.

The archeologists were appalled. My practical approach was to consider the contour of the land and the configuration of village buildings.

These factors led me to a high, level site near the church that was certain not to be flooded with the spring thaws. This, however, did not take into account what lay beneath the earth's surface. As it turned out, I'd chosen a site where the ancient people camped. The birth of a school would mean the death of choice digging grounds.

Climate factors contributed to the difficulty in transporting the school. "I hope the new school is shipped in soon," I wrote my parents. "I'm afraid if they wait much longer that the creek may overflow its banks and run over the runway." Thousands of dollars had been spent on the runway, yet breakup and forthcoming flooding of Contact Creek threatened a wash-out. Although only the breakup of Contact Creek, it might have been the Yukon River for as much excitement as it generated. Each year, at this time, above-freezing temperatures dumped melting snow into the creek, causing it to climb above its banks. Springtime rain clouds threatened to increase the danger.

I'd heard that Wien wanted to extend the airstrip and dig a permanent ditch to divert such threats the following year. It was doubtful that Wien could adequately dike the overflow this season. For the time being, the near-future runaway route of the still-frozen creek kept everyone guessing.

On my birthday, May 10, the creek started flowing. What a wonderful present! Once again, I had running water. No more melting snow. No more straining out foreign substances, such as dog hair. No more adding Clorox to kill bacteria. No more waiting overnight for the Clorox taste to dissipate. I blithely walked to the creek, swinging my pail, and hauled back clean stream water.

My euphoria turned to apprehension when a number of villagers warned, "Miss Bortel, last year water goes in your house." Sure enough, one Sunday afternoon, Nick, with Jane following, came to visit after the Sunday school class children left. We'd just remarked about the wonderful warm temperatures when we saw the creek waters moving steadily in the direction of my house. We grabbed shovels and set to work. Desperately, we chopped the stiff tundra to divert the overflow into channels. We kept glancing over our shoulders to see if we were winning. The tundra held its ground. Children and adults lent their aid. Ever so slowly, and with strained muscles, the water was channeled away.

On the same day of my birthday celebration, a twin-engine plane landed on the airstrip. I thought how at some point the children would never remember when Homer had to put willow markers on the lake when the ice was eight inches thick and substantial enough for a bush plane to land. Nor would they remember when planes could not land and dropped mailbags to the ground. Several weeks later, Bob Sutton announced that the first load of pre-fabricated school construction materials had arrived in Fairbanks. It awaited a larger cargo plane to transport it to our village. Our school was about to fly.

Other things were flying besides planes.

"Miss Bortel!" I heard an excited voice. There stood Danny, holding a dead duck by its webbed feet.

I'd seen the ducks in the creek and observed some schoolboys trying to hit them with slingshots. I'd wished for a duck roast to supplement my steady diet of caribou. My wish had been granted. I thanked Danny, picked up a knife, and went outside to clean my dinner.

A couple days later, Simon invited me to join him and his son, Roosevelt, to check about a hundred snares.

"I could just live off the land like you," I announced boldly.

Simon chuckled. "Do you want your own snares?"

In exchange for a can of milk, he provided me with sinew snares. I set my snares deliberately. Perhaps I'd catch a ground squirrel too, now that they'd come out of hibernation. In the midst of all my other activities, however, I forgot to twice-daily check my prospects. As it turned out, it was a futile effort. I wouldn't be able to live off the land after all.

Besides these springtime delicacies, the caribou remained plentiful. My fourth-grade boys, ages thirteen to fourteen, managed to focus their attention on books and reading groups during school hours, but then, as if spring-loaded, they raced out the door to hunt. I couldn't help but wonder what the city children in the reading books would think of such after-school activities. The spaniel, Spot, and white cat, Puff, probably would have run for their lives.

Not only had the supermarket of the frontier flung wide its doors with all these delicacies, but Mary Darling, Bob Ahgook's sister from Fairbanks, opened a store. Anaktuvuk Pass was rapidly becoming modern. I admired her entrepreneurship, but was doubtful of her success. For one thing, Homer already had his trading post. Then, too, the Nunamiuts had such minimal currency, and unless she was open for bartering, I wasn't sure she'd make anything with such high freight costs.

ABC

"Marie's baby comes now!" exclaimed Jane. "Need supplies."

Her voice was directly above my bed. She'd walked in and awakened me at 6:00 a.m. one Sunday morning. Groggily, I gathered a sterile pad, pills to make the uterus contract, and a cord tie. This would be the first occasion to use the items Ann had left. Even with Jane's skepticism, it appeared she was following instructions for an advanced means of delivery and prenatal care. She went on her way, and I rolled over in bed. I did not embrace mornings.

At about 6:50 a.m., Abraham Kakinya, Marie's husband, burst in. "Drops!" he said.

I shot straight up in bed, rubbed my eyes, and reached for my glasses. I'd forgotten to send the silver nitrate drops along with Jane. Either Abraham wasn't thinking when he barged in or he didn't know I'd requested visitors to knock before entering. Regardless, I was now wide awake.

"Is it a boy or girl?"

"Yes," he replied.

"Is it a boy or girl?"

"Yes," he said again.

I'd have to go find out myself. I carried along the scales, and when I arrived, Jane was scrubbing the squirming infant with Castile soap. She glanced at me out of the corner of her eye. I'd told her not to soap the babies' faces. Simon had already done his part by delivering the baby, and Dora had used the cord tie. Apparently, Marie and Abraham were willing to try the newfangled stuff.

"You do it." Jane and Dora deferred to me for putting in the drops.

"No," I said. "You are the delivery team."

I instructed and encouraged them. Now it was my turn. I set the infant on the scale. The little boy's legs and arms flailed slightly.

"Show me," exclaimed Abraham, leaning toward the weighing device.

I took advantage of his excitement and tried to give him an arithmetic lesson. The baby weighed in at six pounds. A bit small, and it seemed to me that he was a bit blue, reminding me of baby Peter. I wrapped him in a soft flannel gown and held him close.

Marie curled up on a fresh caribou skin. Even though her forehead was still moist from the exertion of labor, she appeared comfortable. The sun seemed to have never slept and shone through a window, warming the sod house. Jane had prepared hot cakes while waiting for the birth, and now we sat on the floor, enjoying an early morning breakfast with fresh coffee.

"Abraham in the Bible had a son named Isaac," I told Abraham.

He repeated the name several times. I assumed this meant the baby had been named.

ABC

Marie's labor was over, but the long labor to birth the school went on. One afternoon, when Andy landed, I, as usual, pulled out my binoculars. He'd dropped off a business-looking man before throttling up and returning to the skies. I could see that Thomas had met the newcomer and now the two were walking back to the village.

Just as I expected, they walked directly up to the school area. After examining the site, they proceeded to pound in stakes where the school building, teacherage, and light plant building would actually be constructed. At this point, I went over to take a look. The dimensions appeared insufficient to me. The entire living quarters would be 16-by-24-feet and would contain one large room, a tiny bedroom, and a minuscule storage room.

My life was about to change drastically. In conjunction with constructing the school building, a second teacher was to be hired. The State Department assigned Angelee Cash, a young, single teacher. She'd be coming from Gustavus, in Southeastern Alaska. That coastal region was nothing like what she was about to encounter in the arctic Interior. I tried to adequately answer her questions in an early springtime letter without painting too bleak a picture. Besides describing the school children's grade categories, I hinted of the rigors in this pass.

Anaktuvuk Pass is located in a windy mountain pass. It snows in September and lasts until May. We had -46 F° this winter, but it does go lower. I don't think one minds the temperatures as much as the wind. Heavy clothing is a necessity. I wear Eskimo clothing part of the time—caribou parka, caribou mukluks, etc.

At the present, I am living in a sod house and have school in a little log Presbyterian Chapel. However, the new school and quarters are to be built this summer.

I guess you know that one makes his own entertainment in a village such as this. The social life consists of church services, a few religious films, and free films put out by oil companies. We will be the only whites in the village.

I also wrote the Juneau office that I did not want to be the head teacher; this position would require that I deal with the maintenance of the light plant. I'd beat on frozen oil lines. I'd run with running water. I'd adjusted to sitting on my caribou-skin-seated outhouse. That was enough. Besides, I cherished my sod house and independence. I did not want to move out of my house to the teacherage, where I would pay rent and still melt snow for water. I would gain the privilege of having electricity, but I desired the freedom of having Sunday school and Bible studies in my own home, which I could not do in the state-owned teacherage.

Angelee and I corresponded back and forth. Her questions about the vast unknown were astute.

Is there electricity? Are dishes furnished in the teacherage? Where is food ordered from? How often does the mail plane fly in? Will I be teaching Eskimos or Indian children? Can I order Eskimo parkas and mukluks or will I need to purchased such clothing in a Fairbank's store?...I have only been in Alaska one year and I surely don't know much about it.

I was jubilant when Angelee wrote back and accepted the head teacher position and said that she had experience working on generators and actually enjoyed it. Of great concern to her was whether or not there would be a long pole available for the antennae she needed for her ham radio transmitter. I couldn't believe my good fortune! It appeared we would be a complementary team.

ABC

Once the school *landed*, innovation was needed to launch construction. When the huge cargo plane circled and lumbered to a stop at the end of our runway, I wasn't sure how the materials and supplies would be transported from point A to point B. All we had was the Cat from Umiat. In this last frontier, I felt sure we'd find a way to reach this impossible goal.

Anaktuvuk Pass School Board Meeting

May 23, 1961

The second meeting of the Anaktuvuk Pass School Board met May 23rd at 8 p.m. at the home of the teacher.

The annual council election was held preceding this meeting. At that election it was voted to have the school term run from September through May. The vote was 30 to 10 in favor of the above term.

A discussion was held concerning the storage of school items. They had just been moved from Zacharias Hugo's tent into his sod house as his family wanted to move into the tent for the summer but he plans to tear down his sod and re-sod the house this summer.

Bob Ahgook suggested that he might be able to store them at his place until the new school is built if his sister is able to move into a tent with her store supplies.

After the meeting was adjourned the party sighted in the teacher's new gun.

LIFE ON SOD BOULEVARD

· ·

"Eat, Anna," said Lela Morry Ahgook as she nodded toward the caribou head that rested on a crudely built table. The entire top section of the head had been removed, and now the brains and tongue were exposed for eating. A number of women had gathered in John and Dora Hugo's home. After taking generous portions, they squatted around the tent, savoring the freshly cooked meat.

I had never witnessed this type of feast, so I sipped a cup of tea and studied the anatomy of the head. It was quite unlike the animals I had worked on in biology classes at Greenville College. Although the head had been cooked, reddish brown hair remained intact on both sides.

Apprehensively, I took an ulu and sliced a small portion of meat from the side of the jaw bone, scooped out a dollop of brains, and shaved off a tidbit of tongue. Tentatively sampling each item, I found this novel fare unexpectedly tasty. Another woman chose a delicacy, the eyeball, her special privilege since it was her father who'd shot the caribou. I observed her utter satisfaction as she bit into it, just as if she'd bitten into a juicy T-bone steak.

I remembered that after my arrival, these people wouldn't have considered sharing these prime selections, and, at that time, I might not have relished the idea myself.

ABC

Simon and the village council agreed that classes would not be held over the summer as they had been the previous year. Therefore, as in a traditional school schedule, in mid-May, classes were winding down. One more holiday remained before closing books and concluding the first school term. Anaktuvuk Pass had never observed Memorial Day. These people, who had hunted and camped around the Anaktuvuk Pass settlement area for nearly ten years, had no servicemen buried in their cemetery. Nor had I heard of anyone here who had been in the armed forces. For me, every Memorial Day held solemn importance.

ABC

In 1939, the world had been a somber place. The Germans were moving their forces toward the Polish border after having annexed Austria a year earlier. As months passed, world conflicts escalated. Adding to the tension in Europe, Japan sought to expand its empire in the Pacific. War loomed on the horizon. At that same time, the war hit closer to home and I said an anxious goodbye to my brother David who went to fight. We clung to one another with uncertainty about our next reunion.

To assist in the war effort, the Heinz Ketchup factory converted their machinery so that they could produce K-rations for the military. During summer vacation, Mother, Millie, and I decided to work for the cause. My job entailed stuffing breakfast boxes as they traveled by on the conveyor belt. One day as I repetitiously placed ham and cheese in the boxes, I said to my partner, "I wonder where these boxes will go and who will get them?"

We speculated for a moment, and then I decided to put my name and address on a slip of paper in some of the boxes. I anticipated a quick reply, but as time passed I stopped hoping.

One blustery March weekend when Millie and I arrived home from teaching in Crissy, Mother said, "Anna, there's a letter for you from a serviceman."

I looked at the postmark: Philippines. After twenty months, my slips of paper had resulted in a response. This first letter came from Eddie. I read it aloud. Letters from other lonely servicemen found their way to my mailbox too. In time, one of my letters to Eddie lay in my mailbox returned, with "Deceased" stamped across the envelope. Eddie had given his life for his country.

Fervently, we prayed for the safety of those young men, and especially those we knew. What a relief when David walked through the door. I praised God for his safe return.

At this point, the people in Anaktuvuk didn't have loved ones who had served in the military, but they did know about death. At some point they'd learn how Alaska had played a strategic part in the war. Regardless of what they knew or didn't know, they had a growing sense of pride about being part of America.

ABC

"Would you please buy green, red, blue, and yellow crepe paper for me?" I wrote Gladys and Ida Mae. "And I need eight stewing chickens and ten large packages of egg noodles."

Not only would school be closed on this national holiday, but the entire village would celebrate.

News of the upcoming observance circulated through the village, and eighteen women and older girls gathered in the chapel one evening to make crepe paper flowers. They caught on quickly and surpassed my designing instructions with their own ingenuity.

On Memorial Day, the villagers assembled at the foot of the hill below the chapel. Two boys, who carried the United States and the Alaska flags, led the procession across the creek to the cemetery. Upon arrival, the large group formed a circle. After a moment of silence, the women stepped out from the circle and placed their array of carefully shaped flowers on the graves of loved ones. Next, Danny and Simon moved forward.

"Originally, Memorial Day, or Decoration Day, held on May 30 in most states of our Union, was an occasion for decorating the graves of soldiers killed in the Civil War," Danny read his part and paused.

Simon had listened carefully and now interpreted these historical facts into Inupiaq.

"But since World War I, it is a day commemorating those who died in later wars. Today, we pay tribute to those who have served in our armed forces to keep our country free. How fortunate we are to live in America." Danny spoke clearly and convincingly.

While Simon translated, I couldn't help wonder what images these words conjured up in the Nunamiuts' minds.

Danny then explained that people now extend the recognition to all deceased loved ones. Simon concluded the solemn aspect of the day and announced that relay races and contests would take place.

Children teased one another as they sprinted up the rise beyond the cemetery. A subtle breeze shooed away the usual plague of mosquitoes. Although only mid-morning, the sun had been overhead for hours, and the villagers began peeling off layers of clothes to participate in the activities. I didn't. Forty degrees still wasn't that warm to me.

Young and old took part in the contests, and the generations enjoyed watching one another compete. One particularly amusing event was the string-and-candy contest. Two people were given 24-inches of string with a piece of candy attached to the middle. A crowd gathered around Elijah and Mae. They each took an end of the string, placed it in their mouth, and hooked their hands behinds their backs; their tongue and teeth reeled in the string, each racing to reach the candy before the other. The men cheered on Elijah, and the women encouraged Mae. *"Ariga,"* ("Good") rang out as Elijah jawed ahead. The winner's eyes wrinkled into an ebullient smile.

After a while, we disbanded to prepare food in our homes. I dumped noodles into the de-boned chicken and broth that I'd left simmering. By 6:00 p.m., the villagers were lined up at the chapel for my entree, along with their standard fare of caribou meat, sourdough hot cakes, and pots of steaming coffee and tea. No one left hungry.

The children's Sunday school program followed, and groups of engaged children proudly said Bible verses and sang songs they'd memorized. Parents were equally proud.

The evening was young, and I pulled out my movie projector. While I threaded in nature movies, the adults stood and stretched before settling back on the floor for more entertainment. Toddlers and babies, tired of the confinement, squalled during much of show, and preschoolers darted in and out of the door, which was open but covered with sheer fabric to fend off the mosquitoes.

For the first time in its history, Anaktuvuk Pass had observed Memorial Day, May 30, 1961.

ABC

"Here, students," I said, passing out paper sacks. "Tomorrow morning, put your meat in here. Be sure to have your mothers cook it."

I'd eaten in a home recently and found maggots cooked right into the chunks of caribou. Oh my! No wonder diarrhea was going around.

The next day, I took graham crackers and spread white frosting between two squares, making crunchy and sweet sandwiches for our end-of-school picnic. The morning schoolwork dragged on for everyone, but finally, it was noon. Away we went, across the wobbly bridge and toward the hills. The children skipped around me, swinging their brown sacks, laughing, singing, and playing tag. I carried a pail of Kool-Aid, which I tried *not* to swing. We settled in a circle on the uneven tundra and leisurely ate lunch. Enormous folded-in-half hot cakes were pulled from many sacks.

"Look?" Children peeled apart their crackers to inspect the frosting.

I'd brought along a ball and bat as well as a larger, plastic ball for the younger kids. For a while, I pitched for the batters, who swung vigorously and then stumbled over the rough ground on their sprints around the bases; occasionally, they fell headfirst and then laughed with their tackler as they rolled about before getting up.

I held in my heart the images of a child tucked under each arm and intermittent imploring of "You stay?" "You be our teacher?"

I'd made it and not only in regard to living and adjusting to the rigors of the far north but as a school teacher. I'd accomplished the task the elders had pleaded for and envisioned and which I'd accepted. Students had remained alert all year and absorbed as much as they could hold of geography, science, nouns and verbs, and the English language. Yes, without a doubt, I'd be their teacher.

ABC

Instead of returning immediately to Ohio for the summer, I remained in the village to wait for the completion of the school and for school equipment and furniture to be moved. Even though I would not be the head teacher for the fall term, I was still responsible during the transition.

Bob Sutton returned to Anaktuvuk after working on other projects during the winter when airstrip progress had frozen to a stop. A second large airplane arrived with four workers who clustered around Bob. A stewardess emerged in her uniform of navy slacks and light gold tunic top with a matching wide, bannerlike scarf. Behind her was a TV announcer who announced his presence as though he was a celebrity.

"Hey! So good to see you. I've been wanting to come here for the past seven years!" His neck tie flew over his shoulder in the wind. He threw his arm around men's shoulders as if he'd known them for years, and he complimented every woman on her atiga.

The stewardess joined in with, "I have senior status and wouldn't let anyone else fly this route until I did. You know, they all want to see this uncivilized place."

"Say, you must be the school teacher." The announcer grabbed my hand and pumped it emphatically.

I stepped back. I was friendly and hospitable by nature, but these two were overstepping their boundaries and presuming familiarity that hadn't been established.

"Could you give us a tour while the plane unloads?"

I felt like a museum curator; a curator who was glad when the tourists climbed back up the steps to the airplane. I imagined the announcer yakked on TV the next day about the primitive people he'd visited.

They were two of many. Anaktuvuk could have used an air control tower with all the aviation activity. Andy flew in with two Yale students. A helicopter brought in Shell Oil officials. I wasn't sure who I'd find using the chapel-school for night's lodging or a place to start up a Coleman stove to cook a meal.

The two transport planes returned and returned. I lost count after six loads. Amid the building supplies and Cat parts were three boxes of used clothing; children's books from the Methodist publishing house; and even bacon and eggs, which I'd jokingly requested of a pilot on his next trip.

With each arrival, there was the dilemma of ground transportation. At long last, someone sent a trailer that could be attached to the Cat. Items were loaded and slowly tugged up the hill to the school site.

One June 21, the longest day of the year, I was fully experiencing the land of the midnight sun. The phenomenon of the never-setting-sun fascinated me. There was no incentive to go to bed, and I wasn't the only one who broke curfew. In winter, the absence of the life-giving sun depressed my energy, but in summer, I, like everyone else, acted like a tireless maniac. Besides, there were no "eight-to-five" jobs to inspire slumber. People slept as needed, regardless of the time of day or night. It was exhilarating for a while, but then I put black paper on my windows to simulate night. That helped me get regular rest, even though much of the time I lived on Eskimo time.

Without lesson plans to prepare and papers to grade, my days were filled with giving girls haircuts, scrubbing clothes on a washboard, baking bread, carrying water from the creek, or bandaging a cut finger.

ABC

"How you make that?"

Several women hung on my elbow and leaned over the table as my knife sliced through the blueberry pie. I followed up an earlier request to teach pie-making. Ten women and older girls filed into my house. They examined the measuring cups, rolling pin, and pastry cloth I'd arranged on the kitchen table and made little comments among themselves. They recognized the sugar, but not the cinnamon.

"Before we start our pie-making, I'm going to read Proverbs 31:10-31 about a woman of strength."

Indeed, these women, who worked so very hard, fit the description of an industrious woman as described by King Lemuel. After the brief devotional, Doris passed out the slips of paper with typed pie crust recipes. Even if a woman couldn't read, most likely she would have a school child who could.

"First, we'll measure out the flour, shortening, salt, and water," I said.

Keen eyes watched every move.

"Do not work the mixture more than necessary," I cautioned.

Several girls edged forward to better view the process.

"Gently roll the dough from the middle out."

Step by step, I demonstrated. *What will they use to roll pie dough out on?* I wondered. Most of them didn't own a table, but set food on a piece of plywood on the willow-bough-covered floor. *They will have to improvise—they are good at that.*

Originally, the request was for blueberry pie; however, blueberries were not available. Occasionally, they had access to dried apples, so prior to the baking lesson, I'd cooked slices in preparation. Now, I showed them how to add sugar and cinnamon and to dot on butter before folding over the top crust. *Will they ever be able to accumulate or afford all these ingredients?* I had to ignore this concern. The cooking crowd tightened around me when I pinched together the edges of the crust. Scraps of floury dough were left on the pastry cloth, and I handed them each a bit to taste. A follow-up pie reinforced the learning experience. Gently, I placed the two pies in my cook-stove oven.

"Any questions?"

The English-speaking cooking students interpreted for the older Eskimos. Then conversation moved to other topics while we waited for the product of the lesson. My house heated up from the oven and the many bodies. Women slid off their chairs and chose the cool floor—their favorite place to sit. The sweet smell of fruity pastry hung in the air.

"Let's see how they're doing," I said. Everyone wanted to peek in, and I mentioned what to watch for when determining the dessert's readiness. The delicately browned pies with sugared tops were perfect. Amidst *oohs, ahhs,* and *mmms,* we sampled success. Even if these Eskimo women never make a pie, the camaraderie and refreshments created pleasurable memories.

ABC

"Maybe something wrong with baby," Simon told me shortly after Isaac's birth.

Simon had delivered many babies in the village and recognized a normal, healthy one. His remark confirmed my doubts about Isaac's physical well-being.

"You know, he was blue," continued Simon.

During the past year, only three of the seven full-term babies were still living. The ones who had died all appeared to have had a heart condition.

The first week of his life, Isaac seemed lifeless and did not want to eat. He experienced difficulty simultaneously coordinating sucking, swallowing, and breathing.

"He must eat. You'll have to work with him," I told Marie.

She borrowed a baby bottle from Ethel Mekiana and put her own milk into it. This required less effort on the child's part, and the infant seemed to respond. To complicate matters, Marie developed a high fever and temporarily had to be put on penicillin.

I continued to check on mother and child. Then, one evening, as I was ready to make loaves out of my rising bread dough, I heard commotion in my entry.

"Come! Isaac forget to live," blurted out Abraham with a shocked look on his face.

"I'll be right over." I put the dough into a larger bowl.

When I entered Abraham's tent, Marie sat on a caribou skin, holding her dying infant and weeping. I sat down beside her. Anna Hugo, who'd been at my house when Abraham knocked, had come along too. Now she joined the company of women who surrounded Marie in this time of sorrow. They ate caribou and drank hot tea in silence. The Eskimos often communicated comfort with their presence rather than words. Only Marie's sobs punctuated the quietness.

After several hours, Marie collapsed, exhausted, on the caribou skins. I put her parka over her shoulders and told her I would hold the baby. Her husband lay down beside her. Abraham's adoptive father, Elijah, dozed off and on in his sleeping bag. His mother, Mae, sat motionless on the other side of the tent, smoking a cigarette.

At times, the poor infant would gasp so hard his entire little body shook. Suddenly, after the young parents had drifted off to sleep, Isaac quit breathing altogether. I aroused his parents. The baby struggled, turned blue, and choked. Marie, overwrought with anguish, could not reach out to him. John Hugo, who had entered the tent, moved beside me and started to massage his abdomen to "bring his stomach down." I didn't know what this meant, but I assumed it was a traditional therapeutic response to such a situation. We worked with him from 1:00 a.m. until his fitful breathing stopped at 2:30 a.m. I cradled the limp, but serene child.

"Isaac's gone." My voice choked, and I felt tears run down my cheeks. No one moved for a few minutes, and the room was silent, peaceful in the sense that the child no longer gasped for breath. Then Marie got up and found material for his burial clothes. Rachel Mekiana set up the sewing machine. The men conversed and pointed to floor boards inside the tent. They pulled out several and went about building a burial box. Ada Rulland took the sourdough starter pot and started making donuts. Everyone knew his or her job in this hour of need.

I was physically and emotionally drained. At about 6:00 a.m., I dragged one foot behind the other, skirted a few remaining snowdrifts, and stumbled home. The abandoned bread dough lay lifeless on the table, but I fell into bed without regarding the matter. After a few hours of fitful sleep, I got up. I contemplated what to do with the dough and finally decided to add more yeast. To my amazement, this brought it back to life. While it rose, I puttered about my house and then shaped two loaves and stuck them in the oven. The comforting smell of freshly baked bread filled the house, and I felt my shoulders relaxing.

I'd just filled my cup with tea and had patted butter onto a warm slice of bread, when two boys called out from my entryway, "They want you."

I surmised that the family wanted a graveside service like I had conducted for Baby Peter. I covered the bread with an embroidered muslin tea towel and found my Eskimo songbook and New Testament Bible.

Although the grave had not been completely dug, most of the villagers had already assembled. Even in June, the frost held firm and the men picked and chopped at the frozen tundra. To pass the time, the women boiled tea and sat eating dried caribou meat. After a while, they started to sing from their hymnals. Their melodious songs merged with the howling wind and drifted over the rolling hills. Two young Yale students stood in the distance and watched soberly.

After several hours of exhausting work, the men placed the burial box in the grave and announced that all was ready. The Eskimos gathered around, and the women sang, "Oh, How Joyful." I read portions of consolation from John chapter 14, a text that speaks of life after death in heaven, and then I offered a prayer. When I opened my eyes, I saw the children leaning over the grave.

"Would you like to gather flowers and place them on baby Isaac's grave?" I asked softly.

While the men filled in clods of frozen dirt, the children scampered about searching for small handfuls of dwarfed yellow and blue flowers. Lovingly, they placed their condolences on the grave. The final shovelful was tossed, the last flower arranged, and we looked up. There in the dark clouds, against the mountains, a rainbow appeared like a heavenly gift in this time of sorrow. For a few moments, we stood still, gazing silently.

ABC

"Elijah, he sick," said a worried voice outside my door.

No time to catch up on my sleep. I dressed quickly and gathered various medical supplies, and then hastened to his tent. Fortunately, the Alaska sun shed plenty of light to jump substantial water puddles.

Old Elijah's temperature was almost 102 degrees, and his pulse worried me. One, two, three, four, *pause*. One, two, three, four, *pause*. I tried to remember anything I'd read or been taught that might shed some light on the problem, but I couldn't put together any pieces to form a diagnosis. The Eskimos didn't volunteer any information, so I asked questions. He hadn't eaten anything all day, so I looked around the tent for any form of nourishment. An opened carton revealed several eggs, so I concocted some eggnog. The old-timer easily finished off the beverage.

Simon had given him penicillin shots, but they didn't seem to have any effect. I was baffled and concerned, but had no idea what to do. Finally, I stopped trying to come up with a medical solution and decided to care for him as I would my own father. I patted his aged and darkened, frostbitten hand, tucked his blankets around him, and sat beside him for a while.

The next morning, I made my rounds. Elijah showed no signs of improvement. About that time, Andy flew in. I walked toward the airstrip, and we met halfway.

"Andy, am I glad to see you! Something is wrong with Elijah. He needs to see a doctor."

Andy tried to radio Tanana from his plane, but couldn't get through. His compassion wouldn't let him give up, and he would not stop trying, but kept messing with the dials. I stood outside the Cessna with my back to the wind. All of a sudden, the door popped open.

"Hey, I reached Barrow!"

That was the complete opposite direction of Tanana; however, their radio had a more powerful signal and thus a stronger signal than his. He requested they contact Tanana Hospital and relay the message that Elijah Kakinya was coming in.

"Okay! Let's do this now!" Andy, usually soft-spoken and unhurried, wanted to leave without delay.

I hastened to Elijah's.

"Maybe I stop," said Elijah, meaning it was time for him to die.

"No, no," I said.

The villagers around him disagreed too and urged him to seek care and live. They bundled caribou skins around him and his cot, and carried their beloved village elder to the airplane. The old man kept trying to be cheerful even though he felt so poorly. I climbed briefly into the airplane and situated him as comfortable as possible; after which Andy secured the door, waved briefly, and started the engine. The prop-wash scarcely made a difference when mixed with the characteristic gusts.

Everyone stood around and watched the plane bounce off the airstrip, and then followed it until it disappeared into the gray-streaked sky. Elijah was a dynamic character in the community, and his absence left a void. I found myself expecting to hear his voice singing in a Sunday service, or joking in group, or walking into the foothills with his gun slung over a shoulder. Whenever Andy returned with mail or supplies, someone would inquire if he'd heard about Elijah.

As it turned out, Elijah had pneumonia. Given proper medical treatment, he recovered and returned to the village and back to his role as astute businessman, or, as I referred to him in some of my letters, "The Man on Wall Street." The bantam village patriarch hung around the school construction site, prepared to claim lumber discards. With the scarcity of wood, these scraps were treasures to be turned into a shelf or a door frame. Only Homer took the initiative to request wood for his tent floor; otherwise, most of the men stood back in typical deferring Eskimo behavior, even though they were obviously being left out. Of course, Elijah got more than his share, and strain mounted with the disparity of the distribution, even though Mr. Thomas, the construction superintendent, assured everyone that there would be plenty of lumber and nails remaining from the project.

"Elijah not poor like us," several villagers complained to me.

I had willingly assumed the position of school teacher and Sunday school teacher. I had been cast in the roles of doctor and funeral director. I did not want to be the judge.

At the same time as this discord, the archeologists were horrified that the school erection was destroying access to artifacts. They worked frantically to secure as much as possible. Jack Campbell, professor from George Washington University, supervised the diggings with the two Yale students, but needed more hands. He'd been granted a generous sum for this summer's dig and paid the Eskimo children for flint arrows and other objects they'd uncover. The researcher dated many of these artifacts back to 3000 BC. Mr. Thomas generated competition when he increased the monetary rewards for specific findings, such as ulus. And so, the village men kept busy procuring wood, and the children dug for artifacts. Everyone benefitted from this unique economy.

Bob Sutton continued to supervise improvements on the airstrip. One day, he mentioned to me, "I met Eddie, the teacher, while working in Kobuk."

I immediately tuned in and looked at Bob with interest, and then felt my cheeks start to blush and turned away.

"I really like him," he added. "He's working at the copper mine this summer and plans to buy an airplane."

Everyone seems to like Eddie. I sure wish I could meet him.

I didn't let it slip out that I'd been corresponding with Eddie the previous months or that Eddie had written he'd like to visit Anaktuvuk Pass.

Through Eddie's letters, I'd learned that besides being a teacher in a small village, he too had driven up the Alcan. Not only did we share the same faith in God, but he'd been a summer counselor at Victory Bible Camp, where friends of mine had sent their children. I absorbed his tidbits about the Nunamiut: "Years ago, the Anaktuvuk people came to Kobuk to trade, but one winter, they got the flu while here and never returned." In our letter discussion, we decided that this decision probably had nothing to do with illness and, most likely, they began to barter with Pat, who had established himself in Anaktuvuk Pass. Thus, we reasoned, there was no longer a need to go to Kobuk for bartering.

At any rate, every time I received an envelope addressed in green ink, I knew it was from Eddie, and my heart beat a bit faster. Still, nothing had actually happened, except for the smile on my face and sensation of floating on cloud nine.

Fairbanks Daily News-Miner

"Anaktuvuk Pass-ages"
Homer Mekiana—*Correspondent*

June 2: Two helicopters land here belong to Pan Am and fuel up and keep on going to Umiat.

A Cessna plane came from Fairbanks with two passengers who are examining the location of the new school building. And the one who was working on the airstrip a mechanic name Bob Sutton went to Fairbanks with them.

June 4: Today the C-46 two motored plane came and brought school buildings, three times today and also brought four men who are going to build a schoolhouse.

June 5: Today the C-46 came again with more load of school building and comes here three more times. The men are hauling the school supplies with tractor trailer up to the site where the school is going to be build. (sic)

June 7: Today a Cessna plane came from Bettles an(sic) brought one woman and four kids. The woman is the wife of a man that is a boss who are (sic) building the schoolhouse. And in the evening the same Cessna plane came again and brought a botanist that is going to work around this place. Also today C-46 brought some caterpillar parts and 10 drums of diesel fuel.

June 8:   Today same plane—Cessna—came from Bettles field and had two passengers. They come from Hal University in New Haven, Connecticut. They are going to look around for old things. During in the evening that same plane came again and brought Professor John Campbell. He used to come here before too before he had that name professor and he come again and looking of more old timers things.

June 15:   Today Norseman's plane from Bettles field came piloted by James Anderson and brought mail.

June 16:   Today a Wien plane Norseman plane came and brought mail and had a person. His name is Oscar Neptune from Allakaket. He is working for Alaska Department of Health and Sanitation.

A PAGE IN THE HISTORY BOOKS

I was about to meet the newest addition to the teaching staff in Anaktuvuk. From my correspondence with Angelee Cash, I expected she was capable, undaunted by hardships, and mechanically adept. When the north winds blew, I doubted she'd take the next plane out of the Pass; she seemed just the kind of teacher we needed.

It was mid-August, and I was in Fairbanks. Ida Mae and Gladys accompanied me the airport. After letter-writing and forming a mental picture of her, I was surprised when we discovered that Angelee was the small, brown-eyed woman wrestling with heavy baggage. Her brown braids swung to and fro with the exertion. We greeted the plucky brunette, and off we went to shop for canned goods, wool socks, and other sundries she'd need for survival in the Pass.

Angelee had grown up in South Dakota and was accustomed to the rigors and responsibilities of country life. As young as she appeared, she'd been teaching for ten years. The next day, with poise and equanimity, she gathered up her loads of suitcases and boxes and flew ahead of me to Anaktuvuk. I was confident the standard welcoming committee would lend a hand and lead her to the brand-spanking-new teacher's quarters.

ABC

Fourteen months earlier, I'd landed on Eleanor/Summit Lake, and *that* had been timed strategically between winter ice and summer break-up. On this trip, when the plane dropped altitude to land, I thought of the many changes that had taken place so quickly: a *real* school building, an additional teacher, radio contact, and an airstrip. These changes not only served Anaktuvuk people, but radiated farther. The radio was a receiver for the village *and* transmitted weather reports to Fairbanks. The landing strip was the only alternate strip between Fairbanks and Barrow that could handle prop-jets, which was of prime importance when there was a weather problem or flying emergency. The ripple effects didn't stop. The full-length strip, adequate for commercial airlines and cargo planes, would also make possible the transportation of fuel oil. Rather than combing the area for willows, an additional heating source would be available for those who could afford it.

I could hardly wait to disembark.

When the children recognized me, they jumped up and down and clapped their hands. "Are you happy?" they asked.

Handshaking began with adults. Tiny tots were pushed forward to greet me in like manner, and I took their little hands in mine. My eyes lingered on the friends and students before me, and then I took in the liberal sky above. The late-summer sunshine felt pleasant on my face, and the unusual absence of wind was a surprise. I felt comfortable in my light sweater. Everything was right in my world.

A procession carried my suitcases. Memories of my early springtime return flashed through my mind, and I felt a perceptible relief when I pulled out my key and *unlocked* the door into my chilly but not frigid house. I wrote my parents, "Although I enjoyed the city, I feel so much more at home in a village…"

ABC

In spring, I'd stayed in Anaktuvuk until I felt confident that everything was lined up for the next year. I'd scrutinized the construction of the school and teacherage and was skeptical about the insulation. I doubted very much that the amount layered in would be adequate protection against the incurable refrigeration of the pass. A baffled construction worker asked, "After we build this nice place for you, aren't you going to live in it?" They'd heard I'd decided to remain in my sod house. He couldn't fathom why I'd give up what he perceived as a castle compared with my sod house.

The painter from Texas agreed with one of my reasons: "It will be warmer in your sod house than in this modern structure."

The plans did not call for an entryway on either the school building or on the teacherage. Without these, cold air would blow in on the tails of whoever came or went. There was no way to trap the unwelcomed air outside. The State of Alaska Department of Public Works sent the architect, George Filler, to inspect and approve the completion of the new school on July 7. He recognized the need for entries and immediately authorized the contractor to proceed with such construction.

While Mr. Filler was there, I learned that by applying for a state radio, we could have much needed radio-telephone communication for our solitary village. Without delay, I filed for a license, and the villagers signed the required petition. I marveled at how this communication would suddenly move the village into quick contact with outside resources. Whereas I had struggled through the year alone with medical decisions, now I would be able to radio the Tanana Hospital for assistance and guidance. The desperate sense of isolation, when faced with an emergency, would dramatically decrease.

ABC

Anchorage Daily Times
July 31, 1961
"Anaktuvuk Gets New School"

There will be school in Anaktuvuk this winter, held in a brand-new building that looks strangely out of place amidst canvas tents and sod huts.

Anaktuvuk is a Nunamiut Eskimo village, started about 12 years ago when a nomadic group of inland Eskimos decided to settle in the heart of Anaktvuk Pass, deep in the Brooks Range of northern Alaska...

All materials for the building, and the teacher's quarters next to it, had to be flown in. There are no roads or water routes reaching the village.

The building is pre-fabricated, and was designed especially for the at area, according to Lee Hayes, area superintendent. Angalee (sic) Cash, White Owl, S.D., will serve her first season starting this fall. Miss Bortel formerly taught at Tanana...

Summer school was conducted locally for several years before the new school was opened.

On September 5, 1961, the Nunamiut village children lined up outside the Anaktuvuk Pass School. This event wrote itself into history books and significantly impacted the Nunamiut Eskimos. The caribou no longer determined their home and hearth, nor was Anaktuvuk Pass village just one of many hunting camps. Pat's trading post and Homer Mekiana's traveling post office were first steps. The chapel in the mountains staked roots in deeper; yet, out of necessity, they'd continued to come and go for timber, meat, and skins. The airstrip changed their isolation and, at least temporarily, their income, but it would be the school that anchored the Nunamiut Eskimos to this very specific spot in the Brooks Range.

On this first day of school, the children only knew of the excitement of a new school building. They didn't realize that they were the first generation to receive education without leaving home. They didn't know that they'd been taught by the first permanent school teacher or that they'd find their school documented in the Congressional Record.[18]

They gazed about in wonderment and, as instructed, hung their assortment of parkas in the narrow hallway between the two classrooms. "E-e-e," ("yes") they squealed, looking at the rooms. I felt the same exhilaration. They tipped up their noses and sniffed the new construction, a blend of sawn lumber, paint, and glue. As for me, I could hardly believe the paste-painted walls, linoleum-tiled floors, and abundant light from the south-facing window. All this would provide a winter tonic for teachers and children. Ample blackboard space warmed my heart, as did bookshelves.

In late spring, I'd written Angelee:

The students range in ages from 6 to 18. By this coming September, there will be another grade since several of the beginners have covered two years of work and will be third graders. You will then have third, fifth, and sixth grades. I will have approximately 13 first and second graders.

My responsibilities were lessened, and in a matter of only a few weeks, I felt an unusual lightheartedness.

ABC

My little pupils were eager to please, yet, at times, were unable to comprehend what I'd say. We'd sit in a reading circle, and when I'd tell them they could return to their desks, they'd remain motionless. Their eyes intently met my gaze, and I knew they wanted to please, but my words hadn't connected. What a challenge to teach children educational basics when they didn't even know the language.

In addition to words, I had to demonstrate. "Put your hands *on* your desk. Put your hands *in* your desk. Put your hands *under* your desk." Every day, they learned more words and more concepts.

The previous year, I had to consider the entire group with multi-ages and multi-learning goals, and I couldn't focus on one skill set or one field trip. This year, I could take my two specific grades on an individual learning experience. A unit on toys provided just the opportunity. I instructed each student to bring a homemade boat to school. Most of the students crafted their own, although two fathers assisted their children and one boy constructed a tiny vessel for his sister.

I combined the toy unit with a nature study. After lunch, we slipped out into the brisk but sunny day. We wandered about the tundra, picking up items. The early snow had not stayed on the ground, and we collected berries, berry leaves turning purple, lichens, moss with spores, and toadstools. Some moments were spent in quiet, wide-eyed investigation, with students squatting near the ground. Other times, the still air was broken by tittering when wild cotton was stroked on their nose or lichens brushed gently on their fingertips.

When we neared the summer-depleted shallow creek, I showed the youngsters how to sail their boats. I couldn't understand what they were saying in Inupiak, but the intonation of their quiet words let me know they were enchanted by this experience. These were opportunities to seize and savor, even though the formal school day had ended. I didn't want to forget this autumn day with Eskimo children in the Arctic pass. Weeks later, they still talked about sailing their boats, and they continued to deposit on my desk their latest finds from the tundra.

ABC

By the end of September, we'd had snow flurries. Already, I'd had a flurry of people sitting at my table or sleeping on my floor. I wrote friends:

> We had three men come to the village who needed a place to eat so I cooked for them. One was a Mr. Kenneth Cohen, a Relocation Officer with the Bureau of Indian Affairs from Fairbanks, who had a meeting and explained that the government would finance relocating interested folks between 18 and 40 if they were interested in going stateside to work, perhaps in the Chicago area. I can't imagine them on big city sidewalks, chasing buses and elevated trains instead of caribou through the Brooks Range mountain passes. As it turned out, only one person showed interest, but he was not a suitable candidate.
>
> Then the nurse came and stayed with me. She had me practice giving shots, one on her, and one on a little boy who needed one. Last night I was brave enough to give one to a baby, whom I'm afraid may have pneumonia. Now I have confidence. These babies go so quick with pneumonia and I'm determined to reduce infant mortality rate.
>
> Oh, Ann, the nurse left on Friday…But she returned last week with the X-ray technician. They came to my room and took X-rays of about 40 people. I had to help them.
>
> I counted dogs. We have 174 and we're ordering rabies and distemper vaccine for about 50—for those 2 yrs. and younger. (We have 105 people.)

ABC

The joys of teaching brought humorous twists. The children were learning new words in English every day. As would be expected, they'd latch onto one specific meaning I gave for a word. Unintentionally, I'd end up using it in a different way, which threw them off, and me.

"Boys and girls, how would you like to have an addition flash card race?" I asked.

Thirteen heads bobbed up and down in agreement. I grouped them into two lines.

"When I hold up the card, the child at the beginning of each line will guess the answer. Whoever answers first gets the card. At the end of the time, the side with the most cards wins the race." I thought these instructions were clear.

Their dark eyes shone in anticipation. I flashed the first card. The first child in each line took off running around the room as fast as he could go. Their teammates cheered them on. I stood dumbfounded. *Race* meant *run* to them. I burst out laughing. I tried again. Pretty soon, we were all laughing. Little tears edged out of their slanted eyes, and I could hardly catch my breath. They'd need more English lessons before we could do *this* arithmetic lesson.

I almost felt guilty having so much fun teaching, so I was glad to hear Angelee was enjoying her class too. She'd been apprehensive about taking the older children since, in her previous position, the FAA teenagers had been disruptive and disrespectful. I'd assured her that none of that behavior would happen with the Anaktuvuk young people, and it didn't.

ABC

In the 5:30 a.m. stillness, I heard a scratching noise between the sod and the cardboard wall, followed by a plop, and then scampering across the linoleum floor. I shot up in bed, my eyes wide open in the darkness. Chills ran down my back, and my hair prickled on the back of my head. I waited. Silence. I let out my breath in little rushes. I hadn't actually seen him, but just the thought of a mouse in my house terrified me. I could eat caribou brains, clean a duck, and shoot a ptarmigan, but I could not cope with mice.

Gingerly, I stuck my feet in my slippers, turned on my flashlight, found some traps, set them, and waited. After drifting in and out of fitful sleep, I got up a second time to check my in-house trap line. I dragged a chair over to the first spot, near the cupboard. To get some distance from the trap, and ensure the critter didn't run over my toes, I climbed on the chair and shone the light down from a waning flashlight on the trap. No mouse.

The second area, the off-set storage space extending out from my kitchen area, had neither mouse *nor* trap.

Oh no! It must have carried off the trap into to a hole under the floor! Nothing could persuade me to hunt for it.

The following day, I went to Mary Darling's store and bought new flashlight batteries, not that I'd be excited to see the nighttime visitors. There, I ran into Angelee.

"I'm scared of mice." I confided. Giggling nervously, I told her about the missing trap.

"I'm not," she said, without any comments about my silly fears. "Do you want me to look for the trap?"

I accepted her offer, but as much as she searched, no mouse or trap could be found. My size ten shoe became my night-time assault weapon, and I kept it near my bed. If I detected the culprit careening across the floor, I'd try to make a hit in the darkness.

Whatever the reason, my threats, my shoe, or death somewhere within the missing trap, the nocturnal visitations ended.

ABC

Indians and Eskimos have a history of fighting and fear. Over the years, some incidences have grown out of proportion. Other incidences are true, such as brutal fighting over traditional hunting grounds. Regardless of truth or fiction, interpretation of neutral events can be influenced by these perspectives.

Take, for instance, the Arctic Health Researchers from Anchorage. Two men came to work on caribou and blood. One was crippled, and he asked me to prepare the Eskimos for seeing his handicap, which I did; however, through the grapevine, the story changed shape until it came back to me that, "A man, maybe Indian, come without legs." Well, I discounted and cleared up that bit of rumor; nevertheless, that didn't stop the spooky stories that circulated. Two hunters returned and warned the community, "Indians near our camp." Had they actually seen anyone? No. But that didn't diminish the Indian scare that floated like a ghost in the air.

ABC

"Oh! I didn't bring along any food."

Mr. G. Lee Hayes from the supervisory office at Anchorage flew in for a lesson on village education. He replaced Miss Lois Morey, who had advised me in Tanana and during my first year here. He was from Oregon and a recent newcomer to Alaska, so he didn't know much about this frontier. Visiting Anaktuvuk Pass School would be an extreme introduction, and I trusted he wouldn't be too shocked.

When he climbed out of the bush plane, he didn't say a word; just stood, blinking his eyes. Then, he pulled his coat more snuggly around his neck and reached into his pocket for gloves. We walked through the village to the school, and he kept staring, not so much at the sod houses but at the mountains that rose up grandly from the flat valley floor.

In short order, he realized there were no restaurants and, with dismay, realized that he should have come more prepared. I had cooked for other state and federal visitors, and they generously paid their per diem allotment for food, so I didn't mind dipping into my winter's supply of groceries. Angelee and I had discussed this kind of situation. She did not feel comfortable cooking, which we knew would be an expectation when education supervisors and such people flew in to check on school and teaching status. Therefore, we had mutually agreed that I would continue this responsibility.

After school, I asked Angelee to join us for supper. At first, she politely declined because she felt like she had eaten too many meals at my place already. I insisted.

"Angelee, you know how far upstream we have to go for water now. Could you please help in that way?"

"Okay," she agreed.

I walked to my home to bake bread and a cherry pie. Mr. Hayes showed up just in time to accompany me to the Rullands' for caribou meat. I admired his gumption and curiosity.

The three of us discussed school business, but then the conversation headed to sod houses, outhouses, no electricity for the villagers, English as a secondary language, and the many uses of caribou. Mr. Hayes took in every word, with comments of incredulity.

The day before Mr. Hayes left, the school generator quit. In other situations, the school fix-and-repair projects had fallen on my shoulders. Not this time. I stood aside while Mr. Hayes and Angelee nonchalantly made the required adjustments. They had no idea what a burden they lifted from me. I didn't care how many times Angelee ate at my house as long as she could keep the generator going. I'd choose making fresh bread and pies over dealing with wrenches and mechanical problems anytime.

Mr. Hayes's parting words were, "Anna, that was some bread you made." I figured we'd passed his inspection and he'd be back.

ABC

"What would you think if I taught the adults to read?" I'd asked Mr. Hayes before he left.

He had no objections. In October, I announced that all adults who wanted to learn to read were to come to the school at 3:00 p.m. That day, like a revolving door, my first and second-graders exited and six to eight nervously excited adults entered the room for an hour of schooling. I divided them into two groups, according to their knowledge of the written word. Each Monday and Wednesday, they arrived promptly and paid close attention to the lessons. Some of the mothers had their children help with reading assignments at home.

After class one day, John Morry walked up to my desk. "Miss Bortel, Don Webster want me teach Eskimo to older people so they can read it. Maybe we have Eskimo New Testament soon."

Apparently, John had received a letter from Don and Thelma Webster, Wycliffe Bible translators. They lived in Wainwright, on the Chukchi (CHUCK-chee) Sea, about 72 miles southwest of Barrow, where they were translating the Bible into the Inupiaq language.

"John, you should talk to Miss Cash about it," I said. "She is the head teacher now."

"She not understand me," he replied with a downcast face. "You go with me."

Together, we went to her classroom, where she was straightening up desks and cleaning the chalkboard. His apprehensions were unfounded. Without hesitation, she agreed for him to hold Eskimo reading classes on

Fridays at 4:00 p.m. John left in good spirits. He too would be an *Ilyisautri* (Eel-yee-SOW-tree)—or teacher. And, indeed, he was a good teacher.

Angelee and I didn't feel right about using the school supplies, so we provided paper and pencils for the classes. Then we traded our roles of teacher for those of student and found ourselves in school desks. Now *we* looked up at the chalkboard.

I received an *A* on most of my spelling papers, but sentence structure was a challenge. For example:

> *angutit tututut:*
> *men caribou they killed*

> *angun tautuka tutu:*
> *men see he/it caribou*

I taped slips of paper around my house with the names for chair, table, and bed. I used frequently the words of *avula* (sugar), *nungarak* (candy), *kalun* (cup), *imik* (water), *imuk* (milk), *taqiuk* (salt) and *ig-nig-vik* (stove). When I visited homes, I tried to use simple sentences, such as, "*Tea tugok' pick*" ("Do you want tea?") and "I *tea tugok' tunga*" ("Yes, I want tea"). One day, I attempted to use a more complex sentence about caribou meat. Lela, in whose home I was having tea, laughed. "Your tongue like stiff willow when you talk Eskimo." I joined her in the amusement.

Time passed. One afternoon, John said seriously, "Ilyisautri, what do we do? Susie can't learn write Eskimo."

"She's having difficulty in my class too, John, but we must be patient," I answered. "Ask Simon to help her."

This dear mother tended to the needs of her large family and, in addition, saw to it that I had warm winter clothing. She was skilled at threading sinew through a bone needle, preparing the softest caribou hides, and flipping the fluffiest hot cakes, but school was difficult for her.

John replied, "I ask Simon, but he want pay."

The previous year, Nick had used grant funds to pay Simon for language studies; now, Simon wanted pay from John to help his own wife learn to read Eskimo. I tried to keep a straight face. No doubt, Simon was well qualified as a tutor of the language.

"Perhaps her children can help her," I told John, "or one of the women in class could be her tutor."

Sometime later, I received a letter from the Websters. They wanted me to assist John in the language classes. They sent along stories, written in three forms, and requested that the Eskimos pick the form they liked best. This input would influence the way they translated the Bible stories. As it turned out, the Eskimo classes had three-fold benefits. It helped us as school teachers better adapt to the culture. It enabled the Eskimos to express themselves in their own tongue. And, the Wycliffe translators could more accurately translate the Bible.

Once or twice a day, John wrote me notes about the Eskimo class and sent them with his children. Sometimes, a child would hand me a note when classes began in the morning. Other times, I'd return from lunch and find a note on my desk. One day, I received the following message:

Ilyisautri Miss Bortel

I ask you about school. When you guys quit English school I would like to know what we do. I would like to quit too because my Eskimo school class some of them (students) quit. Don't like (Eskimo) school. But really like school English. That why make me lazy too. I am hard work too.

Next time (class) we have read Matthew 5:1-11 translated to Eskimo. Also Lord Prayer.

John Morry

This invaluable instructor experienced the same discouragement as any teacher.

The Lord's Prayer—Matthew 6:9-13

Aapavut kilanmiit-tuatiin, Ilivich atkin kiksigi-rauli. Umialgutin kaili. Pisuutin pirauli nunami pirau-rautun kilanmi.
Aitchuk-tigut uumani uvlumi uvlutaugman nikiptinnik,
Suli suliku-tiginaik-kich akiilavut uvagut-tauk suliku-tiginai-kaptigik
Akiilak-tuktivut,
Suli aulla-tinata ikligutchak-tinniagu-tinum aglaan annau-tiluta piluunmin,
Kanuk ilivich pigigin umialgun suannallu kamanaullu isuit-chuamun.

ABC

The previous year, caribou had been scarce. Children and dogs complained of hunger. It broke my heart to hear tummies growl and little eyes watch me eat. Of course, I shared as much as possible, but I couldn't feed an entire village. Men had left the village on hunts. Women had checked snares for ground squirrels. Even when the caribou had migrated through and hopes soared high, there would be an initial day of hunting, but that was followed by weeks of waiting. The older people had experienced this before and set their jaws in determination of survival.

This year was different. October started off with a blizzard, and when it blew in, a storm of caribou appeared with it. For days on end, the caribou remained in the area. I'd try to teach, but then look out the window and see men hiding behind a rise in the foothills. I'd stop in mid-sentence, and the students would follow my gaze. A hush fell over the entire classroom as we watched the caribou approach the hunters, unaware of the ambush. Quietly and quickly, the hunters followed the caribou with their gun sights. Suddenly, a caribou sensed danger and spooked. In a wild rush, the herd reversed directions. Gun shots blasted. My young pupils shouted unheard encouragement to the hunters: their fathers, uncles, and older brothers. Their success meant food and protective clothes to survive the brutal elements.

One man, however, was absent from this subsistence ritual: John Hugo. The men in the village relied on his leadership, but instead of heading up the hunt, he had lain on caribou skins in his sod house, overcome by fever, chills, headache, and overall weakness.

Andy had been contacted for the medical emergency, and John was airlifted to Tanana for medical treatment. Dr. James's diagnosis was brucellosis, also called undulant fever, from which recovery would be gradual.

In the Lower 48, undulant fever is passed from cows to humans through improperly cooked beef or unpasteurized milk. Dr. James wrote me:

> ...As you know by the visit of the personnel from Arctic Health Research, the Public Health Service is interested in this disease and is going to great expense and time to learn more about it and

what efforts could be made to prevent the passage of the disease from caribou to human being…The only suggestion I have to the people of Anaktuvuk Pass to prevent further outbreaks of the disease is to cook all caribou well before eating. The bacteria are thought to reside mainly in the bone marrow and in the udders of the caribou, so these two parts of the animal definitely should be cooked before eating.

Even though John returned to the village, he remained in a weakened condition. He could barely work on repairing dog harnesses, much less go out for a hunt. The people in Anaktuvuk were not on welfare, as were many of the other villages, but when I saw how the Hugo family suffered from John's incapacity to provide, I wrote to Joyce Towne with the Welfare Department.

Would it be possible for John to have a welfare check for the month of November? He is a leader in hunting in our village and the men miss him so much this year. He is not a shirker but brucellosis has stopped him for a while.

This request was acknowledged, and he received checks.

ABC

On a Saturday evening, around 9:00, a mother rapped on my door.

"Jack sick. Maybe die." She burst into tears.

Jack was between fourteen and fifteen years old.

"Where is he sick?" I inquired slowly and distinctly.

She just looked at me. Unable to cross the language barrier, she sobbed hopelessly. I found my first-aid supply kit, which contained spirits of ammonia, antibiotic ointments, aspirin, Band-Aids, bandages, and other basic supplies. I also picked up *Merck's Manual* before bundling my parka around me. The light from my flashlight bobbed up and down as we hurried to her sod house.

I found Jack Morry stretched out unconscious on the floor. One man was massaging his stomach, another man held his hands, and two women were rubbing his feet. I touched his face and arms. He felt deathly cold. My heart thudded hard within my chest. I urged them to wrap him in warm blankets and skins and tried to get the background of what had occurred prior to this state, but my efforts seemed futile. Grasping for clues, I sent for Danny, who had brought Jack home in this grave condition.

Apparently, the two boys had taken seven dogs and gone to Come Out Creek to bring back caribou meat to the village. On their return, they'd stopped by a lake and drank the water. Immediately following this, Jack had felt dizzy. Danny had half carried and half dragged his buddy home. Further details revealed that the boys hadn't eaten during this strenuous several-hour hike and that much of the time they had run alongside the dogs in an effort to make better time getting back to the village.

This sounded to me like exhaustion. I put a cold cloth on Jack's forehead and spirits of ammonia beneath his nose. All the while, I called his name. His family and other villagers watched silently with the expectation Jack would soon regain consciousness. I hoped their faith proved right. After a long hour, Jack moaned; shifted his position; and, bit by bit, opened his eyes. "Water." His mother brought him a cup of strong tea. We'd reached a turning point. I stayed for a while and then, before leaving, prayed for him.

"You come back?" they asked.

I assured them I would return in the morning.

On Sunday, I was thankful to find Jack sitting up and alert. Even though the people credited me, I gave God the praise for these medical recoveries.

Sometimes, it wasn't medication or bed rest that was needed but just basic nutrition. During one school day, I'd received two notes telling me of a sick baby, which turned out to be the *same* baby. I tried to stay focused on my teaching, but when the children turned in their crayons at the end of the day, I followed them down the hill. I stopped at my house and intuitively picked up two cans of milk before continuing on my mission.

Before I even reached the door of the sick child, I could hear hysterical screams of an infant. The emaciated child had a fever and a cold. When I filled a bottle with diluted canned milk and offered it to the baby, he clung tightly to the nipple and sucked strongly. Previously, I'd taken the family canned milk. I looked around. Not a can in sight. I knew they didn't have money to purchase any more. The villager's lack of revenue for primary needs disturbed me greatly.

For a variety of reasons, baby health problems occurred much too frequently in this village. When I informed Dr. James about the high infant mortality rate, he followed up with communication to the Public Health Area Medical Officer in Charge in Anchorage; as a result, he was given permission to pay transportation for all pregnant women in Anaktuvuk Pass to come to the Tanana Hospital to deliver. Furthermore, he recommended they be flown in two weeks before their due date. To ensure this actually happened, he contacted the Wien Airlines agent at Bettles to provide the transportation.

I appreciated his pursuit and persistence through medical channels to address not only this Alaska Native health statistic, but also the heartbreak of illness and death. I'd only been in this village a short time, and the emotional upheaval was wearing me down. I didn't know how the mothers and fathers maintained their hope and optimism during the course of repeated pregnancies and deliveries, many with the same end result.

Fairbanks, Alaska, Monday, November 6, 1961

"Changing Times"

Now things will probably change. Oil will be carried into the village on the big planes where it could not be handled before. The Natives whose basic diet is now caribou, will be having food shipped in from Fairbanks. And who knows, maybe a wash house will come along next summer…Some authorities say the Native culture should not be disturbed. But then there are others who take the opposite position.

NAPIKUK'S
ESKIMO CRAFTS

"I want hot cake," sobbed little four-year-old Rachel Mekiana.

"We don't have flour," her mother, Ethel, reminded her again. "Tomorrow, we have flour."

But still the child cried.

I'd just given the mother payment for a handcrafted mask she'd made me. Tomorrow, she would go to the store to buy a sack of flour. I agonized, *Should I go home now and get flour to give to this family? I know I can't share with all the needy families.*

This wasn't an unfamiliar experience. In the spring, while sipping tea with a student's mother, I'd glanced around and noticed the cupboard box was completely bare. There was no sign of food. I'd seen her teenage son eating in a neighbor's home, and I wondered if the other children were doing the same. The father was out hunting caribou and would stay away until he could bring home meat. I couldn't watch hunger right in front of my face. I left troubled. When I walked into my house, the first thing my eyes focused on was the bag of rice in my pantry box. I couldn't help but sack up a cup and take it back to her.

ABC

I grew up in the Depression. I'd witnessed hunger; although we always had food on our own table. Daddy tried to explain to me about the Depression, and why men were out of work. It wasn't uncommon to hear a rap at our back door. When Daddy wasn't home, I would be frightened and run upstairs to the first landing, and peer out the window. Below, I'd see a hobo. Our house was 500 feet from the New York Central Railroad tracks and seemed to be targeted as a charitable stop. The ragged men with despairing eyes slumped on the cement step between the house and the garage, and quickly and quietly filled their empty stomachs.

One time I saw a hobo's toes poking out of his shoes, which were tied onto his feet with frayed cords. Mother noticed this too.

"Wait here on the steps," she instructed the tattered man.

Within a few moments she was back with some of my father's footwear. Truly, Mother took to heart and demonstrated Matthew 25:35. 'For I was hungry and you gave me something to eat, I was thirsty and you gave me something to drink, I was a stranger and you invited me in, I needed clothes and you clothed me."

Before Mother sent the men on their way, she would hand them a religious magazine, a Sunday school paper, or a story tract. I witnessed her faith in action. That tangible caring had been instilled in me since a child.

ABC

If hunger in this village had been a singular event, I could have let it pass, but now, as I retired for the night, I continued to hear Rachel's pleading cries. I too wanted to cry for the plight of these impoverished friends. The village did not have any jobs aside from those related to the airstrip, and welfare was not a part of their lives. When I'd helped the men apply for social security cards and work on tax returns, I'd become painfully aware of how little income the families had.

"How much more did you make this year besides what you earned from Wien Airlines?" I'd asked one man.

"One wolf," he replied. The State of Alaska offered $50 per wolf for bounty.

Over and over, like a needle stuck on a record, my mind played, *Every child ought to have the right to bread.* In this culture, daily bread meant sour-dough hotcakes.

I couldn't shove aside their plight. I had to do something. *What if there were markets for their crafts? Could I encourage families to make masks and help them develop other marketable craft items?*

ABC

Scientists, healthcare personnel, and bush pilots were infrequent buyers of the Nunamiuts' incidental crafts. But with the consistent people-traffic associated with school-related projects and the increasing ease of access into the village, interest and motivation for revenue-generating crafts took off like a dog fresh in a sled harness.

In early June, I'd shown Anna Hugo the little Eskimo yo-yos I'd bought in Barrow. She easily copied the idea, using scraps of caribou for two weighted fur-fringed faces. Each face was attached to an 18 to 20-inch strand of caribou sinew, one slightly shorter than the other. The two lengths were joined together with a tuft of caribou skin or bone.

Mr. Thomas, the school construction superintendent, and his wife, recognized the economic need, as did his crew. In early summer, Mrs. Thomas had gone around to the homes to see what crafts might be available. She was a quiet, caring soul, and the Eskimos sensed her goodwill. When the school was completed, the Thomases and the work crew bought a number of objects before they left the village.

Visitors assumed that the fascinating, often-elaborate masks among the crafts had originated decades before. Perhaps they'd started with a medicine man, or maybe typified a ceremonial dance, or possibly imbued good luck to hunters. Certainly, the Natives of the Northwest made ceremonial masks that held significance. The creation of masks *was* characteristic of these other Alaska cultures; nevertheless, the Nunamiuts of Anaktuvuk Pass did not have a tradition of mask-making. Furthermore, throughout their migrations, none of the roving bands had ever seen these indigenous masks; therefore, they had no foreknowledge to imitate mask-making.

When a newcomer would inquire about the history of the masks, the villagers would break out in smiles, glance meaningfully at each other, speak a few words in Eskimo, and try to explain in broken English the simple and humorous conception. It was some time until I was able to piece at least most of the story together.

Around 1950, Bob Ahgook and Zaccharias Hugo, both in their twenties, were tending trap lines outside the village one evening at camp and talking about the approaching Christmas holidays. Zaccharias had visited Fairbanks around Halloween and was fascinated by the masks in the stores. That night, the young men decided to make masks and use them as disguises during Christmas celebrations. After much trial and error, they cut out oval pieces of caribou skin for basic face pieces, slit eye holes, and cut pieces for the noses. Caribou fur turned into a mustache, beard, and eyebrows. A perimeter of fur, simulating a parka ruff, completed the design. They used caribou sinew to sew everything together.

On Christmas Eve, the dancing commenced with Eskimos sitting in a circle, drummers beating out a rhythm, and a group chanting in accompaniment. The women were attired in recently sewn atigas. Children joined the merriment, imitating the dancers and drummers. Well into the festivities, the two masked men made a surprise appearance, dancing and teasing their friends. People laughed uproariously, pointed in amusement, and sought to determine the identities of the newcomers.

Following the Christmas event, the masks were hung up in homes and forgotten. No one even thought of selling masks until 1952, when two University of Alaska scientists came through Anaktuvuk and offered $10 per mask. The mask-makers were out of the village, so Simon, who was the chief at that time, negotiated the deal. He didn't want to take advantage of their interest and talked the scientists *down* to $5 apiece. When the young men returned from their hunting camp, they thanked Simon for acting wisely. Once again, mask-making was pushed to the side.

Then, several years later, Ethel Ross-Oliver, a school teacher who had conducted the 1950 census and held a deep affection for the Anaktuvuk Pass people, returned with three women to hold a summer school session. In a show of appreciation, Elijah and Simon bestowed upon the group twelve masks, three for each woman. This time, they were made of wood rather than caribou skin.

Ethel wanted to help market the masks and generate income from them, so she contacted an Anchorage gift shop owner who agreed to pay $20 per mask. When the masks arrived, they were not out of wood, as were the samples Ethel had shown him, but made from caribou skin, like the original ones. Obviously, there was no exact standard for the masks but continued trial and error efforts.

About that time, Justus, known for making the best snowshoes in the village, took it upon himself to perfect the mask-making. He carved a wooden mask and then stretched skin that had been soaked in water, coffee, tea, or blood on top of it. The rudimentary mask with slits cut for the eyes and mouth was then left to dry. Once hardened, the skin was removed from the wooden frame and features were added. This method reduced production time from two days to one. Not feeling the need to have a monopoly, he unrestrictedly carved wooden molds for other mask-makers to use.

In 1959, when I'd visited the village with Doc Gaede, he'd purchased one of Simon's wooden masks, as well as a skin mask. In 1960, when I arrived to teach, sales had once again lulled.

ABC

I tossed and turned in bed. *How could marketing crafts become reality? What if I could get a business license and start a mail order business and advertise in the* Alaska Sportsman Magazine, Fairbank Daily News-Miner, *and* The Anchorage Daily Times? I drifted to sleep, dreaming of children eating stacks of sourdough hot cakes drenched in melting butter and sticky sweet syrup, and women shopping for fabrics for their atigas.

I was always careful that I adhered to my contracted teaching role first and that my other passions and concerns, such as teaching Sunday school, teaching adults to write, and now getting a business license, didn't take away from these responsibilities. I wrote Mr. Hayes for permission to get a business license. He had seen the village and met the people. He supported my efforts.

To my amazement, I received a letter from the Northern Commercial store in Fort Yukon requesting that I send Eskimo-crafted skin masks on a consignment basis. As if this was not exciting enough, they explained that they expected to both display and sell Alaskan Arts and Crafts at the Seattle World's Fair in April 1962. They asked, "Would you have any additional items? Could you send a photograph so that we can carefully consider what to include?" And so it appeared that I was in business for the Anaktuvuk Pass Eskimos. Hopefully all the little children would soon have happy and content tummies and no one would cry for hunger.

This confirmation compelled me forward. I contacted the *Alaska Sportsman* magazine and, using my Eskimo name, composed the following:

FOR SALE: DIRECT from Napikuk's Eskimo Crafts

Anaktuvuk Pass, Alaska

Caribou Skin Masks	$16.00
Wooden Masks	$25.00
Yo Yos	$4.50

Now, instead of making only health-related rounds, I also made rounds to check on craft orders. "Ethel, I need another doll," I'd request, stopping at one house. The going rate for dolls was $10 and $12.50 with postage. Then, dashing to another, I'd say, "Zaccharias, I need two masks—soon!" As fast as they produced crafts, I'd box them up and mail them out to buyers.

Mailing things proved to be an ordeal. Homer had been designated by Wien Airlines to transport the mail from the landing strip. He subsequently opened the post office in his home. In December 1961, I wrote my parents:

> Last week, I had three boxes and Homer had no stamps to send them, so I paid freight. Eek! This week, he said the one box cost over $2 and I never thought anything about it until I started smearing saliva over a sheet of 100 one-cent stamps. I nearly had that box plastered with stamps when I realized it was just going to Anchorage. When I questioned why so much postage, he said, "I thought it was going to the States." Frantically, I started peeling off the stamps. Other times, he doesn't have any stamps and sends me back home to use the ones I have there.

I never know where my mail will end up—found your box up at school. It was delivered by dog team. Other times they'll go right into my house with my things.

During all these transactions, I paid the craftsperson before I saw the actual sales money myself. Sometimes, even after several billings, a purchaser had not sent a check and I took a loss. I kept track of the sales in a brown leather notebook. Each villager who participated could be found in alphabetical order. The date, items, and price were carefully recorded. Initially, the items were pretty much the same for each person; however, along the way, specialties emerged: candleholders, purses, drums, and miniature kayaks were added to masks and ulus. Mittens weren't just mittens; they were "Fox Head Mittens," "Sheep Mittens," or "Wolf Head Mittens." Even a pair of precious ugruk (bearded walrus) mukluks showed up.

Homer Mekiana and helpers loading mail at Anaktuvuk Pass, Alaska. The new school is in the background. The Cat from Umiat is half-buried in snow behind the 55-gallon oil drums, 1961.

Now, mask-makers let their imaginations go. Small, beveled pieces of caribou hooves turned into eyes on the wooden masks. Soon, eyelashes appeared on the skin masks. Instead of using sinew thread exclusively, cotton thread and glue were used too.

Winter blizzards could not bury the elation of moneyed villagers who pushed through the white-coated wind to Homer's store to buy staples, and even luxuries of peanut butter and jelly to put on their hot cakes. I saw one mother, surrounded by glad-sounding children, buying factory-sewn mittens and gloves for her entire brood. When I paid John Morry, our Eskimo teacher, for a little wooden kayak, he bought Kool-Aid and candy bars for his kids.

Later on, when I went to Fairbanks for Christmas, I ordered *Napikuk's Eskimo Crafts* business cards, which I passed out to every visitor in the village, as well as placing in each box of crafts that was mailed out.

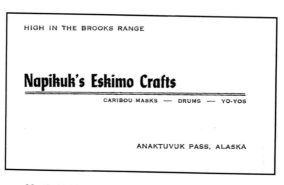

Napikuk's Native Crafts, Anaktuvuk Pass, Alaska, 1962.

As word about these crafts spread, orders increased. When an X-ray technician held clinic in the village, he ordered a caribou sleeping bag. Shortly after, Mt. McKinley mountain climbers sent an order for mukluks, caribou skin socks, and mittens. After their successful climb, they sent letters of appreciation to the villagers. A man at Clear, Alaska, asked for a franchise to market crafts. Sales left the state, and an order for six masks went to a museum in Idaho.

ABC

My life resembled a busy and happy circus. When visitors climbed out of airplanes, my sod house rated second in their curiosity about the Nunamiuts. I figured that after wandering through the village, they'd want a tour of the new school, an odd miracle in this far-flung place; instead, they stopped at the "schoolteacher's house." I jokingly considered charging admission to my humble domicile that now housed wrapping materials, orders to mail out, and increased medical supplies.

Even without out-of-village guests, just the regular traffic practically wore me out. One afternoon, I put a sign on my entry indicating no visiting until the evening. I flopped down on my bed for a much-needed nap. I'd just drifted off when I heard, "Miss Bortel," at my ear. I opened my eyes, and there stood a woman leaning over me, requesting rickrack for her atiga and bias tape for another project. She was scarcely out the door when a teenager wanted to show me a picture she'd made. With only moments between, a young fellow brought me a fish from successful ice fishing. Finally, the last guest of the day came bearing a lamp of caribou antlers.

"Next time, candle holders," said Jack, father of three. "Pretty soon, I get enough money for gun."

Amid this hubbub, one Friday in November, I received a letter from Eddie Hooley asking if he could come for a visit. Finally, I would get to meet the man who everyone seemed to know except me.

The following day, as I was sorting clothing to be given to the Eskimos and mentally composing an affirmative reply to Eddie, I heard the hum of a small plane overhead. Earlier in the day, George Riedel, a pilot for Arctic Research, had flown in. I'd come to recognize all the planes that flew in and out.

Who could this be now? I ran out to look. This most definitely was no one I knew. *Oh no! Could this be Eddie already?* I gasped.

I darted back inside and threw the clothes into boxes and shoved them behind my curtained-off area. I looked in the mirror and gasped in horror. My hair was straight and oily, and I had on old denim jeans. Saturday evenings were hair-washing days, and I had a bucket of snow melting on the stove; even if I could wash my hair, I would need time to set it on pink foam curlers, which would take hours to dry. Usually, I went to bed with a scarf tied around my disciplined locks so as not to lose the spongy rollers. But for this emergency and last-minute first impression, I attempted to *fix up* as best I could and compose myself. I waited. I paced. No one showed up.

I needed to deliver the clothes I'd been sorting to the school, so I loaded them on my big, Eskimo-style sled and headed that direction.

Struggling to get up the hill with my load, I tried to kick foot-holds in the packed snow, all the while watching that my cargo didn't tumble off behind me. I could have used a dog or two to help pull. That pretty well took the breath out of me, but I succeeded.

On my way home, some schoolchildren caught up with me.

"Miss Bortel, Mr. Hooley, the teacher from Kobuk, is here," said one.

"He's having coffee with Jack," chimed in another.

"He landed on the lake," added yet another.

I was grateful for at least a little advance notice. Once more, I endeavored to freshen up.

A knock sounded on the door. My heart beat wildly. I couldn't believe my eyes. Here he was, Eddie Hooley, taller than me, carrying no more weight than necessary, and a kind face.

He looked at me intently. "Is that invitation you gave me a year ago still good?"

I returned his gaze and uncertainly began, "I just received your letter yesterday. We haven't had mail for days. Come on in..."

We had waited a long time to get acquainted face to face, and I was ecstatic but didn't want to appear like a love-struck teenage girl.

"I can't believe I'm in Anaktuvuk Pass, finally," he said slowly, his eyes never leaving mine.

In the middle of an awkward pause, there was a forceful rap at the door. There stood George Riedel, his parka hood sliding off his balding head. He looked as though he'd just pulled his head out of a plane engine, and an oil smear ran along one cheekbone. I couldn't tell if the older man hadn't shaved that morning or if his face was just shadowed with plane innards and blowing snow.

"Could you tell me where I could get some meals?"

Oh no. Just when we finally meet, we are already interrupted. "Right here," I stammered. "But I thought you took off."

"I did. But the weather was terrible. I headed north over the flats to Umiat when I had to turn back. Almost flew up the wrong valley."

Though George's arrival was ill-timed, I didn't feel I could violate the unwritten law of the North to extend hospitality. I invited him in, and the two men sat down in the chairs I'd pulled away from the table. I tried to concentrate on frying crisp the thin caribou steaks, making gravy, and stirring the rice and heating canned peas, but I couldn't help feel Eddie's eyes on me.

I wonder what he thinks of me. I have so many questions to ask him. Why did George have to show up now, of all times?

The two men talked. George had a one-track mind—his own experiences—and he filled the time and air with these until I placed dinner on the table and pulled up another chair. After a quick blessing, there was a brief silence while everyone spooned out the steaming meal.

"Anna, tell me how you ever ended up this far north," said Eddie.

George interrupted, "Talk about north. I was just heading over the flats before Umiat and got into a doozy of storm!"

He was oblivious that Eddie and I were trying to get acquainted, and I suspected that his primary purpose in seeking me out was to find white man food to fill his stomach.

I ignored him and responded to Eddie, "Well, it was a series of steps..."

George reached for the gravy and continued, "I really took a step back when my plane started to shake and I looked down and saw that cabin."

I paused for a moment to eat, thinking how strange this all was. *I've been eager to see Eddie, and I've played over in my mind what it might be like. Certainly nothing like this: stringy hair, close together in my tiny house and just across the small table from each other, which would be intimate, except for...*

"Anna, you were saying..." Eddie was not giving up.

"Boy, these steaks are great!"

I didn't see how George managed to even swallow with so much talking.

"I kept seeing that cabin every time I looked down, so I guessed I wasn't getting anywhere fast. Talk about headwinds!"

I gave up trying to carry on a conversation with Eddie.

"That was probably Elijah Kakinya's. He and Simon Paneak were at Tulugak Lake, in that direction, until we started school here. About fifteen miles away."

"Well, yes, it was about that far. I just know my gas gauge was going down, down, and I figured I'd better get out of there before I went down, too."

Even if Eddie's conversational efforts were thwarted, all the same, he was the perfect guest. "This is the best fried caribou. I'm so enjoying it and everything else you cooked tonight."

I smiled at him and studied his face, trying not to smile too brightly. For a moment, we shut out George and were in our own space.

"Thank you, Eddie," I replied sincerely.

George still was in his own world. "I'm really glad I got back in tonight after flying up a wrong valley! Man, did everything look alike."

One thing I knew: these two men were *not* alike.

Eddie was captivated with the village in the valley, and after supper, I suggested that we walk to Angelee's to see my Anaktuvuk slides. George tailed us. The projector rattled, and within a minute, Eddie had out a screwdriver. A handy man indeed. Throughout the presentation, he complimented me on my photography, which charmed my heart. He'd say things such as, "This is just what people like to see outside," or, "I've never thought of taking one like that." When he turned his head sideways to listen to my reply, he reminded me of my uncle, Newman. I felt my cheeks warming and hoped he didn't notice.

George managed to keep his mouth shut until he jumped up suddenly and said, "Oh, I'd better go check my plane. Those winds are howling." Off he went.

Eddie lifted his eyebrows and looked at me out of the corner of his eyes. After George left, Eddie let out a laugh. "He really likes to talk, doesn't he?"

I liked this man. There was a comfortable familiarity about him.

That night, Eddie and George slept in their sleeping bags in my classroom. The next morning, with temperatures hovering at minus 20 degrees, the men came stomping in the entry for a sausage-and-pancake breakfast.

"Anna, tell me how you got here," said Eddie.

This time, while I told my story, George actually sat quietly. He just drizzled syrup over his pancakes and sausage and stirred sugar in his coffee.

When I was finished, Eddie shook his head and repeated, as he had the day before, "To think! I'm in Anaktuvuk Pass, Anna's pass."

That sounded like poetry, but the words barely rested in the air before George burst out with his you-wouldn't-believe-this-or-that storm tales.

The warm breakfast must have refueled his energy. This last saga led to asking Eddie if he'd like to fly north.

"The end of the lake is the farthest north I want to go," he replied. "But right now, I'd like to take some pictures."

The end-of-November sun couldn't find its way over the mountain ranges, and the hint of light cast long, blurred shadows on the ground. The lack of much depth perception and the abundance of wind caused us both to stagger on the stiff-whipped snow. He snapped pictures the best he could.

Then it was time for Eddie to leave. He knew it would take awhile to warm up his plane, and he had nearly three hours of flying time ahead. He had to take advantage of winter's porthole of light.

"Anna, it is so cold. You don't have to walk out to the lake with me," Eddie said. All the same, he handed me his transistor radio to carry, as if he expected me to join him.

The mile hike would afford more time together, so I layered on clothes to accompany him. We faced directly into the north wind, but even so, we were finally alone. When we'd stop to rest with our backs to the wind, I could see in his eyes and hear in his voice the same feelings that stirred in me.

"Anna, you'd better go back now," he said tenderly. "But may I come visit you again?"

"You have an open invitation," I responded.

With that, we said our good-byes. Chilled to my marrow, I walked home with a warm heart.

George had not left. After teaching afternoon Sunday school, I'd gone over to Angelee's. She had a new Montgomery Ward catalog that I wanted to window shop through. She'd just poured hot water into a cup for some hot Tang when there was a knock at the door.

"Oh, there you are!" George looked straight at me. He had his sleeping bag, and it was apparent that not only had he *not* left but he was looking for bush hospitality. "Could I get another meal? Love your cooking."

I couldn't even be left alone for an evening to relive my memories of Eddie.

"Angelee, why don't you come over for supper?"

241

Both of them were talkers, so I didn't have to say much. I busied myself reheating leftovers and finding another can of vegetables.

"So, George, when do you plan to leave?" I asked.

"Well, what's the hurry? I think I'd just like to spend the winter here."

My goodness! I'd have to change my cooking so it wasn't so inviting, and maybe not wash my hair for a week or two, or more.

ABC

The upcoming holidays would not be happy for everyone.

"Maggie had her baby...it died."

I was on my way to fix supper at Angelee's when Jane found me. I knew the baby wasn't due yet. I also knew it was Maggie Hugo's third baby, all of whom had died in infancy. I felt angry and sad about this reoccurrence and detoured to her house. Jane and I pushed through the door. I expected to find the baby in a cardboard box; instead, Maggie pointed towards a bundle wrapped in paper. Carefully, I unwrapped the infant and examined it, trying to figure out the cause of death.

Her previous babies had blue faces, but this one was blue all over; furthermore, it was malformed. One ear was lopsidedly low, the eyes were hard to make out, and the nose was extremely pug. Blood had seeped out of the tiny infant's mouth. Maggie carried the baby only eight months, but regardless of the early delivery, it was too deformed to have lived. I felt like bawling.

Hungry children. Dying babies. In some ways, life was becoming very modern in Anaktuvuk, and in other, basic ways, it was still locked in tragic historical patterns.

ABC

A plane buzzed overhead, and I looked out the window. I could tell from the pictures Ed Parsons had shown me that it was the new Pilatus Porter, an airplane that had just come out of production. Ed, the superintendent of stations for Wien Airlines and the assistant to President Sig Wien, along with two of his mechanics, had been stranded in the village for four days with flat tires. During this time he'd told me about this recent purchase.

I excitedly instructed, "Children, get your parkas."

They reacted quickly. Down the hill we stumbled and slid on the crusted snow, and over to the runway we raced.

On this inaugural flight into Anaktuvuk Pass, President Sig Wien and Richard Wien had accompanied Ed Parsons. The children walked around the plane and even got to inspect the cockpit and cabin. The turbo-engine, eight-passenger aircraft with wheel-ski combination landing gear was replacing the Wien's four-to-six-place Cessnas. What a beauty. In the Lower 48 States, children went on field trips to zoos and science or history museums. Here, above the Arctic Circle, the airstrip was an outdoor aviation museum.

In most cases, a schoolteacher would have corralled her children and returned to school with souvenir entry-pass tickets or brochures. In my case, Ed hauled out boxes of unexpected groceries for Angelee and me. My mouth dropped open. What an unexpected treat.

He brushed it off as though it was nothing. "You fed us when we got stranded."

Store-bought food *was* something, and especially with Christmas coming. We'd sort through the box together, and who knew what we might find; possibly Strawberry Quick drink mix, olives, Ritz crackers, chicken fryers, real potatoes, or even apples. Canned pumpkin caught my eye, and I thought I saw some jellied cranberries.

"Hey. My wife and I have been handing out Napikuk cards," he told me enthusiastically.

Before he left, he fixed Angelee's ailing radio set and adjusted some of the villager's radio aerials too. Then, as he got ready to fly out, he said, "Anna, how would you like to be a tour guide for Wien during the summer? Think about it."

His kind generosity and support knew no bounds.

Fairbanks, Alaska, Monday, November 1961

"Wien Tests New Swiss Bush Plane"

The Pilatus Porter, new bush plane recently added to the fleet of Wien Alaska Airlines was given a test flight yesterday by Richard and Merrill Wien, sons of Noel Wien of the flying Wien family...Primarily to be used for "bush" operations, the

Pilatus Porter will eventually replace the Norseman and the Cessna 180's and the 185's presently being used for this kind of operation.

The plane will carry a payload of 1,400 pounds and is powered with a 350 horsepower Lycoming engine. When turbo prop engines are installed a later date the horsepower will increase to 520 horsepower. The Pilatus Porter was the first Swiss airplane sold in the United States.

ABC

Visitors continued to drop into Anaktuvuk. One late Thursday morning, within the few hours span when airplanes had visibility to land and take off in the arctic darkness, I heard a plane and watched it land. My primary students lifted their heads from penciling arithmetic worksheets. I reached for my binoculars and saw several people get out. Bags were unloaded.

"I don't know who it is," I answered the students' questioning looks.

Soon, I heard voices outside Angelee's classroom, followed by a knock on my classroom door. There stood two unfamiliar men with friendly smiles surrounded by bags and cameras. Who, in the dead of winter, would have come to Anakatuvuk Pass, Alaska? One of the men, who introduced himself as Don McCune, or "Captain Puget," produced children's TV programs for KOMO-TV out of Seattle. The other man, Dick Cornwell, was from some Expedition Northwest Program.

"We need something different for our Christmas show, and what better place to come for footage than near the North Pole," said the captain, taking off his black-rimmed glasses and defogging them with a handkerchief. His short moustache was snow-frosted.

The charismatic man attracted the children and convinced me that this would be a fun and good idea. He set up bright lights on tripods and took movies of me sitting on a little chair with my students cross-legged on the floor, in a reading circle. Then, we sang, "It's Christmas Time in Anaktuvuk." This was followed by Captain Puget playing his guitar and singing with the students. He'd sing a verse of "Jingle Bells," and the children would join in the chorus. Their eyes sparkled, and heads bobbed. When he stopped, they clapped their hands for more.

Before the duo left, they wanted to see the rest of the school building. Seeing a tub of water on the school stove, Dick Cornwell asked, "What's that for, humidity?"

"No. I plan to do my laundry tonight."

He didn't understand, and I just wasn't up to explaining common practices here in the Bush. I'd been euphoric when the modern pink washing machine had arrived a week before. Since I had no source of electricity, it was kept in the schoolhouse storage room and run off the generator. Regardless, without plumbing and a hot water heater, Angelee and I had to heat water and dump it inside the washer. As laborious a process as this was, it beat hand-scrubbing on a board.

The recordings were to be aired on Captain Puget's TV Christmas programs. After Christmas, I heard from two acquaintances that they'd seen my children on a Seattle TV station. Bill and Bonnie Wartes, who had moved to Washington, after their missionary work in Alaska, were elated when they saw Anaktuvuk children. Truly it was a Christmas gift to them.

Fairbanks Daily News-Miner

"Don McCune Returns to Make Bush Flying Movie"

(circa January 1962)

Don McCune, former manager of KFAR radio and television stations was a Fairbanks visitor yesterday while en route to the bush to make an adventure movie.

He is known to Seattle audience as "Captain Puget" of KOMO-TV...they will visit Anaktuvuk Pass in the Brooks Range for primitive scenes...McCune and Cornwell have sound and a silent camera. Their movies will be released on a children's show with tailored narration to suit a young audience, and Expedition Northwest, an adult show of true life adventures... McCune and Cornwell were met at the Fairbanks International Airport by Noel Wien, pioneer Alaskan aviation figure...

CHRISTMAS MEMORIES

· ·

"E-e-e-e," resounded throughout my classroom as I handed each child a hektographed copy of a Santa's head to color.

"You may color Santa and then paste cotton on for whiskers," I instructed the impatient workers, as more *e-e-e's* ascended.

Since the previous year, the school term had let out for timber time, I hadn't gotten in on Christmas traditions in the village. This year, I indulged in holiday baking. I'd just frosted cut-out sugar cookies when I heard a plane coming in. I recognized it as Andy's and put a package of still-warm cookies into my self-drawn sled and headed toward the airstrip. My mother had always baked cookies for the mailman, and here, my Anaktuvuk Pass mailman certainly deserved extraordinary thanks for delivering much-anticipated letters from friends and family.

"Merry Christmas, Andy," I said. "These started out warm, but with the current 30-below temperatures, they aren't warm anymore."

Andy thanked me and pointed out that I was getting frostbite on my nose. "And, something for you!" He turned around and pulled out bolts of cotton fabric.

In addition to the Fourth of July, Christmas was a major event in Anaktuvuk, and called for sewing new parkas and mukluks for all the celebrations. I'd special-ordered provisions for the woman to make their Christmas atigas. Andy climbed back in his plane, which, at this time of year and this near the North Pole, could have passed for a Santa's sleigh. I pulled my sled back, feeling a bit like Mrs. Santa Claus.

In short order, I heard taps on my door. The women swarmed into my sod house for shopping. They fingered the material, compared their choices with one another, and extended their arms to show how much yardage they needed.

"Just like Fairbanks!" squealed one woman, holding up a length of cranberry-red print against herself.

"Never had so much in Anaktuvuk before," said another, her face glowing with anticipation.

I measured and cut calico and multi-hues of rickrack and named their balance. They meticulously counted out dollar bills. Joy filled my house and their world.

ABC

I wanted our classroom to look festive; after all, this would go down in history as the first school Christmas celebration in Anaktuvuk Pass. The children painstakingly cut and pasted red-and-green construction paper loops to make chains and frequently chewed off dried glue on their fingers. Since the nearest tree was forty miles away, I was amazed when Jack, the new janitor, went to check his trap lines and returned with a Christmas tree. I popped popcorn that the youngsters strung into ropes and popped into their mouths while they worked.

Each day, following the three *R*'s and spelling, more decorations would go up, followed by more Christmas program practice. The small choir worked diligently, learning "Silent Night" and other songs that were new to them. At one point, a little guy got a piece of caribou hair beneath his shirt and kept scratching, almost in time to the music. One of the kids decided to help him find the offender, which tickled him. Pretty soon, the hooting overcame the music, which tickled me.

Several of Angelee's older boys carried the pump organ from the church to her room, and by Friday evening, her room became an auditorium. The Eskimos preferred to sit on the floor, so this eliminated the need for chairs or an elevated stage. Parents' faces radiated with smiles as their offspring performed. Little Myrtle Mekiana sang a Christmas lullaby to her new doll, shifting from side to side as she rocked it in her arms. My class lustily sang an Anaktuvuk adaption of a Tanana Christmas song I'd written.

After singing, they turned away from the audience, and on each of their backs was a letter, joining the other letters to spell *WELCOME*. The people who could read explained the meaning of the letters to those nearby. Following the program, everyone proceeded into my classroom for hot chocolate and cookies.

The day before vacation, Angelee's class joined mine for a party. Their eyes sparkled as they joyously sang, in several-part harmony, a number of newly learned carols around the lighted Christmas tree. This was followed by a gift exchange. My philosophy was that, regardless of how poor one might be, if he or she cared deeply for another, a gift could always be found to share. The children caught the spirit. Their gifts were primarily made from caribou, in the form of yo-yos or pins. Some brought along an old toy. Friends of mine in Hillsdale, Michigan, had sent rag dolls for my girls and toys for the boys. My eyes moistened when I watched the first-grade girls glow with happiness as they lovingly caressed their dollies. I wished my friends could see how much their kind efforts meant to the children.

After juice and cupcakes, little Myrtle, followed by the other girls, came up to me and asked, "Miss Bortel, would you put my baby in the back of my parka?"

They wanted to carry their dollies home just like their mothers would carry real babies. Into the darkness of an arctic afternoon, the happy children walked, singing, "We Wish You a Merry Christmas."

ABC

On Christmas Eve, my boots crunched up the snow-packed hill toward church with my flashlight showing the way on the fresh snow. The organ was back in its original spot, and the villagers gathered to sing carol after carol, some in Eskimo and others in English. I pumped and pumped.

Oh, if only someone could fix the leak in the bellows!

The muscles in my legs ached.

When the singing was over, Homer read the story of Jesus's birth from the book of Luke, first in Inupiaq and then translated into English.

At times, I nearly pinched myself. I was so far from my Ohio home but exactly where I'd dreamed of being *someday*.

Following the traditional service, Santa popped in carrying two huge mail sacks filled with gifts. The children whooped with delight. Most of the gifts, however, were jokes. Over the years, a curious custom had developed. Items lost, misplaced, or left at another person's home became presents since there was no income for purchasing new things. I expected to be an observer, and my mouth dropped open when I was handed a flashlight I'd lost.

That night, I received other gifts as well. When I opened a sugar sack tied with sinew, there was a wolf ruff. When I opened the next package, there was another. I was shocked. These were so very valuable. Each would have brought $15. These friends could have paid for ammunition, food, or fabric. I received other gifts made from caribou too. Finally, John Morry presented me with a mask. On a card in the back, he'd written, "To *Ilyasautri* (teacher), Mary Christmas, From *Ilyasautri* Morry." My heart overflowed with the outpouring of selflessness.

After the celebration, I went to Anna Hugo's home. I was curious how the Nunamiuts spent their Christmas Eve and felt honored they'd invited me. The moon, like a bright street light, illuminated our way, and we easily found our way through the village. The snow-buried sod houses appeared to be what outsiders expected Eskimos to live in—igloos.

The small group told stories about comical gifts they had received on other Christmases. Anna interpreted to me, and we chewed urak (cooked caribou meat) and sipped hot tea. I nearly choked with laughter when one man told of the toenail he'd received in a large box. The hilarity continued late into the night.

Once again, I was struck by how different Anaktuvuk was from Tanana because it was a dry village and alcohol was not a part of their Friday nights or celebrations. In Tanana, as much as I loved the Natives, there weren't many cabins I'd have gone into for Christmas Eve partying. The Nunamiuts' remarkable sense of humor was not the result of anything imbibed.

I'd noticed this quality soon after I'd arrived in Anaktuvuk, and that their good nature transcended generations. It was as if they'd been born with optimism. Scientists who had spent extended time in this culture mentioned it as well. Anyone who had much contact with the Nunamiuts, or knew anything of their history, and the hardships of their survival, would be aware that there was no correlation between wealth and easy living and the full-cup attitudes and good natures.

Just past midnight, I drew my parka around myself and walked home beneath a starlit Christmas Eve sky.

ABC

Repeated tapping on the door roused me from sleep, but I could see nothing in the darkness.

"Anna?" sounded through the door.

I glanced at the clock beside my bed. Oh! I'd invited Angelee for Christmas Day breakfast, and she'd probably been up for hours, waiting for 8:00 a.m. I reached for my flashlight, knocked it over, and felt my way to the door.

"I'm sorry," I apologized to Angelee.

Since there was no sunlight to encourage my departure from bed and I hadn't set my alarm, I'd snuggled down and slept. I understood hibernating bears.

The beam of her flashlight led me to mine, and I then lit my lantern. Lethargically, I washed my face, got dressed, and gathered powdered milk, powdered eggs, and flour for pancakes.

"I know I have sausage here somewhere in the entry," I said to Angela.

Pretty soon, coffee perked noisily in my pot on the stove.

Angelee had nowhere to go and nothing else to do, so she settled on the floor in front of my bookcase. She pulled out a book I'd so enjoyed, *Dayspring on the Kuskokwim* by Anna Buxbaum Schwalbe, about the Moravian missions in Alaska. The greasy-good smell of frying sausage mingled with that of the coffee. After a leisurely meal, we exchanged gifts. Then, since the Christmas Day feast at church would not start until later in the day, we decided to take my .22 and go ptarmigan hunting. We started out confidently in the dim northern daylight. Our confidence eroded when we couldn't differentiate the camouflaged white birds from the dusky background. The bitter wind and subzero temperatures confirmed our decision to return to the warmth of my house. No turkey, ham, or ptarmigan for dinner on this Christmas Day.

We'd just removed our parkas when Amos stopped by to announce, "Feast begins when women finish cooking. Maybe near five."

Angelee decided she'd go back to the teacherage. I sat down in the solitude of my sod house, turned out the lantern, and lit a red Christmas candle. Outside, the wind chased about but couldn't get in. I'd designed a Christmas tree shape on my wall with Christmas cards. The shiny foil and glitter on the greetings reflected the flickering light. Hot water came to a boil on the stove. With a few rare, unstructured hours before me, I made a cup of hot chocolate and reminisced about Christmases past.

ABC

Christmas Day at Grandma and Grandpa Crosby's was a highlight of my childhood. Relatives would arrive with baskets of mouth-watering pumpkin and mince pies, and assorted Christmas cookies and candies. Jars of canned pickles, peaches, and green beans lined the kitchen countertop. Before long, the kitchen shared with the entire house its appetizing odors of scalloped oysters, sweet potatoes, roast chicken, and other tantalizing dishes.

We cousins hung around the tree and plopped on our tummies waiting for the big moment: gift exchange. Uncle Norman, dressed in a Santa suit, ran in the front door, headed for the tree, and handed out the gifts. Happy chaos of wrapping paper and bows littered the room.

The adults retired to the living room and we children closed the bifold doors. Grandma and Grandpa trusted us with the old Victrola and in uneven strokes we took turns winding up "Yes, We Have No Bananas Today" and "On the Sidewalks of New York." Oh, the abundance of childhood energy—and the patience of the adults who loved us. Oh, what worlds away I was now.

My eyes closed and head nodded. Wax puddled around the bottom of the thick candle. My cup, now empty, was outlined with the remains of hot chocolate. A noise at the door called me to out of my reverie. It was Amos announcing that the feast was about to begin. I wrapped up to go out and thought how the people I'd come to *help* had lovingly and lavishly made me feel so much at home.

Outside in the wind, the night was alive with flashlights bouncing up and down, children sliding down the hill, and stars twinkling high above. Inside the school, caribou and all the trimmings of hot cakes, biscuits, tea, and coffee were arranged down the center of the room, on the floor. The people started to sit around the edges. Women dressed in their beautiful atigas moved gracefully, making final touches.

I spotted little Rachel in a corner, holding a rolled-up sourdough hot cake in each hand.

"I have hot cake," she said, looking up at me with a sugary grin.

I hugged her. This elf of a girl was in part responsible for the merriment of the season. Her sobs, months before, had prompted me to find a source of revenue for the Eskimos, and now they had begun to make and sell their crafts. This was truly a Christmas of hope for everyone.

Christmas wouldn't have been complete without an Eskimo dance. Near midnight, the singing and dancing began. Drums beat, a rhythm was set, and dancers moved to the center of the room to gesture and bend as they depicted a successful hunt. During a pause, and knowing I had to leave early in the morning to fly to Fairbanks, I jumped up, imitated a woman's dance, and danced right out the door as everyone cheered and laughed.

PART VI

1962

TEACHER OF THE YEAR NOMINATION

In late November, Andy had dropped off a load of mail, and in my pile, I'd found this startling letter:

State of Alaska

DEPARTMENT OF EDUCATION

JUNEAU, ALASKA

November 29, 1961

Miss Anna Napikuk Bortel
Anaktuvuk Pass School
Anaktuvuk Pass, Alaska

Dear Miss Bortel:
    It has been my pleasure to nominate you as the candidate from Alaska for the 1962 National Teacher of the Year award.

    I am enclosing a copy of the letter of nomination as well as a verifax copy of the instructions from the U.S. Office of Education. You will note that you are to submit an autobiographical statement to the Project Coordinator. Will you please submit it first to this office so that you may use the services of our clerical staff in typing it. We are more than anxious to do anything that we can to help you win.

Sincerely,

Theo Norby
Commissioner of Education

The person who emerged as the winner would go with Mr. Norby to the White House. Someone else might have leaped in ecstasy, but I just shook in my mukluks. *Look Magazine* sponsored the event, and I'd probably get tremendous publicity if I won, but as I wrote my family, *Pray for my defeat. I DON'T WANT TO GO! I just wish they'd leave me alone with my Eskimos.*

Within moments of reading the letter, I tramped up the hill to Angelee's.

"I'd rather get an award for cooking in rustic conditions than a teacher's award," I jokingly told Angelee. Then, more seriously, I continued. "I know I should pray that God's will be done, but I really don't want any part of this."

The relaxed life of the Eskimos agreed with me, and I had no desire to be plunged into the pressures of public life. I didn't have a professional picture to include with the autobiography and hoped that this might disqualify me. I would gain satisfaction and honor enough by just holding in hand the glowing letter of recommendation that Mr. Norby had sent the Chief of Reports at the US Office of Education in Washington DC.

State of Alaska

DEPARTMENT OF EDUCATION
JUNEAU, ALASKA
November 29, 1961

Mr. John H. Lloyd
Chief, Reports Section
U.S. Office of Education
Washington 25, D.C.

Dear Mr. Lloyd:

It is our privilege to nominate Miss Anna Marie Bortel, Head Teacher at the Anaktuvuk Pass School, Alaska, as the 1962 National Teacher of the Year.

Since coming to Alaska as a teacher in 1954, Miss Bortel has performed outstandingly, often under the most primitive conditions...Anaktuvuk Pass is the most primitive and one of the most isolated of all the communities served by the State-operated school system. It is located 261 miles northwest of Fairbanks in the heart of the Brooks Mountain Range and is accessible by air and dog team only. The population is comprised almost exclusively of semi-nomadic Eskimos, many of whom to not speak English...

She is interested in improving not only the educational level of the children in
the village, but also that of the adults; and she devotes as much of her free time to this end...

Sincerely Yours,

Theo Norby
Commissioner of Education

Where might these accolades lead? Halfheartedly, I began filling out an educational and professional autobiography for Mr. Norby, stopping often to recollect what had brought me to this place in life.

FROM: Anna Marie Bortel, Alaskan Nominee
1962 National Teacher of the Year
SUBJECT: Autobiographical Statement

PHILOSOPHY OF LIFE AND EDUCATION

My philosophy of life and education has changed considerable since coming to live with this primitive Eskimo group. When we think of the drive that possessed the founding fathers of our country, and how our lives have been enriched by their sacrifices, what are we doing to enrich the lives of others? Are we dedicated to a noble cause that we feel has power to help those who are less fortunate than we....Are we willing to sacrifice our life of ease and pleasure to help bring a new light...? Certainly I desire, as a teacher in Alaska and my beloved United States, to do all I can to help others to realize the privilege of our American heritage...by imparting in a small way the joy of growth through education.

ACHIEVEMENTS AND COMMUNITY ACTIVITIES

In Anaktuvk Pass...I am conducting adult education classes. Many of the Eskimos have never learned to read or write, and it has been a thrill to see their faces brighten as the learning takes place. I explain letters to the village council; assist the Department of Agriculture by taking a census of village dogs in order to obtain vaccine for rabies and distemper shots; assist the itinerant nurse; teach a teen-age Sunday school class; conduct graveside services for deceased infants; and provide boarding facilities to downed fliers who are sometimes stranded in our village.

One of my greatest desires is to publish a primary songbook of "Children's Songs of Alaska." I have composed a number already and am convinced that children love to sing about experiences that are meaningful to them.

As much as I dragged my muluked feet to accomplish this task, I recognized how my educational experiences, people-loving personality, curiosity, and ability to live with bare necessities had pulled me to Alaska and then pushed me to where I found myself now. The picture made sense. I'd been born at the right time and designed in the right way.

I put my completed autobiography, into an envelope and sealed it. All night I had nightmares about winning and meeting President Kennedy. The fanfare, floodlights, and frenzy, left me searching for a train or airplane – or dogsled to get back to Anaktuvuk Pass.

I thought of the new Wilson School I'd taught at before coming to Alaska. It was a teacher's dream. How very different from where I found myself now, bent over my typewriter at my kitchen table in a sod house with lantern-light casting vacillating shadows on the papered walls. At age thirty-nine, I was in an extremely different teaching location, yet rapidly becoming enviable as well.

HALLOPIAKIPEN!
NAKEWISI?

February 25, 1962

Dear Robiners:

*Hallopakitpin! Nakuvisi? Nakurugut pakmapak. Tuyuksagikoin
naitchuanik asi pianikupkick tuyutitka kuisagitimkilamik.*

How are you? We are fine. I am writing you and hope you
will answer right away.

I was bursting with news to my friends who were in a round-robin circle
of letters; this time, I could show off my new skills in learning the written
Inupiaq.

Breaking down language barriers brought me closer to these people
whom I loved, lived with, and served. The written word enhanced their
lives too. They didn't have to stand on the outside looking in, but would
soon be able to make sense of a newspaper or book and connect with
the world outside the Brooks Range. It worked both ways: the Nunamiuts learned to speak and read English *and* had their own language put
into writing. Translating the Bible into their words was a significant start.
John Morry had worked diligently in conjunction with Don Webster, the

Wycliffe translator in Wainwright, to put the New Testament into Inupiaq. At this point, they were only twelve chapters away from completing the New Testament.

Another door that had opened was that of daylight. I'd been printing spelling words on the chalkboard during a morning class session when I turned around, astonished to see students sliding out of their desks and dancing in the aisles.

"The sun! The sun!" they shouted.

How could I reprimand their disorderly conduct when I felt the same ecstasy? This was the first time since mid-November that the sun had found strength to pull itself over the mountains. As puny as that might be, each day, it would grow stronger and taller. Pretty soon, I wouldn't have to walk home after school with a flashlight in hand.

The Robiners weren't the only letter-writers. Eddie and I exchanged correspondence regularly. However, it seemed we were more like pen pals than two people in a personal relationship. Every time there was the opportunity to be together, such as the teachers' conference in Fairbanks, or even here in little ol' Anaktuvuk, there seemed to be a throng around us. Of course, what should I care? The letters I wrote my sister showed my ambivalence:

> I'll never know Eddie! I suppose we'll correspond 'til retirement age. Ha. Sometimes I feel that I should just devote all energies to working with the Eskimos and a husband would interfere. He signed his letter "Yours." I really do like him...

My letter rambled for a page and a half. I mentioned he'd be coming to Anaktuvuk as soon as he could get his airplane fixed.

Chances were, I wouldn't have him to myself. The Gaedes planned to fly from Soldotna either the weekend of March 31 or April 7. They'd left Alaska for two years, but had been easily lured back by a request for medical assistance on the Kenai Peninsula. In addition, I heard from Ward Wells, a photographer from Anchorage, who said he wanted a few pictures.

No, this wasn't exactly remote living any more with so many people filtering in and out, the radio communication, and more consistent mail service. In fact, who would believe that when I'd bought a pair of caribou hoof sunglasses from Simon just yesterday that we'd be talking politics? Dr. Milo Fritz, an eye, ear, nose, and throat specialist in Anchorage, was running for governor. Somewhere along the line, he'd met Simon and now sent Simon political materials. Simon showed me a book he'd just received.

"See. He send me Barry Goldwater book. That Dr. Fritz must be smart. He's head doctor."

Simon had started reading the book and proceeded to give his interpretation and opinion. I always enjoyed talking with him and hearing his views, whether they were about the natural environment or the United States as a whole.

We sipped tea and let the minutes pass.

A few weeks later, he asked me to help fill out a form. He handed me a three-fold layer of papers, which I examine with some amusement: Peace Corps Application.

"Simon, where did you get this?"

"Homer sent it with my kids coming from school," he replied.

I paused, uncertain of what to say next. "Do you want to go to Africa?"

He cocked his head to the side and answered seriously, "No. It is too hot."

Obviously, he knew something about the environment outside of Alaska *and* of North America. I explained to him what the form was about and that he didn't need to sign it.

ABC

Even though Anaktuvuk had the start of a runway, pilots other than Wien Airlines needed permission and had to pay a fee to land on the uncompleted strip. Wien airplanes landed on the runway with a combination wheel-ski gear. Bush planes landed with skis on the lake. First Eddie touched down in his Cessna 140, and then Doc's red Piper PA-14 landed nearby. Although it was the end of March, and could be considered springtime, wind scuffed up snow and the temperatures were below zero.

Ruby and I hugged one another. "Anna, I can't believe I'm here. Now I can see what you've been writing about!"

I was distracted by Eddie, just a few feet away, but couldn't say much more than, "Eddie how was your flight in your new plane?"

His look lingered, but he didn't say a word. I would have given anything to know what he was thinking, but then Doc walked between us and stuck his head under the opened engine cowling to see what Eddie was tinkering with.

The Gaedes were only five people since they'd left Mishal (Mish-shell), who they'd adopted in Tanana, at home. Naomi would be twelve on April 2, Ruth turned eleven in the summer, and Mark was six. The children put their backs to the wind and pulled their parka ruffs around their faces for the walk to the village. I turned for a quick look at Eddie. His parka ruff blew in front of his face. He and Doc were still diagnosing the malady.

Most of the adults remembered Dr. Gaede from his medical field trip three years prior and greeted him cordially. I'd let out the word that there would be a singspiration that evening at the chapel, and a large number of villagers exuberantly showed up. The Gaede family sang, and Ruby played the chapel pump organ. I sang in a trio, and then the congregation sang as a whole.

For school, I baked a birthday cake for Naomi, and the students sang "Happy Birthday" and encircled her tightly when she blew out the candles. They treated both girls as if they were breakable china dolls, although after school, all three Gaede kids tumbled and slid down the hill with the others and didn't break.

Doc and Eddie slept at the schoolhouse, and Ruby and the children slept in my house. I'd borrowed caribou skins for the floor and had a slumber party with the youngsters while Ruby slept on my roll-away bed. Even with the lack of much privacy or time alone, Ruby and I managed to get in a good share of gabbing about this and that and divulged for-your-ears-only conversation.

A time or two, Eddie and I found ourselves alone in the school hallway or walking between it and the chapel. At those moments, I forgot everything else and blurted out excitedly, "Eddie…" At the same instance, he'd say my name in his slow, engaging way, "Anna," as if it were a musical note. But then someone would show up and burst our bubble with concerns such as did Eddie need assistance with his airplane or did I needed chairs set up for this or that. My head justified the interruptions as acceptable or necessary, but I swallowed disappointment.

"If women could only know the score with men," Ruby empathized.

Doc and Ruby visited some of the homes and, in typical northern hospitality, were offered thick tea, which they took in stride and with appreciation. They weren't offered any food, and that was probably for the best.

After they left, I had a curious culinary experience that perplexed me even though I'd lived in the village for nearly two years and thought I'd seen and tried about everything. Roseanna invited Angelee and me to supper. Our selection was caribou jaws with hide and hair—and tongue, and ptarmigan with heads and anus intact. I didn't quite know what to do with the head, so I decided to pick at it. When I put pressure near the windpipe, it squeaked with a rush of air, and when I shifted my hand and squeezed near the head, juice squirted out of the eyes. Well, that pretty well finished me off on that bird.

That occasion would have made for some remarkable pictures, but it was not what Ward Wells had come for a month before. At the end of April, I received a letter explaining his impromptu arrival and quick departure.

> April 23, 1962
> Dear Miss Bortel:
> I want to thank you for giving me a chance to take a few photographs in your classroom...As LOOK MAGAZINE are (sic) quite interested in education and schools and people...I hope they can use a series from above the Arctic Circle...I have done some photography in the past for Miss Toni Taylor, editor of the GRAND TEACHER MAGAZINE, and I am hoping that I can get her to use a few photographs in a future issue...
> Sincerely,
> Ward W. Wells, Photographer, Owner

ABC

"School will soon be over, and vacation will begin," I told my adult English class.

No cheers with this announcement. They wanted to learn more. Just the night before, we'd worked with the value of a penny, nickel, dime, and so on. It was hard to imagine that women between ages twenty and forty did not have those concepts. They would not quite complete first grade work by the end of the school year, but I was very pleased with their progress with only once-weekly lessons.

For my younger students, the year concluded with a program and then a picnic.

One of them had blurted out in class, "Soon, we'll empty our books," meaning, "Soon we'll be finished."

If that implied they'd emptied the contents of their texts into their minds, how truly satisfied I'd be.

I felt good about the job I'd done as an educator, but I was tired. Perhaps it was because the snow seemed to be lasting much longer than the year before, which the schoolboys thought was terrific since they could still get around by dog team. I didn't share their enthusiasm. Winter seemed stuck in this pass.

Nearing the end of May, the creek was still frozen. In years past, that would have meant continuing to collect snow to melt or chopping ice in the lake. The education department, however, had contracted with the Natives to bring ice from the lake to provide water for the school and for the two of us teachers. For this I was grateful. I didn't know how I could deal with the extra effort at this time. I counted down until I'd fly out for the summer. Perhaps more sunshine and less snow would revive me.

In spite of the dreary-to-me elements, at the end of May, I took my class on a picnic. We hiked through ankle-deep snow and over partially packed drifts until we found a bare spot on the frozen tundra. I built a small fire with twigs and paper I'd brought along, and then demonstrated threading a wiener onto a willow bough and cooking it near the leaping flames. The kiddies stood transfixed by the extraordinary-to-them display and then, with twitchy anticipation, reached out and wrapped their hands around the fleshy meat and angled it onto roasting sticks. At first, they were dismayed when the hot dogs caught on fire, but after a while, they whooped and hollered when the hot dog would blister or burst into flames. I crouched low beside the short blaze, holding my hands out for extra warmth, offering encouragement at their mishaps of dropped hot dogs and broken sticks.

First-ever school wiener roast in Anaktuvuk Pass, Alaska, Anaktuvuk Pass, Alaska, 1962.

ABC

Before I returned to the sunshine of Ohio, the kinship of family, and the ease of everyday living, I accepted the invitation of John Chambers to chaperone the girls at his second annual Arctic Youth Camp. John picked me up in Anaktuvuk and then flew in young people from Wainwright, which was a little less than 100 miles down the coast, to join the youth from Barrow. The camp was to be held at an abandoned coal camp on the Meade River, where the former owner had built a large frame house. This destination was 70 miles over the tundra from Barrow.

We traveled by Cat train. The Cat pulled three large sleds. A tent was pitched on the first; supplies, including barrels of airplane gas, were stashed on the second; and a wannigan squatted on the third. The wannigan resembled a short, stocky Quonset set on skids, or an Alaska version of a Wild West covered wagon. I was in charge of twenty-five chattering, giggling girls between the ages of fifteen and twenty. There were nearly that many boys, plus four of us leaders. Since there was not a passenger car on this train, and not everyone could fit into the tent, some of the kids wrapped themselves in blankets and jostled on top of the canned peaches, sacks of flours, bags of rice, tins of coffee, jars of peanut butter, and boxes of Pilot Boy crackers. Others crawled inside the wannigan but soon climbed back out since the rocking and swaying motion of the tail-end sled produced motion sickness.

At one point during the twenty-six hours of travel, we got stuck in the snow and ice crossing a river. The water started rising and pushed up the floor covering. Kids yelled, and I shouted, "Grab your sleeping bags! Get your overnight things!"

In a stampede, we jumped ship onto the shore, where our screaming turned to comic relief and hilarity over the near disaster. The Cat pulled itself and its train out of the water, and we continued on.

I taught two Bible classes. The evening messages were given by John Chambers; Reverend Paul Moyer, a pastor of the United Protestant church in Palmer, Alaska; Reverend Roy Ahmaogak, the Eskimo pastor from Wainwright; and Reverend Samuel Simmonds, who was John Chambers assistant at the Barrow Presbyterian Church.

In one of my last letters to my parents before I flew home, I wrote, with amazement, "I'll never attend another camp like this—I'm sure—nothing could ever be like this!"

ABC

I left for the summer with a feeling of fulfillment. I left without hearing about the Teacher of the Year Award. I left and didn't communicate much with Eddie Hooley again.

During the summer, I felt listless and experienced dizzy spells and thought it was the humid heat. I fought to think clearly, but my mind was fuzzy. Tears flowed uncontrollably. Unexpectedly and out of character, I told my father, "I don't know how I can return to Anaktuvuk and keep the pace I started."

I went in for a medical examination. The physician advised me strongly not to return to Anaktuvuk.

"Your body is telling you something," she said. "As much as you love those Native people, you are worn out from the pressure of so many responsibilities, rigors of daily living, and isolation. Your heart and soul might be ready to return, but your body says otherwise."

I was heartbroken. At the same time, I was relieved. I was sad because I wouldn't be returning to my sod house with all its simplicity or to the people whose friendship and culture I'd come to love. I was relieved that I wouldn't be returning to my little musty cabin with no plumbing, electricity, or running water.

I thought back to that last evening up north. After the youth camp, John Chambers had flown me to Wainwright to visit the Websters. They had asked me to speak at the Sunday evening service, through an interpreter. I'd chosen passages from the New Testament book of Ephesians, chapters four and five, a message written by the Apostle Paul. The interpretation would have been something like Eugene Peterson would paraphrase in his book *The Message.*

> I want you to get out and walk—better yet, run!—on the road God called you to travel. I don't want you sitting around on your hands. I don't want anyone strolling off, down some path that goes nowhere. And mark that you do this with humility and discipline—not in fits and starts, but steadily pouring yourselves out for each other in acts of love...
>
> You have one Master, one faith, one baptism, one God and Father of all, who rules over all, works through all, and is present in all...
>
> But that doesn't mean you should all look and speak and act the same. Out of the generosity of Christ, each of us is given his own gift...He handed out gifts of apostle, prophet, evangelist, teacher...

That evening, the incredible Alaska sun had shone and reflected off the Arctic Ocean and streamed through the chapel windows. Yes, I'd walked—and run—up the road from Ohio to Alaska. When roads vanished, I'd climbed into an airplane and ventured farther north. Finally, I'd steadily pushed higher, to a place where dogsleds made paths. Yes, I'd been gifted by God to be a teacher. Now, I trusted that Anaktuvuk would not be the end of the path, but that I'd be directed to another. How could I think otherwise?

EPILOGUE

....

Anna never heard back about the Teacher of the Year award. She moved to Anchorage and taught first grade at a new school in Eagle River, about fourteen miles northeast of Anchorage. The following summer, she was asked to take a teaching position at the Alaska Native Services Hospital in Anchorage, which provided education for Native children who were ill—many with mastoiditis and some with tuberculosis. She joined the teaching team of Pauline Burkher, Vera Keith, and George Allen. Some children attended classes on gurneys and wheelchairs; those too ill had bedside lessons. At Christmas, Anna sewed four-year-old Dora a red dress and took the small child home with her. Dora had leukemia. It was her last Christmas.

Anna and roommate-teacher Phyllis Matheny rented an apartment. When both women planned to go home for the summer, Bob and Darlene Church, a young couple who were friends, asked if they could sublet the apartment for his parents and twin sisters, Mary and Margaret, who were coming from Oregon to visit. En route on the ship, Bob's mother passed away. Two years later, Bob's father, Henry, came to spend Christmas with Bob and Darleen. Anna met this widower, eleven years her senior, who had spent his life in the wood products industry. She was struck by his kindness and consideration. After he departed, his letters filled her mailbox, flowers arrived, and love filled her heart. Following Anna's visit to

Oregon, the two were engaged. They were married on August 5, 1967, in the Free Methodist Church in Salem, Oregon. At age forty-four, the single, pioneer school teacher found herself with three adult children.

Henry retired, and the newlyweds returned to Alaska, where Anna taught until 1973. The couple moved to Newberg, Oregon, in 1981. Henry passed away in October 2003. Anna lives in Friendsview Manor in Newberg and delights in visits from Bob (Darleen) Church, Mary (Roy) Skinner, and Margaret (Bob) McCormick, along with six grandchildren and twelve great-grandchildren.

ABC

In May 1962, Old Elijah, ever the opportunist, pitched a tent by the runway, put in a willow floor, and opened a coffee shop. He died in 1986 at the age of ninety-one.

Anna Hugo became the first person from Anaktuvuk Pass to graduate from college. She obtained her teaching certificate and married James Nageak from Barrow. She returned to Anaktuvuk Pass and taught another generation of the Nunamiut Eskimos.

Anna Bortel revisited her dear friends in Anaktuvuk in1966 and stayed with Ruth Rulland in her summer tent.

Simon Paneak estimated that by 1964, 1000 masks had been made and sold. Paneak died in 1975 at the age of seventy-five. The Simon Paneak Museum was constructed in his honor and sits on the hill near the original Chapel of the Mountains. The museum displays Nunamiut Eskimo history and traditions through exhibits of tools, clothing, trading, hunting, and trapping. Native crafts and gift items are available for purchase. At the University of Alaska's Museum of the North, in Fairbanks, visitors can view dolls and caribou mittens made by Simon and Susie Paneak. Anaktuvuk Pass village is still accessible only by air and is a novelty day trip for tourists. In 2012, the population was 324.

In 1968, the tiny Chapel of the Mountains was outgrown and a larger meeting place was constructed next door. The original chapel was used for Sunday school, Bible studies, prayer groups, and general meetings. In 1994 and again in 2004, the old chapel was renovated. On August 27-29, 2009, a 50th anniversary of the dedication of the first chapel was held, with the acknowledgment, "May we renew the vision of our early founders to be a light in our village and on the North Slope." Among the attendees were Reverend John Chambers, Bonnie Wartes with Mark and Denise Wartes, Merrily (Wartes) and Steve Lowry with granddaughter Erin Goyins, and Marti (Wartes) Bennett.

Naomi returned to Anaktuvuk Pass in1984 and in 2009. At the later date, she was deeply touched to met Rhoda Ahgook, Anna Hugo, "Little" Elmer, and other people who remembered her father, Dr. Elmer Gaede, and Anna Bortel.

Rhoda Ahgook and Naomi Gaede-Penner in Anaktuvuk Pass, AK 2009.

ABC

It is our hope that these stories will help pass on to future Nunamiut generations their rich Native heritage; document the determination of scientists to learn more about the vast, unknown, and frozen Alaska Territory; celebrate school teachers who go beyond words and numbers to educate children; and inspire ordinary people to use their gifts in extraordinary ways.

Anna Bortel Church
Naomi Gaede-Penner

MORE PRESCRIPTIONS FOR ADVENTURE

You just met Anna, who has even more adventures to share. She, in turn, introduced you to the Gaedes: Doc, Ruby, Naomi, Ruth, Mark, and Mishal. You can read about these characters and experience life in Alaska from their perspective.

'A' is for Alaska: Teacher to the Territory

Just as the Alaska spawning salmon swim upstream, so did this Anna Bortel swim against the current of a society that expected her to fit the mold of wife and mother. Instead of bemoaning her singlehood, in 1954, this young schoolteacher drove up the Alaska-Canada Highway from Ohio to Valdez, where snow was measured in feet and an Easter egg hunt unheard of event.

Her curiosity wasn't quelled. She pushed farther north to an isolated Athabascan village along the Yukon River. Teaching and living in drafty Quonset huts with freezing oil lines at 50-below zero added to her teaching rigors. Discouraged? Yes. Daunted? No.

You'll smile, laugh, and shake your head in amazement as you read these heartwarming, inspiring, and captivating stories of teaching in the Territory of Alaska.

From Kansas Wheat Fields to Alaska Tundra: A Mennonite Family Finds Home

Take Naomi Gaede, a young Mennonite girl, and transplant her from the flatland prairies of Kansas. Give her village potlatches, school in a Quonset hut, the fragrance of wood smoke, Native friends, a doctor for a father who creates hunting tales and medical adventures with a bush plane, a mother who makes the tastiest moose roasts and has the grit to be a homesteader, and throw in a batch of siblings. Weave into her journey the perspectives of her family members and have them face the lack of conveniences, isolation from extended family, freezing temperatures, and unknown hardships. Mix all these together with an attitude of humor, ingenuity, optimism, and you'll get a sense of adventure! (Reviewed as the *next* Little House on the Prairie.)

Alaska Bush Pilot Doctor

Dr. Elmer Gaede expected to follow in the footsteps of his Mennonite farming family. He never imagined that during the 1950s and '60s he'd fly with other legendary bush pilots, such as Babe Alsworth, Andy Anderson, Fred and John Chambers, Don Sheldon, Don Stickman, and Noel Wien. Or that he'd be counted among the early Alaska physicians in Interior Alaska.

Fasten your seatbelt for Bush flying crack-ups, fly-in house calls in 50-below temperatures, hunting adventures, and a psychotic woman climbing out of his small Piper aircraft, 2000 feet above the Yukon River.

Pack your sense of humor for a monkey in Doc's clinic waiting room, misjudged bush landings, delivering a baby during the 1964 Good Friday earthquake, and more.

Hang on for the thrills and the rigors of life in the Last Frontier. What's next?

- Ruby Gaede tells *her* side of the story, how she met a farm boy and expected a peaceful life on the Kansas prairie, and how her world got turned upside down when she discovered he preferred flying, medicine, and the Last Frontier to milking cows and harvesting wheat.

- Mark Gaede gives his humorous account of growing up in the backseat of his father's airplanes, carrying a gun bigger than he, and by age twelve shooting a moose, mountain goat, sheep, and caribou. Flying a plane before legal age came with the territory.
- The Gaede kids grow up and invite you to follow them as they try their hands at homesteading—with exasperation, surprises, and laughter.

To be the first to know about a new book in the Prescription for Adventure series, to purchase a DVD of Anna Bortel Church recounting her remarkable stories, to learn about the Alaska Unit Study Guide for students—or families planning a vacation to Alaska who want to learn more about the state—or to request a speaking engagement, go to http//:www. prescriptionforadventure.com. Your comments and reviews are welcomed. Send to npenn@prescriptionforadventure.com. For more Alaska facts, fun, and mini-prescriptions for adventure, find Prescription for Adventure on Facebook and read about Naomi's current Alaska adventures at http://blog. prescriptionforadventure.com/

GLOSSARY

· ·

Aleut—the Native people who lived in the Aleutian Chain. This people group was nearly devastated by contact with the whites, as well as relocation to internment camps in Southeast Alaska during World War II.

Alcan—the Alaska-Canada Highway. See Endnote for more information.

Athabascan—Indians who were traditionally nomadic and lived in a vast area of Interior Alaska, and into Canada as well as along the shores of the Cook Inlet.

Atiga—a cloth garment that covers the raw hide of a parka when the fur side is worn toward the body. Conversely, when the fur is worn toward the outside, it protects the fur. Men's atigas and parkas are usually shorter than women's, and made from solid, darker colors of corduroy or other heavy fabric. Women's atigas are nearer to the knee, sewn from brightly colored cotton prints, and decorated with rick-rack. In the summer, women and children will wear atigas without a parka beneath. The long-sleeves and a hood help protect against mosquitoes.

Bureau of Indian Affairs (BIA)—a federal agency that ran educational and health programs for the Natives starting in 1931. In 1954, that function was transferred to the US Department of Health, Education, and Welfare, now known as the Department of Health and

Human Services or the Indian Health Services (HIS.)

Blazo—a brand of white gas that came in five-gallon cans packed in wooden crates. Both empty cans and crates were used for a variety of household purposes in remote villages.

Blue baby—layman's term for a baby born with cyanotic heart defects, that result in lips and fingertips that are constantly blue, because his or her blood does not contain enough oxygen.

Borough—Alaska is divided into boroughs rather than counties or parishes.

Brucellosis (also called undulant fever)—a disease passed from cows to humans through improperly cooked beef or unpasteurized milk. In this case, it appeared to be passed through caribou. The bacteria are thought to reside mainly in the bone marrow and in the udders of the caribou. The Nunamiuts sometimes ate their meat raw. To prevent the disease, meat needs to be thoroughly cooked before eating.

Bunny boots—large, army-issue boots that, in the '50s and '60s, had white felt exteriors and smooth, slick-bottomed soles. They were intended to keep a soldier's feet warm for four hours at minus 50 degrees.

Bush—any part of Alaska that is inaccessible by roads or rail and accessible only by boat, airplane, sled, or snow machine.

CAA/FAA—Civil Aeronautical Authority, which, in 1958, later became Federal Aviation Agency (FAA).

Cat—Alaskans refer to any caterpillar or bulldozer piece of equipment as a Cat.

Cabin fever—a psychological state characterized by depression, restlessness, and sometimes violence. This is credited to the effects of being both housebound and locked in the dark, deep freeze of winter and from the resulting deprivation of sensory variety, physical mobility, and physical activity.

Cache—a structure built to protect food from animals. In some instances, the cache resembles a small log cabin on stilts. In Anaktuvuk Pass village, it was a platform on tall legs.

Daveno or davenport—a sofa or couch. Term used in the 1950s.

Dry village—not allowing the legal sale of alcoholic beverages in the village.

Fizzies—effervescent tablets that, when dropped into water, fizzed like an anti-acid drink. These were introduced in 1957. Initially, fizzies came in flavors of grape, orange, cherry, lemon-lime, strawberry, and root beer.

Igloo or iglu—a house or home. A round, snow-block structure is used by Eskimos for temporary on-the-trail shelter. Most indigenous dwellings follow a dome shape but are constructed with sod, with whale bone or wood supports for the roof.

Honey Pot—another name for chamber pot

Inupiat—one of the two Eskimo groups in Alaska. Both live along the coast: the Yupik along the Bering Sea and the Inupiat along Arctic Ocean. Each differs from the other linguistically and culturally. The spoken language is Inupiaq.

Mantle—aids in the combustion process and resembles a small net bag. Once the lantern is lit for the first time, the mantel shrinks and becomes very fragile.

Mastoiditis—an infection of the temporal bone of the skull behind the ear, which is usually caused by untreated middle-ear infection. It is a leading cause of child mortality; however, with the development of antibiotics, it has become rare in developed countries. Mastoiditis is treated with medications and/or surgery.

Northern Lights (*aurora borealis*)—a spectacular display of natural light, observed at night, and set off by electrical activity of sun spots.

Orienteer—orienteering includes a variety of activities that require navigational skills such as use of maps and compass to find points in unfamiliar terrain.

Pilot Boy Crackers (Sailor Boy Pilot Bread Crackers)—Ship pilots used these at sea when they couldn't get bread, hence the term *pilot* bread. These saltless four-inch-round, thick crackers serve a number of purposes in Alaska: emergency gear for hunters or for bush pilots, after-school snacks with peanut butter, and teething crackers for babies. They seem to be consistently stale yet *never too old* to use. In the villages, everyone has a reserve of these rations. They come in a long, rectangular box with white sailor boys skipping across the blue-papered box, and are in all rural stores in Alaska, as well as available for purchase at Costco in Anchorage, Alaska.

Teacherage—name of the dwelling in which teachers lived; sometimes attached to a school building, usually near the school building. In the same way a parson lived in a parsonage, a teacher lived in a teacherage.

Toni hair permanents—"Permanent wave" hair treatments for women were very popular in the late 1940s and '50s, when curled hair was the rage. Those who couldn't afford a professional perm in a salon used home permanent kits, which included strong-smelling chemicals and perm curling rods. Mothers would give perms to their daughters, and friends would give them to one another. The first popular home permanent kit was the Toni brand. The Toni company used a set of twins to advertise their products.

Tundra—a treeless area covered with low-lying vegetation (small flowers, mosses, and lichens), under which is permanently frozen sub-soil.

Ulu—a knife with a fan-shaped blade and bone or stone handle, used for cutting meat and scraping skin.

SUGGESTED READING

The *Alaska Almanac*. Portland, Oregon: Alaska Northwest Books, 1976-2010.

Anderson, Andy and Jim Rearden. *Arctic Bush Pilot.* Kenmore, Washington: Epicenter Press, 2000.

Blackman, M. B. *Upside Down: Seasons Among the Nunamiut.* Lincoln, Nebraska: University of Nebraska Press, 1990.

Breu, Mary. *Last Letters from Attu: The True Story of Etta Jones, Alaska Pioneer and Japanese P.O.W.* Anchorage/Portland: Alaska Northwest Books, 2009.

Campbell, J. M. (ed.). *Northern Alaska Chronicles: Essays by Simon Paneak.* Fairbanks, Alaska: University of Alaska Press, 2004.

Campbell, J. M. (ed.). *North Alaska Chronicle: Notes From the End of Time.* Santa Fe, New Mexico: Museum of New Mexico Press, 1998.

Chambers, John. *Arctic Bush Missionary: The Experiences of a Missionary Bush Pilot in the Far North.* Seattle, Washington: Superior Publishing Co., 1970.

Cline, Michael. *Tannik School: The Impact of Education on the Eskimos of Anaktuvuk Pass.* Anchorage, AK: Alaska Methodist University Press, 1975.

Feyes, Claire. *Villagers: Athabaskan Indian Life Along the Yukon River.* New York: Random House, 1981.

Gaede-Penner, Naomi. *Alaska Bush Pilot Doctor.* Mustang, OK: Tate Publishing, 2012.

Gaede-Penner, Naomi. *'A' is for Alaska: Teacher to the Territory.* Mustang, OK: Tate Publishing, 2011.

Gaede-Penner, Naomi. *From Kansas Wheat Fields to Alaska Tundra: A Mennonite Family Finds Home.* Mustang, OK: Tate Publishing, 2011.

Gubser, Nicholas. *The Nunamiut Eskimos: Hunters of Caribou.* New Haven and London: Yale University Press, 1965.

Harkey, Ira. *Noel Wien: Alaska Pioneer Bush Pilot.* Fairbanks, Alaska: University of Alaska Press, 1974.

Instad, Helge. *Nunamiut: Among Alaska's Inland Eskimos.* Oslo, Norway: 1951. Woodstock, VT: The Countryman Press, 1954.

Jacobs, Jane. *A Schoolteacher in Old Alaska: The Story of Hannah Breece.* New York: Vintage Press, 1995.

Madenwald, Abbie Morgan. *Arctic School Teacher: Kulukak, Alaska 1931-1933.* Norman, OK: University of Oklahoma Press, 1992.

Movius, Phyllis Demuth (ed.). *When the Geese Come: The Journals of a Moravian Missionary, Ella Mae Ervin Romig, 1889-1905, Southwest Alaska.* Fairbanks, Alaska: University of Alaska Press, 1997.

Persons, Jean. *From Dog Sleds to Float Planes: Alaskan Adventures in Medicine.* Eagle River, AK: Northbooks, 2007.

Schwalbe, Anna Buxbaum. *Dayspring on the Kuskokwim: The Story of Moravian Missions in Alaska.* Bethlehem, PA: Moravian Press, 1951.

Stuck, Hudson. *Ten Thousand Miles with a Dog Sled.* Lincoln, NE: University of Nebraska Press, 1988.

http://uaf-db.uaf.edu/Jukebox/PJWeb/pjcontact.htm

http://www.adn.com/ (*Alaska Daily News*)

http://alaskamagazine.com (*Alaska Magazine*)

http://newsminer.com/ (*Fairbanks Daily News-Miner*)

http://www.commerce.state.ak.us/dca/commdb/CF_CIS.htm

READER'S GUIDE

1. What was one of the first incidences where Anna stretched herself from her familiar and comfortable way of life?

2. What is a comfort zone? What comfort zones did Anna move herself out from or into? What were the results for her personally, as well as for individuals around her? Discuss.

   -Personal conveniences

   -Work and career

   -Friends and family

   -Environment

   -Roles and responsibilities

   -Other_____

3. What comfort zones would be challenged if you were to have lived in her situations? What comfort zones have you moved from in the past five years? What were your feelings? Your fears? Responses by other people to your decisions?

4. Anna is portrayed as whole-heartedly embraced by the

Natives in Tanana and in Anaktuvuk. What might have been other reactions by the people? Why?

5. How did Valdez and Tanana prepare her for Anaktuvuk Pass?

6. Discuss what it would be like if you were without roads, air travel, or boat travel—and without television, radio, Internet, and phone service.

7. What part did getting mail play in Anna's life? Relationally? Emotionally? Mentally?

8. Anna was the first permanent school teacher for the Nunamiut Eskimos. What qualities did she have that enabled her to carry through with the responsibilities this required?

9. Anna faced a number of disturbing issues, including but not limited to high infant mortality, lack of accessible health-care, primitive economy, community hunger, and survival in a harsh environment. Not only did she step forward to be the school teacher, but she became inextricably involved in the community. Review how the above issues, and others you can identify, were ameliorated because of her. Do you think Simon Paneak and the elders had any idea how wide-reaching their demands for a school teacher would be? Why? Why not? How?

10. What qualities do you think the Nunamiuts had to survive in their way of life and culture? What would you consider "unsurvivable" in a situation?

11. What draws people together in difficult and demanding environments?

12. Why was Anna drawn farther north?

13. What intangible gifts did the people in Tanana and Anaktuvuk give to her?

14. What did you enjoy most about Anna's story?

15. What is *your* prescription for adventure? After reading '*A*' is for Anaktuvuk: Teacher to the Nunamiut Eskimos, what are you motivated to do?

- Use your natural abilities and individual passions with the result of an adventure

- Do something outside your comfort zone

- Explore the unknown: wilderness, mountaintop, ocean, third-world country, inner city

- Do some kind of volunteer service

- Live in an environment conducive to adventures

- Read more adventure stories

- Try something new

- Pursue some activity or trip that you've been contemplating

- Watch for the extraordinary to pop into an ordinary day

- Pass along this book to someone else to enjoy

Don't be left out. Live life like an adventure!

Census of Anaktuvuk Pass 1960 by Anna Bortel

Close to the foot of the mountain held

ANAKTUVUK PASS CENSUS

Ahgook, Ben	2-18-22	
Elizabeth	4-21-26	
Jacob	5-19-49	
Amanilla	2-9-52	
Ben, Jr.	12-10-53	
Vera	12-19-55	
dorothy	4-24-58	
Philip		
Ahgook, Bob	9-18-29	
Rhoda	2-20-30	
Minnie	8-14-56	
James	6-10-58	
Ahgook, Jessie	6-17-82	
Jonas	2-27-19	
Hugo, Clyde	1-14-15	
Helen	4-10-23	
Daniel	8-3-44	
Martena	8-11-49	
Harry	5-18-51	
Pat	7-29-53	
Alice	8-14-55	
Willie	10-28-56	
Charlie	7-29-58	
Elmer		
Hugo, Inalurok	12- -85	
Sarah	9-15-10	
Hugo, Zacharias	9- -31	
Elizabeth	2-14-36	
Margaret		
Raymond Paul		
Hugo, John	4-15-23	
Dora	6-7-22	
Anna	9-11-44	
Henry	10-8-51	
Alice	8-14-55	
Kakinya, Elijah	4-27-93	
May	-98	
Ruth	6-4-38	
Kakinya, Abraham	12-24-32	
Marie	7-4-34	
Betty	4-24-58	
Mantigak, Morrie	84	
Amos	3-1-29	
Mekiana, Homer	5-504	
Rebecca	9-10-19	
Doris	1-10-36	
Rachel	3-5-41	
Joseph	12-16-41	
David	2-10-43	
Cyrus	12-9-49	
Chris	10-13-51	
Kenton	4-30-53	
Patrick	3-5-55	

Mekiana, Justus	725-28	
Ethel	11-18-34	
Myrtle	10-25-53	
Justus Jr.	10-14-55	
Rachel	10-14-57	
July		
Morrie, Billy	10-10-14	
Olive	7-4-22	
Lula	2-5-48	
Larry	9-28-50	99
Hattie	11-14-53	
Stanley	3-4-56	
Minnie	3-19-59	
Morrie, John	12-25-11	
Alice	8-1-24	
Lela	8-1-40	
Riley	10-5-42	
Mark	3-18-44	
Anna	10-28-45	
Susan	12-5-49	
Paneak, Simon	4-23-00	
Susie	1-15-19	
Robert	3-19-38	
Raymond	6-17-40	
Mabel	9-23-42	
Roosevelt	7-24-46	
George	2-1-49	
Allen	9-23-56	
Rulland, Frank	1-22-00	
Vera	?	
Jane	1-7-28	
Johnnie	6-4-39	
Lazarus	1-17-30	
Thomas	12-11-33	
Rulland, Joshua	2-26-38	
Ida	6-16-39	
Rose Ann	10-5-42	
Laura Lou	7-26-50	
Samuel	2-8-51	
Laura Lou	1-1-52. Feb. 25 '53	
O'Bonnel, Patrick	60 yrs. (white)	
Morrie, Amos	3-1-29	
Maggie	5- -27	
Jack	2-9-47	
Hattie	10-19-56	
Ahgook, Jack	8-16-32	
Mekiana, Mollie	8-14-33	
Esther	2-4-58	
Ada	5- -57	
Hugo, Jack Zacharias	9-15-1931	
Doris	1- - 36	

288

Congressional Records

succeeded in getting Don C. Foster, then general superintendent of the Alaska Native Service and the superintendent of the Alaska Native Service school at Barrow to send a young couple into Anaktuvuk Pass for 6 weeks. Unfortunately, unfamiliarity with the North and the primitive living conditions hampered their teaching efficiency and they had to give up their plan to start educating the children. Nor did the native service provide teacher replacements.

Three years passed. During this time a post office was established. In 1953 territorial Senator William Beltz, of Nome, an Eskimo, tried to get a school started at the pass but it was denied by the native service on the grounds that the people were nomadic. Finally, in the absence of any other means of providing education, the Alaska Native Service transported several children to southeastern Alaska to boarding schools. However, this substitute for a school at home failed to meet the educational needs of these Eskimos, for though the children were not particularly unhappy, they were not eager to return to school the following year. They missed their families, familiar foods, and their own environment. It became evident that this experiment would not work.

Finally in 1959 the dream of the citizens of Anaktuvuk Pass showed promise of coming true. As the arctic winter lessened its hard hold upon the community, anticipation and determination, far stronger forces, took hold. It seemed that success was in sight.

This success, however, was not imminent. As more people looked into the matter and tried to form definite plans, more and more difficulties presented themselves. It was certainly evident that the living conditions for the school's teacher would be rugged. Whoever was to be finally chosen for the job must be someone prepared to sacrifice unstintingly his or her personal comfort for the good of her school, someone who was intimately acquainted with the ways of life of the Eskimos and their attitudes toward learning, someone who could adjust to this different way of life without sacrificing teaching efficiency.

There were other obstacles. In the Anaktuvuk Pass region there were no building materials. All materials for the construction of the school would have to be flown in. And again there being no wood to speak of, there would be no way of heating the school once it was built, short of flying in fuel oil. Costs here, since Anaktuvuk Pass is served by no airline, would be prohibitive. On top of all this the supplies could not be flown directly into Anaktuvuk Pass, but would have to be transported 15 miles over rugged country. Of course there were no mechanized vehicles in this roadless area.

Even the revelation of so many problems did not dampen the enthusiasm of the folks of the village. For they persuaded Anna Bortel, who had been head teacher at Tanana School, to teach them in their church. In Miss Bortel they had found the ideal teacher, one able to comprehend their problems, one kind and sympathetic, and above all one able to

adjust to all conditions that might face her.

School had finally started, the Eskimos were finally on their way to the knowledgeable state that they had been dreaming of for years. Men and boys, women and children flocked to learn. Whenever their normal daily efforts to survive and provide themselves with food and shelter could spare them, they went to the school. But even now our determined students were not satisfied. They wished a real schoolhouse for themselves, something that could be revered as the seat of learning and knowledge in their village. A monument to knowledge—small, unpainted, wooden—but a monument just the same.

Pursuing this aim with the same determination they had evidenced in a decade of struggle, the village council, the guiding body of Anaktuvuk Pass, wrote to Howard A. Matthews, Alaska commissioner of education, I would like to read their marvelous expression of determination and sincerity to my colleagues:

OCTOBER 20, 1959.

DEAR MR. MATTHEWS: We are writing and asking you for a school at Anaktuvuk Pass, Alaska. We have quite a few kids here that are of school age and they are waiting for the schoolhouse at the Pass. They want a school as soon as possible. We want a school up here, too.

We want our children to be like us who don't know how to write one word. We have two men here who do our writing for us when we want to do some writing, and we don't want our children to do the same. That is why we want the school to be put up here. Why don't we have a school here? We are American citizens. Our children need schooling. After reading this letter that we have written to you, after finding out two people here who do this writing for us, maybe you will start thinking of us as poor people who grow old without knowing how to write (our children will be like us). No, we don't want our children to be like us.

When are we going to have a school? We want to know when and what kind. We will be expecting an answer from you, we will answer you if you write.

Sincerely yours,

THE VILLAGE COUNCIL OF ANAKTUVUK PASS.

The determination of the Eskimos finally began to bring results. Wein Airlines started construction of a good airplane runway only one-half mile from the proposed school site. The Alaska Department of Public Works sent representatives in to arrange for the building of the schoolhouse. Another year passed but finally the school was built. At long last ambition was fulfilled.

Today under the able guidance of teachers like Anna Bortel, schools like Anaktuvuk Pass are in session across Alaska. They face many problems and much expense, but they carry on, sure of what they want.

It seems to me, Mr. President, that I have just told in very specific terms the story of Alaska as a whole. For we Alaskans know what we want and we will struggle until we get it. We have accomplished much in our strivings, not the least of which was statehood, and we will accomplish more—much more. With citizens of ambition and determi-

nation like those of Anaktuvuk Pass we will forge ahead to develop our resources, attract new industry, complete the transformation of Alaska from wilderness to prosperous statehood.

My reason, Mr. President, for calling the attention of the Senate today to the inspiring story of the people of Anaktuvuk Pass and their efforts to obtain an education is to remind the Congress of the overwhelming importance of enacting, at this session of Congress, legislation to provide Federal aid to the schools of this Nation.

It may be recalled that, during the debate in this Chamber on S. 1021, the School Assistance Act, I pointed to the exceptionally high costs of providing an education to the children of Anaktuvuk Pass as an example of the reasons Alaska must have more assistance from the Federal Government if we are to have a good school system in my State. I then referred to the fact that, at Anaktuvuk Pass, the cost of heating the school, alone, is more than $6,000 a year. To provide fuel for the 30 children who go to this school it is necessary to fly in some 75 barrels of fuel oil during the winter, as the lack of any other form of transportation makes this expensive means of transporting supplies necessary.

While the high costs of education at Anaktuvuk Pass may be exceptional as compared with costs in other parts of the United States, I believe the desire for an adequate education for one's children is as strong in all States of the Union, as it is in Alaska, and at Anaktuvuk Pass. Every State in the Union needs to help that can be provided by enactment of legislation to provide Federal aid to education. I hope the story of the children of Anaktuvuk Pass will provide encouragement for the enactment of such legislation.

SELTZER SEES NO WAR IN 1961

Mr. YOUNG of Ohio. Mr. President, a very important article was published in yesterday's edition of the Cleveland Press entitled "Seltzer Sees No War in 1961,—Cites Errors Made by Khrushchev." The article is a most timely one written by Louis B. Seltzer, editor of the Cleveland Press.

Louis B. Seltzer is one of the great newspaper editors of this Nation. He is probably the only newspaper editor in the United States who has ever been offered appointment as a U.S. Senator by a Governor of his State and who declined the appointment because he wanted to continue in newspaper work.

The Cleveland Press is a paper of great circulation and prestige. It is the original newspaper in the Nation founded by E. W. Scripps. It is one of the greatest, if not the greatest, newspaper in the present Scripps-Howard chain.

The article to which I have referred, in which the editor sees no war in 1961, is in accord with my own thinking. It is phrased in a masterly fashion which I could not undertake to equal. It is of such importance that I ask unanimous consent that it be printed in the RECORD as a part of my remarks.

Congressional Records

Bewanee, Tenn., $125,000; Olustee, Fla., $70,000; Alexandria, La., $200,000; Warren, Pa., $300,000; and Madison, Wis., $300,000, a preplanning item.

The West Thornton, N.H., project was reduced by $350,000 to $50,000.

As much as I would have liked to have seen congressional approval of these six projects—for they are all very necessary—I commend the members of the conference committee for the fine treatment they have given our forestry research items. I was especially disappointed that funds were not included for the highly important project at Madison, Wis. We must make a special effort to obtain this item in 1962. This Forest Projects Laboratory at Madison is a national, not a local, institution.

Funds included in the bill this year will provide for construction of 16 urgently needed laboratories, as follows:

1. Riverside, Calif., Forest Fire Laboratory, $975,000.
2. West Thornton, N.H., Forest Watershed Management Laboratory, $50,000.
3. Gulfport, Miss., insectary for insect research, $25,000.
4. Grand Rapids, Minn., greenhouse and headhouse, $25,000.
5. Bozeman, Mont., Forest and Range Management Laboratory, $175,000.
6. Wenatchee, Wash., Forest Soils and Hydrology Laboratory, $300,000.
7. Flagstaff, Ariz., Ponderosa Pine Silviculture Laboratory, $150,000.
8. Moscow, Idaho, White Pine Disease and Silviculture Laboratory, $300,000.
9. Fairbanks, Alaska, Forest Protection and Silviculture Laboratory, $350,000.
10. Laramie, Wyo., Range and Watershed Management Laboratory, $150,000.
11. Bend, Oreg., Silviculture and Wildlife Management Laboratory, $150,000.
12. Bottineau, N. Dak., Plains Shelterbelt Laboratory, $130,000.
13. St. Paul, Minn., regional headquarters office and laboratories for Lake States forest experiment station, $1,250,000.
14. Crossett, Ark., Loblolly Pine Silviculture, Laboratory, $50,000.
15. Athens, Ga., laboratory facilities for research on insects and diseases, forest products utilization, and silviculture studies, $665,000.
16. Bluefield-Princeton, W. Va., market development center and related experimental-demonstration forest, $450,000.

Many times I have emphasized, on the Senate floor and in committee, the need for these facilities in bringing about a dynamic and effective research program. Senators have heard me say, and I repeat:

Let us take our scientists out of the woodsheds.

Many Senators have joined me in this appeal. Not long ago I visited a new forest laboratory where forest geneticists are breeding superior pine trees. Only a short time earlier I had seen those same well-trained scientists attempting to do valuable and essential research in makeshift quarters without even the minimum required modern equipment. It is heartening to see—even miraculous—the more rapid progress made possible through modern laboratories and facilities.

Increased funds appropriated this year for forestry research will permit a stronger and more rapid attack on critical tree insect and disease pests. Two serious diseases of the southern pine—a damaging stem rust and a root rot—will be brought under control more quickly as a result of this increase.

Critical forest fire problems can be attacked with greater vigor and more knowledge.

Needed acceleration of watershed and range forage research will be possible.

The tempo of research on wildlife habitat and forest recreation problems can be brought up nearer to the necessary levels the problems justify.

Research on wood utilization will find new and improved uses for forest products that will make for a greater utilization, a richer economy, and added employment benefits that flow from increased forest industry.

And research on marketing problems will aid our small forest landowners throughout the Nation.

The foregoing are some of the concrete results which will flow from increased forestry research and these new and modern laboratories.

I wish it were possible to move even faster in providing these vital research facilities, and I regret the 1-year delay in the cutback of funds for the six projects mentioned earlier. In my judgment, this is false economy. Nevertheless, I am proud that we have made a reasonable gain this year in equipping our scientists with more adequate facilities for this vital research.

I highly commend those who have joined with me in sponsoring this national program, and I urge every member of the Senate to support this vital program to its fulfillment.

This approved program is a splendid expression of confidence by the Congress in the National Forest Service and their fine personnel. It is also a challenge to the Forest Service to strengthen their forward strides in meeting the opportunities and the demands of our times. I trust that the President will promptly authorize the expenditures of those funds.

A UNIQUE AMERICAN EDUCATIONAL VENTURE IN ALASKA'S FAR NORTH

Mr. GRUENING. Mr. President, today in Alaska there exists a unique school system, unparalleled anywhere in the United States. Because of its great size, scattered population, and lack of transportation facilities, Alaska faces enormous difficulties in trying to provide a public education to all its citizens. For many years the able educators who head Alaska's State Department of Education have been working to combat this problem, which especially affects Alaska's 37,000 Indians, Eskimos, and Aleuts. They have made tremendous strides in setting up schools in remote places. It has been a hard task, which has required persistence, devotion, and courage. But in another sense this task has been easy, for in every area in which a school has been built the school officials involved have had the unwavering and strong encouragement of the people for whom the schools were provided. These ambitious folk have lent their homes, their food, and their strong backs to this cause. Unstintingly they have given in order that they might learn.

And they have been rewarded. For in every corner of the huge State of Alaska small but comfortable schoolhouses, staffed by dedicated teachers, pupiled by interested students, stand through the long summer days and cold winter nights as shining bastions against the wind of ignorance.

I have in my hands today proof of the accomplishments of one of these schools. I would like to relate to you its story, for it typifies the founding of similar schools all over Alaska.

Prior to 1945 the 65 Nunamuit Eskimos who inhabited the area around Anaktuvuk Pass, Alaska, had little contact with white men and the outside world. They were dependent upon migrating caribou herds for their living, just as their ancestors had been for centuries. Caribou was their staff of life. It provided food, shelter, clothing, and tools. Their only cash income came from bounties paid by the Government for the killing of the wolves which prey upon the caribou. This provided guns, ammunition, flour, tea, and tobacco. There were no permanent homes, no school, and no post office. In winter the people broke up into small family groups separated from one another by 20 or 30 miles. This was made necessary because the caribou herds broke into smaller groups which moved into the mountain passes where constant winds kept the mosses and lichens on which they fed relatively free of snow.

In summer, however, the people came together at Tulugak Lake on the northern arctic slope some 16 miles from the summit of Anaktuvuk Pass. Here they fished, made winter equipment and lived throughout the short arctic summer much as their ancestors had in the same area for some thousands of years. Thus their existence passed, unchanged.

But this was not to say that they could not change. For after 1945, with the spreading out of white settlements in Alaska's far north, an occasional pilot, geologist, or health official visited them briefly. With the coming of the white man came an increased awareness of the outside world. Idens of advancement and self-improvement began to form in their minds. Two of their number managed to pick up English. In 1950 a U.S. census enumerator, Ethel Oliver, in fact the first white woman ever to visit the area, came to Anaktuvuk. Her presence, especially when the Eskimos learned that she was also a teacher, stimulated the desire for education and advancement.

We will build a school—

They said—

If we can get 10 pounds of oil and some canvas.

They also asked Mrs. Oliver to help them find a teacher.

Mrs. Oliver saw the enthusiasm and great desire of these people to become more educated and to learn more about the other parts of Alaska—a feeling, I might add which pervades all the Eskimos, Indians, and Aleuts of Alaska—and she attempted to help them. She

Songs and Music Sheets

The Ptarmigan

The Ptarmigan*

Raymond Joseph

Ptar-mi-gan are white as snow

When the win-ter winds do blow.

But their fea-thers turn to brown

When the spring-time comes a-round.

Northern Lights

Napikuk

Shim-mer-ing a - cross the sky,

Pret-ty lights oh, tell us why,

Are you poin-ting out the way

Where the cari-bou go to play?

INDEX

ENDNOTES

1   The town as described here was wiped out by a tsunami generated by the 9.2 Good Friday Earthquake of 1964. The current town sits on the side of Valdez Arm, rather than at the end as did the old town

2   Bill Egan was Alaska's first governor, serving from 1959-1966 and again from 1970-1974. He was affectionately known to all as "Governor Bill."

3   Andy Anderson frequented Anaktuvuk Pass regularly. He served as the mail carrier, brought in scientists, and transported patients to the Tanana PHS hospital. To read more about Andy Anderson, see *Arctic Bush Pilot* by Andy Anderson and Jim Rearden.

4   *Arctic Bush Mission: The Experiences of a Missionary Bush Pilot in the Far North*, by John Chambers.

5   Anaktuvuk River is a shallow river of about 135 miles, originating from a glacier near the Endicott Mountains and running south to the Colville River.

6   Tail-dragger—aircraft with the two main wheels toward the front of the aircraft and a smaller single wheel at the tail. This type of landing gear is considered to be the most durable for landing on uneven and/or unpaved surfaces—such as bush landings in Alaska. The configuration has also been called "conventional" landing gear.

7   DC-3—a twin-engine propeller aircraft that first flew in 1935 and a favorite of pilots both in and out of the military because of its large payload, short airstrip requirements, ability to land on dirt or grass, and general ruggedness. In the 1950s, the DC-3 and DC-4 were the most commonly used airplanes in Alaska, both for passengers and freight.

8   Firearms were introduced to the Native people in the latter half of the nineteenth century, first flintlocks and then muzzle-loaders. In 1900, the rifle had become their primary hunting weapon. By1960, the Nunamiut's favorite .30-30, one of the most common deer hunting cartridges in North America, had been replaced with smaller caliber and higher velocity guns.

9   Hugo Enualurak—his children took his first name as their last name.

10   See *In a Hungry Country: Essays by Simon Paneak*, ed. by John Martin Campbell, p.111.

11   The Beaver was a tough, single-engine, high-wing aircraft developed by de Havilland in Canada. The small aircraft held six passengers plus the pilot. Its multipurpose capability of carrying passengers or large quantities of freight earned it the nickname of "Workhorse of the North."

12   The Fairbanks radio, KFAR, routinely broadcast news from the villages. The Anaktuvuk Pass correspondent asked the teenage students to write about Danny's party. When it was aired, Anna and

her students crowded around the radio at Ethel Mekiana's and listened to the announcer. At the end, he asked the students to write in again. They were so excited.

13   Kivik and Ihyanituk were areas, not villages.

14   Harvey Restaurants—Fred Harvey opened two railroad eating houses in 1875. For the next near century, his company brought high-quality restaurants to the travelling public throughout the Southwest. Harvey is credited with creating the first restaurant chain in the United States.

15   Publatook—an area, not a village.

16   Dr. Lawrence Irving was the advisory scientific director and professor of zoophysiology at the University of Alaska in Fairbanks. "With his graduate fellows, Dr. Irving was working on the puzzle of how naked seal flippers, caribou noses, beaver tails, wolf pads, and bird legs operate at temperatures too low for nerve function in warm-blooded animals." (*National Geographic*, ALASKA.)

17   To read more about Bill and Bonnie Wartes' ministry in Alaska, contact Denise Wartes at denisewartes@yahoo.com or 1713 Central Avenue, Fairbanks, AK 99709.

18   Congressional Record, Senate #13201 by Mr. Gruening.